The Cambridge Introduction to
Twentieth-Century American Poetry

The Cambridge Introduction to Twentieth-Century American Poetry is designed to give readers a brief but thorough introduction to the various movements, schools, and groups of American poets in the twentieth century. It will help readers to understand and analyze modern and contemporary poems. The first part of the book deals with the transition from the nineteenth-century lyric to the modernist poem, focusing on the work of major modernists such as Robert Frost, T. S. Eliot, Ezra Pound, Wallace Stevens, Marianne Moore, and William Carlos Williams. In the second half of the book, the focus is on groups such as the poets of the Harlem Renaissance, the New Critics, the Confessionals, and the Beats. In each chapter, discussions of the most important poems are placed in the larger context of literary, cultural, and social history. This volume will be invaluable for students and teachers alike.

CHRISTOPHER BEACH is Adjunct Assistant Professor at Claremont Graduate University. He is the author of several books in the field of American poetry and one book on American cinema. His most recent books are *Poetic Culture: Contemporary American Poetry between Community and Institution* and *Class, Language, and American Film Comedy*. He is also the editor of *Artifice and Indeterminacy: an Anthology of New Poetics*.

The Cambridge Introduction to
Twentieth-Century
American Poetry

CHRISTOPHER BEACH

CAMBRIDGE
UNIVERSITY PRESS

PUBLISHED BY THE PRESS SYNDICATE OF THE UNIVERSITY OF CAMBRIDGE
The Pitt Building, Trumpington Street, Cambridge CB2 1RP, United Kingdom

CAMBRIDGE UNIVERSITY PRESS
The Edinburgh Building, Cambridge, CB2 2RU, UK
40 West 20th Street, New York, NY 10011–4211, USA
477 Williamstown Road, Port Melbourne, VIC 3207, Australia
Ruiz de Alarcón 13, 28014 Madrid, Spain
Dock House, The Waterfront, Cape Town 8001, South Africa

http://www.cambridge.org

First published 2003

Printed in the United Kingdom at the University Press, Cambridge

Typefaces Bembo 11/12.5 pt., Plantin, Univers   *System* LATEX 2ε   [TB]

A catalogue record for this book is available from the British Library

Library of Congress Cataloguing in Publication data
Beach, Christopher.
The Cambridge introduction to twentieth-century American poetry / by Christopher
Beach.
   p.   cm.
Includes bibliographical references and index.
ISBN 0 521 81469 3 (hardback) – ISBN 0 521 89149 3 (paperback)
I. Title.
PS323.5.B387 2003
811′.509 – dc21   2003043580

ISBN 0 521 81469 3 hardback
ISBN 0 521 89149 3 paperback

For my father, Northrop Beach 1912–2002

Contents

Introduction

A century is a considerable period of time in the development of any literary genre. This is especially true in the case of American poetry, which began the twentieth century as an enervated literary exercise and ended it as a vital form of cultural expression. American poets of the twentieth century pushed the limits of poetic composition, asking fundamental questions about what poetry is and how it should be written. Is poetry the product of an interaction between the real world and the artistic imagination? Or is it a self-contained artistic object with little relevance to the world outside its borders? Is the poem an intimate speech act linking poet and reader in a private encounter? Or can poetry contribute to new forms of social and political awareness?

This book will address such questions in an attempt to provide a better understanding of the poems, poets, and poetic movements of the last hundred years. The primary focus of the book is on the close reading of individual poems. These readings should provide keys to the understanding of each poet's work; at the same time, they should serve as examples of poetic explication and interpretation that can help the reader to articulate his or her own responses to poetry in general. The discussion of selected poems in each chapter will be supplemented by a presentation of the cultural, sociological, and intellectual contexts of twentieth-century American poetry.

As the twentieth century began, poetry was greatly overshadowed by the novel. During the period from the end of the Civil War until World War I, the United States experienced explosive population growth and a powerfully expanding economy. As a result, the nation was focused on pragmatic matters that absorbed its immediate attention: American society had little energy to devote to the cultivation of poetry, which was often relegated to the status of a "genteel" pastime with little relevance to modern-day life. The so-called "Age of Realism" (1870–1910) was a high point in the development of the American novel; American poetry, on the other hand, lingered in the twilight of the late nineteenth century, unable to enter the modern world or break with the conventional formulas and sentimental diction of earlier decades.

It was not until the second decade of the century that poets began to come to terms with the important social and economic changes of the modern era, such as the introduction of new technologies into all areas of industry and commerce and the increasingly urban character of American life. The first generation of American poets to respond to this modern world included Robert Frost, Wallace Stevens, Ezra Pound, William Carlos Williams, T. S. Eliot, E. E. Cummings, and Marianne Moore. It was with this generation – all of whom published their first books between 1908 and 1923 – that the artistic achievement of American poetic writing was clearly established.

Among these poets, Pound was perhaps the most strident voice for a poetry that would serve as a central expression of the new "modernist" aesthetic. In a 1912 essay, Pound declared "the imminence of an American Risorgimento," a renaissance in American intellectual and artistic life that would lift the country out of its "Dark Ages" and propel it into contemporary civilization. Such a renaissance was indeed to take place, largely as a result of the discovery of European culture by American poets. Those responding to American provinciality and cultural isolationism by leaving America for sojourns in Paris or London included Gertrude Stein, Pound, Eliot, Frost, Cummings, H. D. (Hilda Doolittle), and Langston Hughes. While Stein, Pound, Eliot, and H. D. became permanent expatriates, the others returned to the United States, bringing with them an enlarged sense of European culture. American poets found a more receptive audience for their works in Europe than in the United States: the first books of Pound, Frost, and Moore were all published abroad, where the public was more prepared for writing that did not conform to conventional nineteenth-century norms.

The experience of World War I, which brought many Americans into contact with Europe for the first time, further bridged the gap between American and European culture, and it prepared the ground for an international modernism in which Americans would play a crucial part. The war was traumatic not only for the soldiers in the trenches but also for artists and writers whose sensitivity to the effects of warfare made them, as Pound put it, the "antennae of the race." In T. S. Eliot's epoch-marking poem *The Waste Land*, he evoked a postwar world in which traditional systems of belief and established social structures had been radically altered. The changed understanding of human society and human nature brought about by the war contributed to the large-scale literary and artistic movement known as "modernism." As James Longenbach suggests, the war "presented a generation of judiciously limited lyric poets with an epic subject."[1] The realities of war caused a total rethinking of the purpose of poetry in the twentieth century. During the years 1920–26 alone, American poets produced an extraordinary body of work, including Pound's "Hugh Selwyn Mauberly" and *Cantos I-XVI*, Eliot's *The Waste Land*, Stevens' *Harmonium*, Williams' *Spring and All*, Moore's *Observations* and *Poems*, Hughes' *The Weary Blues*, H. D.'s *Collected Poems*, Cummings' *Tulips and Chimneys*, and Hart Crane's *White Buildings*.

World War II represented another watershed in the development of American poetry, marking a definitive historical and generational break with modernism. The postwar poets of the 1950s and 1960s took a number of different guises: there were the academic formalists following the tenets of the New Criticism; there were the "confessionals" with their more intensely personal approach to the poem; and there were the Beats and other countercultural movements which sought to liberate poetry from what they saw as the rigidity of academic verse. Against the political, social, and cultural conservatism of the postwar era, the poetry of the New American Poets took on a subversive aura in the 1950s, serving as a forerunner to the larger social movements of the 1960s.

In the 1970s and 1980s, American poetry entered its third generational phase. During this period, the number of published poets continued to grow, bolstered by a burgeoning network of journals, presses, and academic creative-writing programs. Despite worries about the "death of poetry," movements such as the avant-garde "Language Poetry" and the "New Formalism" helped revitalize American poetry. In the final decades of the century, two other tendencies emerged in American poetry. The first of these was the turn toward oral and performance poetries; the second was the increasing use of computer-assisted technologies for generating poetic texts. The new performance poetry, or "Spoken Word," as it is sometimes called, began as a localized movement in the 1980s and gained tremendous popularity in the 1990s, with readings and "poetry slams" held at venues like the Nuyorican Poets Cafe in New York's lower east side. The use of computers and the internet in what has variously been called "cyber-poetry," "e-poetry," "digital poetry," or "new media poetry" was in the early stages of its development at century's end, and it is still too soon to say what its long-term significance will be.

The first fact to be remembered in any assessment of American poetry is that it has had a relatively short history. Though poetry has been written in North America for over 350 years – since Anne Bradstreet first penned her verses about life in Puritan New England – it was not until the almost simultaneous appearance of Walt Whitman and Emily Dickinson in the mid-nineteenth century that American poetry began to rival European national poetries in originality and literary significance. Until Whitman and Dickinson, American poets were generally paler imitations of their English counterparts, and few of them thought of seeking an original language or form in which to express themselves.

The term "American poetry" is itself something of an oxymoron, juxtaposing the idea of "America" as a new-found land of pure potential and the concept of "poetry," a literary genre defined over hundreds of years of European civilization. One of the central projects for American poets – from the seventeenth-century Puritans to the twentieth-century modernists – was to determine their relation to English and other European poetic traditions. In his 1825 "Lectures on Poetry," William Cullen Bryant argued against the attempt to formulate a new poetic language for American poetry: "If a new language were to arise among us in our present condition of society, I fear that it would derive too many of its words from the roots used to signify canals, railroads, and steamboats." Even as late as 1891, Walt Whitman declared in his provocatively titled essay "American National Literature: Is There Such a Thing – Or Can There Ever Be?" that "the United States do not so far utter poetry, first-rate literature, or any of the so-call'd arts, to any lofty admiration or advantage."

Writing in an inherited language but on a new continent, American poets have always been forced to make difficult decisions about language, form, and subject matter. The poet in England, France, Germany, or Italy has a lineage established throughout the centuries by the corpus of "great works" that constitutes the "canon" of a national literature. In England, for example, a twentieth-century poet could look back through the work of Victorians like Robert Browning and Matthew Arnold to the poetry of Romantics like William Wordsworth and John Keats, and from there back to the even more firmly established canon of John Milton, William Shakespeare, and Geoffrey Chaucer. American poets lack such an easily identifiable canon: with the exception of Whitman and Dickinson, there were few poets before the twentieth century who could serve as important models for modern and contemporary writers.

What, then, is the significance of tradition for American poets? On the one hand, American poetry is formulated as a rejection of the tradition of self-consciously literary writing associated with English poetry. Whitman exemplified this anti-traditional stance, calling for a "national, idiomatic" poetry free from the "genteel laws" of Anglo-European verse. On the other hand, tradition can function as a chosen lineage for an American poet in which he or she can discover sources of inspiration and the presence of kindred spirits. We often speak of a Whitmanic tradition (open, democratic, celebratory), a Poundian tradition (modernist, experimental) or a Dickinsonian tradition (woman-centered, personal, formal), using these terms as a shorthand for an entire stance toward the writing of poetry.

American poetry has a complex heritage, deriving from both literary and popular sources. If the roots of American poetry can be found in Puritan meditative writing, eighteenth-century verse satire, and the Romantic lyric, they can equally well be discovered in slave songs, captivity narratives, and Protestant hymns. Lacking a ready-made literary tradition, American poets have gone far and wide in search of their influences and inspirations. Whitman sought material for his poetry in popular oratory, journalism, and street slang. The modernists found sources in Egyptian mythology, the Hindu Upanishads, and Chinese ideograms. More recently, eclectic sources have become the norm rather than the exception, as poets have found inspiration for their work in various forms of music (jazz, blues, rap), in the visual arts (Abstract Expressionism, Pop Art), and in alternative philosophical and spiritual traditions (Zen Buddhism, Native American mythology).

Poetry in America has rarely been granted the cultural importance it enjoys in countries such as England, France, and Germany. For this reason, as Roy Harvey Pearce observed, the American poet has always felt a compulsion "to justify his existence as poet."[2] Poetry, at least as it is traditionally conceived, deals with the imagination, the emotions, and the appreciation of beauty rather than with a realistic treatment of everyday life. Americans have tended to view the novel, rather than poetry, as the literary genre best suited to the experience of a newer, more pragmatically minded nation. The familiar model of the young writer setting out to write the "Great American Novel" (never the "Great American Poem") is emblematic of this fact. In American literary life, novelists are the celebrated "stars" of the profession while poets are too often relegated to the cultural sidelines.

In many cases, Americans have failed even to recognize the genius of their own best poets. Whitman, later embraced as "America's Bard" and the "Good Gray Poet," was throughout most of his life villified by critics, shunned by his fellow writers, and excluded from contemporary anthologies. Dickinson – profoundly misunderstood even by those closest to her – published only a handful of poems during her lifetime and did not receive a complete edition of her work until nearly seventy years after her death. William Carlos Williams, now recognized as one of the leaders of the modernist movement and one of the central poets of the first half of the twentieth century, was underappreciated and rarely taught until the 1960s. Even Wallace Stevens, now probably more secure in his literary status than any other American poet of this century, was generally regarded during his lifetime as a quirky literary eccentric rather than a major poet. In fact, apart from T. S. Eliot, it is difficult to think of an American poet of the past two centuries whose reputation has not at some point fallen undeservedly low.

With the passage of time, it becomes easier to make definitive judgments about the relative importance of different poets. We can now say with some assurance that Whitman and Dickinson are the two centrally important American poets of the nineteenth century. That is, while it is still possible that a currently underrated poet will rise in our critical estimation, there is general consensus on the part of most poets, critics, and readers about the unique literary value of Dickinson's and Whitman's poems. In the first half of the twentieth century, such critical consensus becomes somewhat more difficult, though there is still a relatively small group of poets who dominate critical discussions of American poetic modernism. There may be admirers of Stevens and Frost who think less highly of the work of Pound and Eliot, and vice versa, but by and large the study of modernist American poetry has focused on a "canon" of five or six central poets.

As we approach the present day, however, there is far less consensus about who the major poets are. It is still difficult at this juncture to refer to a "canon" of postwar American poetry, although poets like Robert Lowell, Elizabeth Bishop, and John Ashbery would certainly come close to qualifying. Not only are there more poets writing and publishing than ever before, but there is also a far more diverse mix of poetic subcultures dividing the available attention of readers. No other country has produced a comparable range of poetry by writers with a greater diversity of backgrounds. Each region of the country celebrates its own school of poets, as does each ethnic and racial group. Poetry anthologies are now devoted to African American poetry, Latino poetry, Asian American poetry, and Native American poetry. Poets of other ethnic identities – including Italian American, Jewish American, and Arab American – are celebrated for their alternative visions of American life, and poetic groupings are made on the basis of such factors as sexual preference and life and work experience (Vietnam veterans, prisoners, children of Holocaust survivors) as well as stylistic and formal considerations (formalist poetry, experimental poetry, mainstream lyric poetry, spoken-word poetry, visual poetry). Although no introductory guide of this length can do justice to both the range and the artistic achievement of American poetry in the twentieth century, my goal in this book has been to include a broad enough spectrum of poets to demonstrate the diversity of American poetic writing, while still providing a useful guide to the achievements of individual poets.

Chapter 1

A new century: from the genteel poets to Robinson and Frost

With the deaths of both Walt Whitman and John Greenleaf Whittier in 1892, an era in American poetry came to a close. Practically the entire generation which had defined American poetry in the latter half of the nineteenth century was now gone, such grey eminences as Ralph Waldo Emerson, Henry Wadsworth Longfellow, and James Russell Lowell having passed away in the preceeding decade. Yet if the major American poets of the nineteenth century had departed, the first important generation of twentieth-century poets was still far from its maturity. Edwin Arlington Robinson was an undergraduate student at Harvard, four years away from publishing his first book of verse; Robert Frost was two years away from his first published poem and over two decades from his first volume; and Wallace Stevens was a thirteen-year-old schoolboy, three decades from the publication of his first book.

The years from 1880 to 1910 were something of a dark age for American poetry. During a time when the novels of Mark Twain, Henry James, William Dean Howells, Theodore Dreiser, Stephen Crane, and Edith Wharton established the undeniable importance of American fiction, poetry was pushed to the margins of the literary world. Not able to compete with novelists in terms of popularity, and not willing to risk moving beyond the familiar models of nineteenth-century verse, poets settled for an uncontroversial mediocrity of idea, form, and rhetoric. As Ezra Pound later put it in his harshly critical appraisal of the era, it was a time of "pseudo-artists" working under a stultifying system of control by the major publishers. Indeed, under the editorial reign of the large-circulation magazines that published poetry – such as *Harper's*, *The Century*, and *The Atlantic* – the prevailing poetic style progressed little between the 1870s and the early 1910s. There was no room in America for a poet who sought to become, in Pound's terms, a "serious artist."

In order to embark on a modern poetic career, poets like Frost, Pound and T. S. Eliot would be obliged to go abroad. To a great extent, as David Perkins has suggested, it was still London and not New York or Boston that served as the cultural capital of the United States: it was the poems of the London avant-garde and not those of the American magazines that "commanded the attention of American literary undergraduates."[1] Still more provocative for young Americans was the literature of France, including the fiction of Gustave Flaubert and Emile Zola, the essays of Théophile Gautier, and the poems of Charles Baudelaire, Paul Verlaine, Arthur Rimbaud, and Stéphane Mallarmé.

However, the number of American poets of the period who looked to the contemporary literature of London or Paris for inspiration was still relatively small. On the whole, younger poets embraced the dominant poetic mode of the American "genteel tradition." The genteel poets – whom E. A. Robinson called the "little sonnet men" and Whitman derided as the "tea-pot poets" – wrote sonnets, odes, and dramatic monologues in imitation of English Victorian poetry, expressing what Pound would characterize as "nice domestic sentiments inoffensively versified." According to Henry Adams – one of the more astute cultural commentators of his day – poetry had become so artificial and removed from social reality that it no longer served as a "natural expression of society itself."[2] Instead, poetry now functioned both as a refuge from contemporary society – with its growing cities, massive immigration, capitalist greed, and political corruption – and as a reaction against the realist and naturalist fiction that attempted to depict that society.

The most prominent of the genteel poets were those of the so-called "Harvard School," which included George Santayana, William Vaughan Moody, Trumbull Stickney, and George Cabot Lodge. The Harvard poets were an extremely cultivated and erudite group: Santayana was a Harvard professor and one of the most prominent American philosophers of his day; Moody taught literature at both Harvard and the University of Chicago; Stickney was the first American ever to earn a doctorate in letters from the Sorbonne in Paris; Lodge, the son of the prominent United States senator Henry Cabot Lodge, studied Schopenhauer in Berlin as well as classics and Romance languages in Paris. Cultivated as they were, however, these poets displayed little true originality; they were, as Larzer Ziff suggests, a school of poets "held in suspension," still tied to past models and unable to articulate a viable American poetics for the next century.[3] Though they were skilled versifiers, the Harvard poets had nothing new to say: as a result, their poems quickly fell into a relative obscurity.

The Harvard poets were dedicated to what they considered a "balanced" attitude in art and literature and to an avoidance of all extremes. While they respected Whitman, they did not attempt to imitate the power of his style. Instead, they emulated the dominant style of Victorian poetry: earnest, traditional, elegiac, formally crafted, and often highly sentimental. Santayana's most famous poem, the sonnet "O World, thou choosest not the better part" (1894) concludes with the following lines:

> Our knowledge is a torch of smoky pine
> That lights the pathway but one step ahead
> Across a void of mystery and dread.
> Bid, then, the tender light of faith to shine
> By which alone the mortal heart is led
> Unto the thinking of the thought divine.

The metaphor of human or worldly knowledge as a smoky torch unable to light the way through life is quite effective, but the overall power of the image is weakened by the sentimental language and the artificial syntax of the subsequent lines. Constructions such as "void of mystery and dread," "the tender light of faith," and "the thinking of the thought divine" express what were relatively hackneyed ideas by the end of the nineteenth century.

Edwin Arlington Robinson

Robinson was born in 1869, making him the oldest of the American poets who successfully made the transition into the twentieth century. Robinson's poetry was, as the poet Louise Bogan later observed in an essay entitled "Tilbury Town and Beyond" (1931), "one of the hinges upon which American poetry was able to turn from the sentimentality of the nineties toward modern veracity and psychological truth." Robinson's poetic output was considerable, and not all of it was of the highest quality, but his best poems are masterpieces of concision and rhetoric. Though he is often ignored in discussions of modern American poetry, Robinson was certainly America's most important poet during the period from the 1890s until the mid-1910s.

Robinson grew up in Gardiner, Maine, which became the model for "Tilbury Town," the fictional setting of many of his poems. Though he spent two years at Harvard University in the early 1890s, Robinson never became part of the Harvard School of poets. Instead, he returned to Gardiner after the death of his father and began to write the poems that would eventually be published in *The Torrent and the Night Before* (1896) and *The Children of the Night* (1897). Robinson had a difficult, lonely, and depressing life, which surely contributed to the underlying pessimism of his poetry. A keenly sensitive individual (born "with my skin inside out," as he liked to say), Robinson experienced neither love nor marriage. He suffered from chronic mastoiditis, a painful malady that ultimately left him deaf in one ear. Further, his family was highly dysfunctional: his father died bankrupt, leaving him in desperate financial straits and obliging him to take a series of demeaning jobs; one of his brothers was addicted to morphine and another to alcohol. Robinson's own road to poetic success was a long and hard one, and it was not until his poems were discovered by President Theodore Roosevelt in 1905 that he began to be recognized as an important poet. The townspeople of Gardiner on whom his poems are based appear to have suffered from many of the same problems as Robinson himself: suicide, alcoholism, tragic loneliness, and a general sense of failure and unfulfilled promise.

While he was an admirer of Wordsworth, Robinson was by no means a nature poet. Commenting on the hackneyed natural imagery of most contemporary verse, he wrote to a friend in 1896 that his first volume contained "very little tinkling water, and . . . not a red-bellied robin in the whole collection." Instead, Robinson was interested in the personal histories of the people he encountered, and in using these portraits to reflect the hypocrisy and spiritual void of his times. In Robinson's most famous poem, "Richard Cory" (1897), we find one of his characteristically ironic portrayals. A paragon of material success, admired and envied by the towns-people, Cory went home one "one calm summer night" and "put a bullet through his head." The ironies here are verbal as well as dramatic: the language used to describe the town's adulation of its first citizen ("imperially slim" and "admirably schooled in every grace") is undercut by the sudden and unadorned description of Cory's suicide.

Robinson established his career with his next three volumes: *Captain Craig* (1902), *The Town Down the River* (1910), and *The Man Against the Sky* (1916). While he was also skilled at longer narrative poems in blank verse, such as "Isaac and Archibald" (1902), Robinson's fame rests on his shorter, metrically formal lyrics. A poem like "Miniver Cheevy" (1910) uses both its metrical form and allusions to classical, medieval, and renaissance life for highly ironic effect, anticipating the ironic use of stanzaic form by modernists like Pound and Eliot. The poem's first stanza introduces the subject of the portrait in brilliantly understated fashion:

> Miniver Cheevy, child of scorn,
> Grew lean while he assailed the seasons;
> He wept that he was ever born,
> And he had reasons.

The final line of the stanza, with its anticlimactic five beat rhythm and its deflatingly colloquial turn of phrase, presents an ironic contrast to the exaggeratedly dramatic presentation of Cheevy in the first three lines. After the somewhat enigmatic first line (what exactly is a "child of scorn"?) and the hyperbolic diction of the second ("assailed the seasons") we find the melodramatic cliché of "He wept that he was ever born" (a line that may also reflect the reality of Robinson's own worldview). Robinson also uses sound very effectively here, repeating certain vowels as a means of further diminishing the self-importance of Cheevy. The "ee" sound, repeated through "Cheevy," "lean," "he," "seasons," "he," "he," and "reasons," emphasizes the narrow and somewhat pitiful circumstances of Cheevy's life.

The poem's ending, however, catches the reader by surprise with a final note of grim authenticity:

> Miniver Cheevy, born too late,
>   Scratched his head and kept on thinking,
> Miniver coughed, and called it fate,
>   And kept on drinking.

Here the final line is used with devastating skill to complete the portrait of Cheevy, who is not only a dreamer but an alcoholic. The rhyme of "thinking" and "drinking" – again playing with the thin vowel sounds of Miniver's name – encapsulates the difference between what Cheevy is and what he would like to be.

"Eros Turannos" (1913) is another quintessential Robinson poem. Its title, meaning "The Tyrant Love," refers to the situation of a woman in an unhappy marriage from which she cannot escape.

> She fears him, and will always ask
>   What fated her to choose him;
> She meets in his engaging mask
>   All reasons to refuse him;
> But what she meets and what she fears
> Are less than are the downward years,
> Drawn slowly to the foamless weirs
>   Of age, were she to lose him.

"Eros Turannos" is Robinson's most important poem, and one of the greatest American lyrics of the first two decades of the century. Like "Miniver Cheevy," the poem presents a protagonist who is a failure and who lives in isolation from the community as a whole; but here the portrait is sympathetic rather than ironic. While the poem's speaker is still distanced from his subject, the woman is memorialized and universalized (she is never given a name in the poem) rather than ironized or satirized.

In the first stanza we find the basic portrait of the wife, a genteel and sensitive woman now advancing in years, who may have been based on the wife of Robinson's brother. The wife is torn in a tragic dilemma between two fears: that of her husband and that of her old age "were she to lose him." The last two lines of the stanza introduce the image of "foamless weirs of age"; with this metaphor comparing the inevitable entry into a lonely old age to a slow drifting into a weir (a kind of fence placed across a river to catch fish), Robinson widens his scope to include the symbolic aspect of the situation. The figurative language, rhymes, and stanzaic structure all work to memorialize the figure of the woman. The initial rhyme of "ask" and "mask" presents the theme of communication denied, and the heavy rhyme of "fears," "years," and "weirs" emphasizes the sadness and isolation of the protagonist.

Each stanza functions somewhat like a chapter in a short novel or a scene in a tragic drama. In the second stanza we learn two further reasons for the woman's acceptance of the situation: her pride (she refuses to discuss her situation with the townspeople) and the fact that love blurs the perception of her husband's weaknesses. The third stanza moves to the perspective of the complacent husband, who is so enveloped by "a sense of ocean and old trees" and by "tradition" (perhaps the New England tradition of a cold and passionless marriage) that he fails to take note of his wife's suffering. In the powerful fourth stanza, Robinson again uses natural images to capture the psychological state of the woman:

> The falling leaf inaugurates
>   The reign of her confusion.
> The pounding wave reverberates
>   The dirge of her illusion;
> And home, where passion lived and died,
> Becomes a place where she can hide,
> While all the town and harbor side
>   Vibrate with her seclusion.

While the husband is reassured by the trees and ocean that encircle their private lives, the wife sees the "falling leaves" as indicating the inexorable passage of time and hears the ocean waves only as a "dirge." The elevated language of the stanza – relying heavily on latinate diction – sets off the moving simplicity of the fifth and sixth lines, "And home, where passion lived and died / Becomes a place where she can hide."

In the final two stanzas, the poem moves outside the home to include the townspeople, who act as a kind of Greek chorus to comment on the situation. The "we" of stanza V suggests the pressure of the public world on the private self, as the town tries to understand the woman's predicament:

> We tell you, tapping on our brows,
>   The story as it should be, –
> As if the story of a house
>   Were told, or ever could be;

Neither the townspeople nor the poet can tell the "real" story of a house and its inhabitants; they can only tell a fictional version of it, "the story as it should be." The poem ends with a series of similes comparing the state of marriage to various natural images. Only in the final comparison does Robinson express his pessimistic vision of marital love:

> Though like waves breaking it may be
> Or like a changed familiar tree,
> Or like a stairway to the sea
>   Where down the blind are driven.

Robinson's language remains old-fashioned in comparison with that of Frost or Stevens, and the syntax of his lines lacks the natural fluidity of Frost's best writing, yet there is a rare power in these lines. In the first line, a spondee in the second foot interrupts the iambic beat of the meter, imitating a wave breaking on the coast; in the final line, the inverted syntax works to enhance the image of being driven blindly down a stairway to the rough sea.

Robert Frost

If Robinson brought American poetry into the twentieth century, it was his fellow New Englander Robert Frost who would make the decisive break from the inflated style of Victorian and genteel poetry. Where Robinson's poems remain highly "literary" in their diction and syntax, Frost adopts the idiosyncratic, colloquial, and locally inflected voice of the New England farmer. Where Robinson made brilliant use of sound and meter to emphasize the meanings of his poems, Frost articulated a more theoretical formulation of the connection between sound and meaning.

In his most famous critical formulation, Frost advocated what he called the "sound of sense," by which he meant that poetry should communicate through its sound even before we grasp its semantic meaning. He wrote to his friend John Bartlett in 1913 that the best way to hear the sound of sense is to listen to "voices behind a door that cut off the words." If a poet can succeed in capturing this "abstract vitality of speech," the specific denotation of the words is less important than the way the language moves to the "mind's ear."

Frost also applied the "sound of sense" to the use of poetic meter. For Frost, the poetry in a line comes not from fitting words into the preexisting metrical structure, but from "skillfully breaking the sounds of sense with all their irregularity of accent across the regular beat of the meter." In this way, the poem can be made to sound natural (or at least as natural as any transcription of actual speech) at the same time that it achieves the heightened musical quality of lyric. Frost's theory allowed him to introduce a rural New England dialect that had never been used in poetry before, and it made possible the use of flexible rhythms within a regular metrical structure.

Like Robinson, Frost had a difficult early life. He was born in San Francisco in 1874, but his impulsive and alcoholic father died in 1885 at the age of thirty-four and the family moved to Lawrence, Massachusetts. Frost entered Dartmouth College in 1892 but dropped out after one semester; five years later he was able to enter Harvard as a special student, but once again withdrew before completing his education. On the advice of his doctor, Frost bought a farm in Derry, New Hampshire, hoping the country air would benefit his health. But providing for himself and his growing family as a chicken farmer (supplemented by a small bequest from his grandfather) was a constant struggle. As a result of the constant shortage of money and the isolation of rural life, Frost at times contemplated suicide. Frost spent eleven years in Derry, engaging in many of the activities described in his poems: mowing fields, mending walls, hiking, blueberrying, and cutting wood. The authenticity of this outdoor experience was itself to make him a very different poet from his more "genteel" contemporaries. He rejected the insipid romanticism of most American verse of the time, and he set out to write a poetry more grounded in the reality of rural life and the immediacy of its spoken language. As a result of Frost's unconventional approach, his poetry was not easily accepted in his own country. By the age of thirty-eight, he had yet to publish a book of his verse and had succeeded in placing only a few of his poems in magazines. Frost decided to move to England, where he felt his poetry might find greater acceptance.

With the help of Ezra Pound, already part of the English literary scene, Frost was able to gain access to London literary circles and place *A Boy's Will* with an English press: it was published in London in 1913. *North of Boston* appeared the following year, and when Frost returned to America in 1915 he arranged for the book's American publication. Frost's third volume, *Mountain Interval*, came out in 1916, firmly establishing him as one of the foremost American poets of his generation.

Though Frost went on to publish many more books of poetry and remained one of America's most widely read and admired poets until his death in 1963, this chapter will focus on the poems of the first three volumes. It was during the brief moment from 1913 to 1916 – before the emergence of a full-blown modernist movement – that Frost's most significant impact on American poetry was to be felt.

Frost's relationship to the modernist movement in American poetry was a rather distant one: his friendship with Pound lasted only a few weeks and he hardly knew Eliot or Williams. Frost ridiculed the route of modernist experimentation followed by Pound, Eliot, Williams, and Cummings, preferring to adhere to more traditional forms of poetry. During his stay in England,

Frost explicitly rejected the tenets of Imagism, the movement often seen as the inaugural phase of Anglo-American literary modernism. Though both Pound and F. S. Flint, another of the leaders of the Imagist movement, responded enthusiastically to *A Boy's Will* when it appeared in April 1913, and Pound encouraged Frost to write his next book in free verse, Frost decided by the summer of 1914 that he was most interested in cultivating "the hearing imagination" rather than "the kind that merely sees things." Frost's characterization of Imagism as concerned exclusively with the visual was clearly an oversimplification – given the fact that Pound's Imagist tenets included prescriptions for the use of sound and rhythm as well as the treatment of the visual object – but it allowed Frost to distance himself from what was happening in the poetic avant-garde and thus to formulate his own poetic theories.

Frost's poetry differed from that of the modernists in several respects: in its adherence to a traditional formalism (as opposed to the formal dislocations and direct challenges to conventional forms found in much modernist writing); in the ordinariness and rustic simplicity of its subject matter; in its resolutely narrative quality; and in its lack of what modernists like Eliot, Stevens, or Crane might consider the transformative power of the poetic imagination. Stevens, for example, denigrated Frost for writing poems about "things," suggesting that Frost's poems remained too closely attached to a description of the real world as we perceive it rather than attempting to transform or transcend our everyday experience of that world.

The chief hallmark of Frost's style, particularly in the early volumes, is its simplicity. Frost tends to use a plain and idiomatic language marked by a lack of multisyllable words, a relative avoidance of formal or literary diction, and a generally straightforward syntax. Words of Latinate or Romance origin, which generally indicate a formality, abstractness or ornateness of diction, are relatively uncommon in Frost's poems. Frost also uses a highly colloquial style, avoiding words that would seem unusual or unnatural in actual speech and attempting instead to duplicate the rhythm and syntax of speech. Frost claimed the simplicity of his language as one of the great virtues of his poetry, boasting that he had "dropped to an everyday level of diction that even Wordsworth kept above." If we look at the word choice in a poem like "Mending Wall" (1914), one of Frost's most famous lyrics, we see what he means by an "everyday level of diction."

> Something there is that doesn't love a wall,
> That sends the frozen-ground-swell under it,
> And spills the upper boulders in the sun;
> And makes gaps even two can pass abreast.
> The work of hungers is another thing:
> I have come after them and made repair

Where they have left not one stone on a stone,
But they would have the rabbit out of hiding,
To please the yelping dogs. The gaps I mean,
No one has seen them made or heard them made,
But at spring mending-time we find them there.
I let my neighbor know beyond the hill;
And on a day we meet to walk the line
And set the wall between us once again.
We keep the wall between us as we go.
To each the boulders that have fallen to each.
And some are loaves and some so nearly balls
We have to use a spell to make them balance:
"Stay where you are until our backs are turned!"
We wear our fingers rough with handling them.
Oh, just another kind of outdoor game,
One on a side. It comes to little more:
There where it is we do not need the wall:
He is all pine and I am apple orchard.
My apple trees will never get across
And eat the cones under his pines, I tell him,
He only says, "Good fences make good neighbors."
Spring is the mischief in me, and I wonder
If I could put a notion into his head:
"Why do they make good neighbors? Isn't it
Where there are cows? But here there are no cows.
Before I built a wall I'd ask to know
What I was walling in or walling out,
And to whom I was like to give offense.
Something there is that doesn't love a wall,
That wants it down." I could say "Elves" to him,
But it's not elves exactly, and I'd rather
He said it for himself. I see him there
Bringing a stone grasped firmly by the top
In each hand, like an old-stone savage armed.
He moves in darkness as it seems to me,
Not of woods only and the shade or trees.
He will not go behind his father's saying,
And he likes having thought of it so well
He says again, "Good fences make good neighbors."

The poem is filled with concrete descriptive words that provide a simple and easily comprehensible picture of the scene being presented: wall, ground, boulders, gaps, hunters, stone, dogs, spring, neighbor, hill, line, cones, pines, loaves, balls, fingers, game, fences, apple, orchard, trees, cows, elves, woods, shade. None of these nouns presents any difficulty for the reader; none requires the use of a dictionary or presents a challenging ambiguity of meaning. On the level of word length, we find a striking preponderance of monosyllabic words and a total absence of words of more than two syllables. A line composed entirely of monosyllables such as line 7 – "Where they have left not one stone on a stone" – would have been considered ungraceful, perhaps even unpoetic, by the accepted literary standards of the day, but it sounds fresher to our ears today than many of the overburdened lines of Tennyson or Swinburne.

Furthermore, there is an unusual amount of repetition of the words and phrases Frost uses: "wall" occurs no less than six times (not including the participle "walling"); "stone" occurs four times; "neighbor(s)" is used three times; and "gaps," "spring," "boulders," "fences," "trees," "apple," "pine," "cows," and "elves" twice each. The opening line, "Something there is that doesn't love a wall," is repeated, as is the phrase "Good fences make good neighbors." Clearly, the effect of repetition is important to the theme of the poem (the idea of doubling, dividing, or opposition symbolized by the wall) but the repetition also serves to emphasize the simplicity and clarity of Frost's vocabulary, a vocabulary that seems extremely limited in comparison with that of poets like Stevens, Pound, Eliot, or Crane. The simple language of the poem is established from the very first line: as Marie Borroff suggests, rewriting the line as "There exists an antipathy toward barriers" would create an entirely different expectation for the language and tone of the poem.[4]

Frost's use of syntax also contributes to this feeling of simplicity and colloquialism. In the opening line, the use of the contraction "doesn't" introduces a colloquial style that is in marked contrast to the self-consciously poetic style of most post-Victorian poetry; Frost's use of contractions continues in phrases such as "Isn't it where there are cows?" "I'd ask to know," and "it's not elves exactly." This colloquial, conversational style is typified by the fifth line, "The work of hunters is another thing." Here we have a feeling of a speaker addressing the reader directly and sharing his thoughts, rather than a poet trying to elevate his language to the most refined level. The reader is pulled into the poem and made to feel comfortable in a way not possible with the poems of Santayana and the other "genteel" poets. This impression is heightened at moments when Frost appears to interrupt the flow of his own thoughts and clarify something he has previously said, much as one might do in actual speech. "The gaps I mean," at the end of line 9, pulls us gently back from the digression about hunters and returns us to the main thread of the poem, at the same time reminding us that someone is speaking. The predominance of sentences constructed around simple connectives ("and" and "but") also suggests the presence of an actual speaker rather than a more distanced and controlling authorial voice. Eight of the poem's lines begin with "And" and another three begin with "But," giving the impression of a speaker spontaneously working through his thoughts and establishing connections even as he speaks the poem. The alternation of simple declarative sentences that fit cleanly within the line and sentences that are made to spill over several lines not only keeps the poem's syntax relatively simple, but it also makes the poem more rhythmically interesting. On a thematic level, this alternation also reenacts the fate of the wall itself, which is built and rebuilt only to be toppled over by hunters or the forces of nature.

Despite all of these examples of colloquialism and apparent simplicity in Frost's poetry, we should not be deceived into thinking of Frost as a rustic or a primitive. On the contrary, Frost was a sophisticated writer who was well versed in Latin poetry and who knew as well as any poet of his time how to make effective use of formal and rhetorical strategies. From his early career on, Frost prided himself on being "one of the most notable craftsmen of my time," as he wrote in his 1913 letter to John Bartlett. Frost's style is dualistic rather than simplistic: he uses the poetic form to hold thematic dualities in ironic tension, while at the same time using formal devices to create tensions or ironies within the language of the poem. Frost is a master at embedding rhetorical devices within apparently simple poems, making effective use of punning and word play, repetition, prosody (the use of rhythm and meter), and metaphor.

In "Mending Wall" for example, Frost skillfully highlights the relation between form and content. We have already seen this relation established through his use of repetition and syntax, but it is also apparent in his prosody. Throughout the poem, lines in blank verse (unrhymed iambic pentameter) play both within and against the metrical and structural impositions of the form. In the opening lines, the speaker's energies disturb formal walls and boundaries: here, we find enjambment (run-on lines) and caesura (breaks within the line), as well as metrical variations which contribute to the theme of the lines. The poem begins with a trochaic substitution ("Something") and contains spondees is lines 2, 4, and 7, emphasizing the powerful destructive forces at work on the wall. Frost uses his versification to create subtle tensions between form and idea, as for example when he uses the enjambment between lines 6 and 7 to break his description of repairing the wall destroyed by hunters: "and made repair / Where they have left not one stone on a stone." But in the lines where Frost describes the annual ritual of rebuilding the wall with his neighbor, the rhythms become more consistently iambic and the lines more often end-stopped. Just as the speaker of the poem describes the act of wall-mending as "another kind of outdoor game," Frost plays a little game with the reader, replicating the changing state of the wall within the form of the poem itself.

Frost also embeds a substantial amount of figurative language in the poem, though he does so in such as way as to make the figures of speech seem rustic and natural rather than abstruse and literary. He refers metaphorically to the wall's stones as "loaves" and "balls"; he uses metonymy to compare the respective orchards with their owners – "He is all pine and I am apple orchard"; he jokingly personifies the apple trees – "My apple trees will never get across / And eat the cones under his pines"; and he uses a simile to compare his somewhat primitive neighbor to "an old-stone savage armed." Only in the final figure of the poem does Frost move to a level of symbolic ambiguity: "He moves in darkness as it seems to me, / Not of woods only and the shade of trees." Frost remains deliberately vague about exactly what this "darkness" is, though we can gather that it is the darkness of a confining tradition ("his father's saying") and the resultant lack of the neighbor's capacity for play or imagination.

The difference between the two men in the poem lies in the fact that while the neighbor participates in the wall's construction only as a necessary and repetitive chore, the speaker (a version of Frost himself) uses it as an occasion for imaginative play. The narrator does not mind building the wall, but it is clear that his sympathies lie more with the "something" that wants it down (whether elves, nature, or his own sense of "mischief") than with the neighbor's unthinking need to repair it. The neighbor is an "old-stone savage" not because he wants to maintain the wall between them, but because he can think of no reason for doing so other than his father's proverb. The poem is in part an allegory for the poetic process itself: as a poet, Frost needs to keep himself open to all forms of experience, and he must be constantly vigilant about what he is "walling in or walling out." The physical wall in the poem is a wall of the psyche, a barrier to human understanding, connection, and communication.

Frost was a nature poet, but not in the naively romantic sense of a poet who celebrates the beauty or pastoral simplicity of nature. Instead, he uses the rural world as a source of emblems and symbols, creating *paysages moralisés* through the use of complex images and extended metaphors. Frost, who in later life described himself as "a confirmed symbolist," could find in almost any natural or man-made object an apt symbol, or emblem, for a more general idea. Such emblems include the scythe in "Mowing," the wall in "Mending Wall," the apple tree in "After Apple-Picking," the woodpile in "The Wood-Pile," the burnt-down farmhouse in "The Need of Being Versed in Country Things," the trees in "Birches," the pitchfork in "Putting in the Seed," the well in "For Once, Then, Something," and the isolated woods in "Stopping by Woods on a Snowy Evening."

As an illustration of the way in which Frost used such symbols from the pastoral landscape to comment on more universal human concerns, let us look at "Birches" (1916), another of Frost's most deservedly famous poems. The poem opens with a series of strong visual images suggesting that Frost was as deeply engaged with the visual imagination as with the auditory "sound of sense":

> When I see birches bend to left and right
> Across the lines of straighter darker trees,
> I like to think some boy's been swinging them.
> But swinging doesn't bend them down to stay
> As ice-storms do. Often you must have seen them
> Loaded with ice a sunny winter morning
> After a rain. They click upon themselves
> As the breeze rises, and turn many-colored
> As the stir cracks and crazes their enamel.

"Birches" is more elegiac and less playful in tone than "Mending Wall," and while it retains the conversational voice of a first-person speaker its language is somewhat more elevated and less colloquial. According to Frank Lentricchia, it was in "Birches" that Frost began "to probe the power of his redemptive imagination," moving from playfulness toward transcendence.[5] The birch trees, with their brilliant white bark and pliable trunks that "bend to left and right," are contrasted in the first two lines with the "straighter darker trees" that form a kind of mysterious background behind them. Unlike birches, which can be manipulated by men (and boys) as well as the forces of nature, these straight and dark trees are a somewhat ominous presence which resists human interpretation. In lines 3–5, Frost introduces a second opposition: between the actions of boys swinging on birches (bending them temporarily but not putting them "down to stay") and the power of a natural force, the ice-storm. Frost appeals to the reader to imagine with him the sight of the trees "loaded with ice" and the sound of them "click[ing] upon themselves." So great is his appreciation of the scene that he aestheticizes the ice-covered trees by comparing them to a work of human creation: the cracking and crazing of the enamel on a piece of pottery. This comparison in turn takes the speaker to an even more dramatic image, as his imagination transforms the pieces of ice shed by the trees into "crystal shells," shards of "broken glass," and finally fragments of "the inner dome of heaven."

Even in these opening lines, we have already come far from an ordinary pastoral or natural landscape. The images and metaphors Frost chooses enact a fusion of the natural world and the realm of human artifice (pottery, glass, crystal, a cathedral dome), suggesting a possible transcendence of brute nature into an imaginative realm. But Frost cannot settle on a single symbolic register for the trees. The next three lines focus not on the transcendent beauty of the scene but on the oppressive weight of the ice:

> They are dragged to the withered bracken by the load,
> And they seem not to break, though once they are bowed
> So low for long, they never right themselves:

Here again, Frost makes skilled use of versification to enhance his description: the lines are lengthened (eleven and twelve syllables instead of ten) and they depart radically from the iambic meter of the opening lines. Frost uses sound to make us feel the heaviness of the ice-covered trees in the drawn-out vowels of words like "dragged," "bracken," "load," "bowed," and "low." The downward movement of these lines concludes with an evocative simile comparing the trailing branches of the trees to "girls on hands and knees that throw their hair / Before them over their heads."

As brilliant as these descriptions are, however, they are not the main point of Frost's poem, as the speaker goes on to explain:

> But I was going to say when Truth broke in
> With all her matter-of-fact about the ice-storm
> I should prefer to have some boy bend them
> As he went out and in to fetch the cows –
> Some boy too far from town to learn baseball,
> Whose only play was what he found himself,
> Summer and winter, and could play alone.

As in "Mending Wall," where Frost used the stone walls of rural New England to explore the more general idea of boundaries and borders in human life, here he uses the birches to create a complex symbolic landscape. Frost prefers the birches to the other trees because they are flexible enough to move in different directions: either "toward heaven," as he says near the end of the poem, or down to the earth. Frost also uses the pliable nature of the birch to suggest the form of his poem: he "swings" from one subject to another, moving from a description of ice-storms to a narrative of a boy bending the trees on his father's farm. The image of the farm-boy playing on the trees is clearly a vision of the poet as well. Like the boy, he works ("plays") in solitude, far from human society; just as the boy attempts to "subdue" and "conquer" his father's trees, the poet tries to bend and shape nature within an artistic form; just as the boy keeps his "poise" while climbing the tree, the poet focuses all his attention on his task; just as the boy swings out, "feet first, with a swish, / Kicking his way down through the air to the ground," the poet swings on an imaginative arc into a state of absolute freedom from earthly concerns.

But the speaker realizes that his "dream" of being a "swinger of birches" cannot always be realized:

> It's when I'm weary of considerations,
> And life is too much like a pathless wood
> Where your face burns and tickles with the cobwebs
> Broken across it, and one eye is weeping
> From a twig's having lashed it open.
> I'd like to get away from earth awhile
> And then come back to it and begin over.

Those transcendent moments of swinging on birches and creating poetry are unfortunately not the whole of life: there is also the mundane reality of "considerations," those details of everyday existence that seem to thwart our imaginative freedom. The simile comparing life to a "pathless wood" is hardly original, but Frost uses it very effectively to make us sympathize with his desire to "get away from earth awhile." The speaker's concerns are universal: we can all relate to the kind of setbacks and irritations represented by the cobwebs on the face and the twigs unexpectedly lashing the eye.

But despite these "considerations," the speaker does not choose to leave earth entirely; instead, he recognizes that "Earth's the right place for love." In the final lines of the poem, he returns to the birch once again in order to establish a balance between the groundedness of daily life and the dream of absolute freedom:

> I'd like to go by climbing a birch tree,
> And climb black branches up a snow-white trunk
> Toward heaven, till the tree could bear no more,
> But dipped its top and set me down again.
> That would be good both going and coming back,
> One could do worse than be a swinger of birches.

Frost ends the poem with typical understatement. After all, as he put it in "The Oven Bird," the question raised by poetry in the modern age is "what to make of a diminished thing." By "diminished thing," Frost means human life as we live it on a daily level, diminished from the romantic dreams of transcendence we all entertain at certain privileged moments. Frost never attempted to make of poetry the kind of epic quest for meaning sought by many other modern poets; as he stated in an essay "The Figure a Poem Makes" (1939), he preferred to set himself the more modest goal of finding in poetry a "momentary stay against confusion." If poetry "plays perilously between truth and make-believe," as Frost once wrote, he preferred to stay slightly to the side of "truth," allowing into his poems only as much "make-believe" as the creative act required.

Chapter 2

Modernist expatriates: Ezra Pound and T. S. Eliot

The poetry of Robinson and Frost suggested one possible direction for American poets in the twentieth century: a reworking of traditional lyric forms that would require no radical break from nineteenth-century poetic convention. In the eyes of some modern poets, however, the work of Frost and Robinson did not go far enough in the direction of a stylistic, formal, or conceptual breakthrough. Poets who participated in the poetic avant-garde of the 1910s and early 1920s, such as Ezra Pound, William Carlos Williams, T. S. Eliot, and Marianne Moore, saw the poetry of Robinson and Frost as merely continuing an outworn tradition of verse. For these self-declared "modernists," poetry needed to undergo the same kind of transformative process that was taking place in the other arts: cubism and collage in painting, chromaticism and atonality in music, and functionalism in architecture. Further, poetry had to reflect the reality of a rapidly changing modern world, a world which the works of Frost and Robinson in large part ignored. Though Pound had been supportive of Frost's early work, by 1915 he had lost interest in the kind of poetry Frost was writing.

The world had indeed changed a great deal since the end of the nineteenth century. First of all, there was the new urban landscape and the increasing speed of communication and transportation. The construction of bridges, skyscrapers, and factories was radically altering the American landscape, while the radio, the telephone, the trolley, the subway train, and the automobile were transforming American life. Though airplanes were not yet a viable means of transportation, the flights of the Wright brothers in 1903 ushered in a new era of aerial travel, while faster trains increased the convenience of intercity and interstate travel.

The changes in consciousness brought about by these new technologies, by a devastating world war, and by crucial developments in the fields of psychology, philosophy, and the natural sciences challenged many of the underlying assumptions of nineteenth-century thought. It was in Europe, and especially in London and Paris, that American poets first came into contact with the new ideas and artistic movements of the early century, such as symbolism, cubism, futurism, and expressionism. From the time Pound first arrived in London in 1908 until the publication of Eliot's *The*

Waste Land in 1922, there was a constant effort by American poets to absorb and put into practice the ideas of the European avant-garde. Gertrude Stein had become an expatriate writer even earlier, having settled in Paris in 1903. H. D. (Hilda Doolittle) arrived in London in 1912, and Eliot two years later. As Pound put it in a 1919 letter to William Carlos Williams, "London, deah old London, is the place for poesy."

Ezra Pound and the modernist image

In many ways, Ezra Pound epitomizes the avant-garde modernist poet: out-spoken, experimental, and fiercely iconoclastic. Pound had the most con-troversial career of any twentieth-century poet, and his overall place in American literature is more controversial than that of any other modernist. As a poet, a critic, and a promoter of other writers, Pound was central to the development of modernist poetry. T. S. Eliot, in dedicating his poem *The Waste Land* to Pound, called him "the better craftsman" ("*il miglior fabbro*"). Yet at the same time Pound was a literary vagabond who never felt entirely at home in any culture. Pound's restless energy led him to London in 1908, to Paris in 1920, and then to Rapallo, Italy, in 1925, where he would re-main until the end of World War II. An exile who embraced Italian Fascism during the war and who was later indicted for treason, Pound was unique among American writers in the extent of his involvement not only with the art and literature of his time, but also with the events of world history in the first half of the twentieth century.

Pound's comfortable early life in suburban Philadelphia and his education at Hamilton College and the University of Pennsylvania would have seemed to prepare him more for the traditional career of a man of letters than for that of a poetic revolutionary. In both college and graduate school, Pound studied Romance languages and literature: he was strongly drawn to the poetry of the Provençal troubadours, as well as to the work of Dante. He took a master of arts degree from the University of Pennsylvania in 1905, and the following year he won a fellowship for travel to Italy and Spain in preparation for a doctoral dissertation on the playwright Lope de Vega.

On his return from Europe, Pound took a post as an instructor of Romance Languages at Wabash College in Indiana. It was his dismissal from Wabash (on the grounds of having kept a young woman overnight in his rooms) that convinced Pound of his unsuitability for academic life. Pound used the rest of his year's salary to travel to Gibraltar and Venice, where he published his first volume of poetry, *A Lume Spento* (1908). This was soon followed by several more volumes: *A Quinzaine for This Yule* (1908), *Personae* (1909), *Exultations* (1909), and *Canzoni* (1911). Pound would later refer to the poems of these early books as "stale creampuffs," but it was through these poems, many of them either translations or imitations of other poets, that he perfected his craft and developed his fine ear for the rhythmic and tonal effects of poetry. Pound experimented in this early work with a wide range of poetic modes, including the dramatic monologue ("Cino"), the troubadour love song ("Na Audiart"), the poem of Ovidian metamorphosis ("The Tree"), the "Villonaud" (a form based on the work of Villon), the Yeatsian symbolist lyric ("The White Stag"), the sestina ("Sestina: Altaforte"), the ballad ("Ballad for the Goodly Fere"), the elegy ("Planh for the Young English King"), the Pre-Raphaelite portrait ("The House of Splendour"), and the verse parody ("Song in the Manner of Housman"). As a developing poet who had spent years training himself as a scholar of comparative literature, it was only natural that Pound's first instinct was to try out as many different styles as possible, imitating the work of great poets from the past before embarking on his own, more personalized poetic project. As opposed to poets like Frost and Robinson, Pound did not confine his reading to the English-language canon, but read widely in the poetry of Italian, Greek, Latin, Provençal, French, German, and later Chinese masters.

Soon after Pound's arrival in London in 1908, his association with the literary magazine *The New Age* brought him into contact with important writers, artists, and critics as well as economists and politicians. By 1912, when he published *Ripostes*, Pound had firmly established himself in London literary circles and had become an important figure in the artistic avant-garde. Along with two other expatriate poets, H. D. and Richard Aldington, Pound put in place a program for what he called "Imagism," a movement which would have several major tenets. The first of these was that the poem should always involve a "direct treatment of the thing," as opposed to the romanticized or symbolic treatment favored by nineteenth-century poets. Pound sought to avoid the vagueness or abstraction of much post-symbolist verse: "Don't use such an expression as 'dim lands of peace,' " he wrote in *Poetry* (March 1913). "It mixes an abstraction with the concrete. It comes from the writer's not realizing that the natural object is always the adequate symbol."

Pound's second rule was that the poem should use no word that was not absolutely necessary to its composition. Pound wanted to follow French prose writers like Gustave Flaubert and Guy de Maupassant in finding *le mot juste* (the right word) rather than adopting the overly wordy style of Victorian poets like Alfred Lord Tennyson and Algernon Swinburne. "Poetry should be as well written as prose," Pound wrote to poet and editor Harriet Monroe, "departing in no way from speech save by a heightened intensity (i.e. simplicity)." Most Imagist poems were short, offering the virtue of concision (and, it was hoped, precision) instead of the verbosity that had often been a substitute for careful writing in the work of the Victorian and

Georgian poets. The attention to the "image" would help the poet focus his language; rather than presenting a generalized poetic sentiment, the poet could create "an intellectual and emotional complex in an instant of time."

The third and final rule of Imagism was that poetry should be composed "in the sequence of the musical phrase" rather than that of the "metronome." Pound rejected what he considered the stifling constraint of monotonous pentameter rhythms. As Pound's collaborator Aldington put it in an essay entitled "Modern Poetry and the Imagists" (1914), the poet should seek "to create new rhythms – as the expression of new moods – and not to copy old rhythms, which merely echo old moods." Though the Imagists would not insist absolutely on the use of free verse, they felt strongly that free verse allowed a greater originality of expression than conventional metrical and stanzaic forms.

With these rules in place, Pound began his two-pronged initiative: both to "modernize" poetry in his own work, and to encourage the work of other poets – Eliot, William Carlos Williams, and H. D., for example – whom he believed capable of modern writing. Pound edited an anthology of Imagist verse, *Des Imagistes* (1915), which contained the work of H. D., Aldington, Yeats, and others. He also began writing a radically different kind of poetry which was at once more visual and more concise than his earlier work.

This change can easily be seen in Pound's most famous Imagist poem, "In a Station of the Metro" (1913):

> The apparition of these faces in the crowd;
> Petals on a wet, black bough.

Pound himself attached a good deal of importance to this brief poem as an exemplar of the Imagist method: he even supplied an explanatory account of its composition in an essay entitled "How I Began" (1913). On leaving the Paris metro one day, Pound claims, he saw a number of beautiful faces: the "sudden emotion" of seeing these faces against the backdrop of the metro station led him to an "equation . . . not in speech, but in little splotches of color." He proceeded to write a thirty-line poem, which he then cut in half, and then finally succeeded in compressing into one "hokku-like sentence." The "one-image poem" which resulted was "a form of super-position, that is to say, it is one idea set on top of another"; Pound attempted in the poem to record "the precise instant when a thing outward and objective transforms itself . . . into a thing inward and subjective." In his typically synthetic manner, Pound had managed something entirely new in poetry, bringing together the form of the Japanese haiku with an aesthetic theory taken from recent developments in the visual arts.

The success of Pound's poem depends not only on its single image – which strikingly links the natural world of petals and boughs with the modern urban environment of the metro station – but also on its highly effective use of sound and rhythm. The poem's verbal energy can be attributed to its forceful refusal of iambic meter – especially in the second line – and to its progression from the percussive consonants of "petals" to the three mono-syllables of "wet, black bough." The second line is as musically evocative as it is visually precise: the dense repetition of vowels and consonants here reinforces the visual effect of the image itself. As Hugh Kenner notes: "The words so raised by prosody to attention assert themselves *as words* . . . from which visual, tactile and mythic associations radiate."[1] The poem is a signifi-cant step in the development of modernist poetry. First of all, its compression was unprecedented: no English poem had been expected to carry so much meaning in so few words. Secondly, by simply juxtaposing two complex images without comment and leaving the reader to establish a relation be-tween them, the poem allows for an extremely open-ended set of possible meanings. As Kenner suggests, the crowd of passengers in the Paris under-ground can be related to the mythic underworld visited by Odysseus and Orpheus, and the word "apparition" in the first line can suggest phantoms as well as living people.

On the eve of World War I, however, Pound saw the limitations of the Imagist movement, which he felt had been coopted and sentimentalized by the poet Amy Lowell (who published several Imagist anthologies of her own). Along with the sculptor Henri Gaudier-Brzeska and the painter and novelist Wyndham Lewis, Pound helped found a new movement called Vorticism. The Vorticists encouraged a more dynamic approach to poetry, seeking the hardness and precision of sculpture rather than the static beauty of the image. The movement was to be short-lived – its journal *Blast* folded after two issues and Gaudier-Brzeska was killed in the war – but it added to Pound's growing reputation as a literary provocateur. Pound also established relationships with various journals – including *The Little Review*, *Poetry*, and *The Egoist* – and with other writers, including Eliot and Frost.

Another event that had a transforming influence on Pound's poetry and poetic ideas was his discovery of the manuscripts of Ernest Fenellosa, an American scholar who had lived in Japan and worked on the translation of Chinese and Japanese poetry. Fenellosa's notebooks and other manuscripts contained unpublished translations of Japanese Noh drama and Chinese poetry. Pound used the notebooks as a basis for his 1915 volume *Cathay*, a series of loose poetic adaptations of Chinese poems based on Fenellosa's notes. *Cathay* contained some of Pound's strongest work to date and rep-resented a new style of modern poem, one combining the simplicity and directness of Imagist poetics with the intense lyricism of the Chinese origi-nals. The most successful poems in *Cathay* – such as "The River Merchant's Wife: Letter," "Song of the Bowmen of Shu," "Lament of the Frontier

Guard," "Poem by the Bridge at Ten-Shin," and "Exile's Return" – achieve an effect unlike anything to be found in English poetry at the time.

"Song of the Bowmen of Shu" was based on a poem written by a Chinese general at the end of the Yin dynasty (1401–1121 B.C.), when the Emperor's troops were sent north to subdue the invasions of "barbarian" tribes. Pound was clearly aware of the parallel between the situation of the Chinese archers and the British soldiers in the battlefields of World War I: he sent the poem along with two others to Gaudier-Brzeska, who was stationed at the front. The poem begins with a direct presentation of the bowmen in idiomatic language and with understated emotion:

> Here we are, picking the first fern-shoots
> And saying: When shall we get back to our country?

The bowmen are isolated at the front and so hungry they are forced to rely on fern-shoots (and later "old fern-stalks") for sustenance. As the poem ends, Pound adopts more evocative imagery to suggest a realization of the time that has passed and the anonymity under which the soldiers serve their rulers:

> When we set out, the willows were drooping with spring,
> We come back in the snow,
> We go slowly, we are hungry and thirsty,
> Our mind is full of sorrow, who shall know of our grief?

Pound creates a verbal energy through a series of clear, direct statements, allowing thoughts and images to emerge free of poetic embellishment. The willows form an imagistic counterpoint to the fern-shoots of the first lines, as Pound holds to his Imagist rule of the "direct treatment" of both objects and emotions. Pound also obeys the Imagist dictum concerning concision, presenting a scene in the fewest possible words.

Finally, the rhythms of the *Cathay* poems owe more to the model of Anglo-Saxon accentual meter than to iambic pentameter; these meters sounded fresh to modern readers, contributing to the spare but evocative nature of the poems. In an example like the following one from "The Lament of the Frontier Guard," we can see how the spondaic and trochaic rhythms reinforce the imagery:

> There is no wall left to this village.
> Bones white with a thousand frosts,
> High heaps, covered with trees and grass.

These lines cannot be read fast. They are weighted down by the heavily accented rhythms (both the second and third lines begin with a spondee), and by the predominance of monosyllables and the lack of verbs (in the three lines, the only verb is the weak copula "is"). The slow progression of the lines functions as a verbal equivalent for the lives of the frontier guards themselves, who must stand and wait "by the North Gate."

Along with the texts of the Chinese poems themselves, Pound also took from Fenellosa the notion of the "ideogram," the term Fenellosa used to describe the "simple, original pictures" formed by Chinese characters. Pound responded immediately to the ideogram, or what he later called the "ideogrammatic method," as a way of bringing visual images together within the written form of language itself. The ideogrammatic method could be seen as an extension of Pound's Imagist ideal of the "direct treatment of the thing," and it also provided a structural basis for Pound's composition of longer poetic works. The importance of the ideogram, in the theory expressed by Fenellosa and accepted by Pound, was that since the Chinese characters were at their root composed of actual pictures they were by nature more concrete, expressive, and poetic than alphabetic writing. So, for example, in reading the character for "sunset," the Chinese reader would actually see the descending sun in the tree's branches. Though this theory of Chinese writing has been discredited by scholars – who argue that the Chinese no more "see" the sun in their character than English readers do in theirs – it provided a powerful ideal for Pound's own poetry, which he sought to make as concrete and direct as possible.

In 1917, Pound began working on a long poem that would eventually become *The Cantos*, and that would take as its primary compositional structure the "ideogrammatic" combination or juxtaposition of different images, ideas, narratives, characters, and historical events. Pound had already experimented in his 1916 volume *Lustra* with longer historical poems, such as "Near Perigord" and "Provincia Deserta," but in his plan for *The Cantos* he was far more ambitious, hoping to create a modern epic or "poem including history." But after completing the original version of the first three "Cantos" (often referred to as the "Ur-Cantos") Pound turned his attention to two other projects.

Homage to Sextus Propertius (1919) is a free translation from the Latin which cast the poet Propertius as a persona who could express Pound's own dissatisfaction with contemporary society. It may appear surprising for an experimental modernist poet to have turned to a model from classical antiquity, but Pound very deliberately chooses a neglected Latin poet – a contemporary of Virgil, Horace, and Ovid who failed to achieve their degree of literary fame – whose work can be dusted off and presented in an entirely fresh and modern way. The style of Pound's poem prepares the way for *The Cantos*, mixing erudite allusions to Roman history and mythology with colloquial speech, anachronistic images (Propertius speaks of not having a "frigidaire" in his cellar), and etymological puns. The poem scandalized classical scholars, who pointed out its numerous "howlers" of mistranslation; but such critiques missed the point of Pound's exercise, which was not to render a literal translation but instead to capture in contemporary form the ironic and satiric feeling of Propertius' original. Like Pound in twentieth-century London, Propertius was an anti-establishment poet, rejecting the heroic mode of poetry which sought to celebrate the imperial affairs of Rome, and "tying blue ribbons in the tails of Virgil and Horace." Pound's poem could hardly be read as a "translation," he points out, since it contained a mention of Wordsworth and a parodied line from Yeats, among other anachronisms. Instead, it is something between a paraphrase, an imitation, and an entirely new poem which seeks to resuscitate an unfairly neglected poet while aligning Pound's own career with that of an earlier master.

Pound's second poetic project of the late 1910s was *Hugh Selwyn Mauberly*. Published in 1920, the poem was a sequence of shorter lyrics tracing the life and career of a poet based on Pound himself. In a 1922 letter to Felix Schelling, Pound called *Hugh Selwyn Mauberly* "an attempt to condense the [Henry] James novel in verse": it is both a poetic autobiography and a terse and ironic commentary on the situation of the poet and English society after World War I. Pound's most ambitious poem to that point, it is an elegy both for those who died in the war ("There died a myriad, / And of the best, among them") and for his own misguided attempts, in his prewar writings, "to resuscitate the dead art of poetry." In the poem, Pound bids farewell to the aestheticism of his earlier work, but he also comments on the degeneration of modern society, which he believed had replaced true art with commercialism and a debased form of mass art. One example of Pound's ironic commentary on the modern world comes at the beginning of section III:

> The tea-rose tea-gown etc.
> Supplants the mousseline of Cos,
> The pianola "replaces"
> Sappho's barbitos.

In comparing the products of modern industrial society with the poetry of Sappho, Pound supplies a kind of ideogrammatic picture of the decay of Western culture. On the one hand we find the "tea-rose," the "tea-gown," and the "pianola," all faddish consumer objects that represent either decadent triviality or mechanical versions of real instruments. On the other hand, there is the genuine work of art or craft: the fine light cloth, for which Pound adopts the French word "mousseline," produced on the Greek island of Cos, and the "barbitos," or lyre, of the ancient Greek poet Sappho. Unlike the tea-gown, which expresses the "tawdry cheapness" of modern culture, the simple muslin cloth of ancient dress was classically pure; unlike the pianola, which plays from a roll of perforated paper and is thus divorced from any contact with the musician, the "barbitos" represents the harmonious unity of the human voice and music. Pound drives home the ironic point of the stanza through the use of anti-poetic diction, such as the "etc." at the end of the first line, and the use of quotation marks on "replaces." Clearly, the new forms of culture cannot "replace" the old in any real sense; they only fulfill an equivalent if debased function.

The poem begins with an "ode" to Mauberly, and to the younger Pound:

> For three years, out of key with his time,
> He strove to resuscitate the dead art
> Of poetry; to maintain "the sublime"
> In the old sense. Wrong from the start –
>
> No, hardly, but seeing he had been born
> In a half savage country, out of date;
> Bent resolutely on wringing lilies from the acorn;
> Capaneus; trout for factitious bait;

In a mock funeral oration for the dead poet, the opening section compares Mauberly (and by extension Pound himself) to several heroic figures. The tone of the poem is complex, because Pound's persona is at once heroic in his attempt to "maintain the sublime" in the midst of mediocrity and a failure in his inability to do so successfully.

An understanding of Pound's allusions to figures such as Capaneus, Odysseus, and Villon also helps us to grasp the meaning of these densely compressed stanzas. Capaneus was one of the "Seven against Thebes," a tragic Greek hero who was arrogant enough to defy the wishes of Zeus and who remained defiant when he reappeared in Canto XIV of Dante's *Inferno*. Capaneus' attack on Thebes could be compared to Pound's own assault on the London poetry world of the early 1910s; Pound fails because he is taken in by the "factitious bait" (i.e. the artificial fly) of a decadent Pre-Raphaelite sensibility. Mauberly/Pound is also compared to Odysseus, who escaped the sirens by plugging his ears with wax, and was later detained by the seductress Circe. Pound feels that he was seduced by an outmoded poetic expression, and as a result was unable to make the necessary transition to a poetic idiom more in "key with his time." Just as Odysseus took ten years to return to his Penelope, Pound needed a decade of writing to find that his "true Penelope was Flaubert," the French novelist who supplied his rationale for the Imagist concision of language. Finally, the protagonist is compared to the fifteenth-century French poet François Villon, another Poundian figure of heroic defiance. Pound identifies with Villon, who published his *Testament* in "the thirtieth year of his age" ("l'an trentuniesme / De son âge") and was later arrested and sentenced to death before being banished from Paris.

Unlike Villon, however, Pound feels he has not yet distinguished himself in his poetry: he has left "no adjunct to the Muses' diadem," no new jewels of verse to adorn poetry's crown.

Rather than the free verse of his Imagist phase, Pound adopts the rhyming quatrains he had learned from Théophile Gautier's stanzas. Pound saw the quatrain as a corrective to the "floppiness" he felt had taken over contemporary free verse. Though Pound would return to free verse in *The Cantos*, here he makes brilliantly ironic use of the stanzaic form, creating unexpected and humorous rhymes and playing with a variety of metrical forms. Despite their formality, the quatrains of *Hugh Selwyn Mauberly* are decidedly modern: no previous poet would have had the audacity to rhyme "lee-way" with the Greek "Troie," or "Pisastratus" with "over us." Pound also seeks to create as much variety in the rhythms as possible, as if to carve out of these stanzas what he calls in section II "the 'sculpture' of rhyme." With these hard-edged lines, Pound sought to reject both the "metronome" and what he referred to as "the slushiness and swishiness of the post-Swinburnian British line."

When Pound left England in 1920 and moved to Paris, *The Cantos* was to become his lifetime poetic work. He would continue to write new Cantos and publish them as separate volumes over the next half century. A work of over 800 pages, *The Cantos* is both lyrical and discursive, a multilingual and allusive modern epic which uses ideogrammatic linkages to combine literary and mythic elements (including a Homeric descent to the underworld and Ovidian metamorphoses) with impressions of such disparate historical figures as the Chinese philosopher Confucius, American presidents Thomas Jefferson and John Quincy Adams, the Italian Renaissance prince Sigismundo Malatesta, the Fascist leader Benito Mussolini, and the economist Major C. H. Douglas. Since a close reading of *The Cantos* is impossible in the space available, and the poem's difficulty and complexity prohibit anything more than a cursory description here, we will have to settle for a general overview of Pound's "epic" rather than a detailed analysis. After all, *The Cantos*, at roughly 23,000 lines, is over twice the length of Milton's *Paradise Lost* and fifty times the length of Eliot's *The Waste Land*.

Though Pound finally admitted that he could not "make it cohere," he sought a philosophical structure for *The Cantos*, which he defined as being "between KUNG and ELEUSIS." By this elliptical phrase Pound meant that the poem was balanced between an ethic of order and rationality as established by Confucian doctrine and a frenetic celebration of birth, death, and regeneration as represented by the Eleusinian mysteries, ancient Greek rites involving the story of the birth of Dionysus. Formally, Pound conceived of *The Cantos* both as a fugue, in which recurring themes are variously rephrased ("the repeat in history") and as an epic on the model of Dante's *Divine Comedy*, with an Inferno, Purgatorio, and Paradiso. Finally, *The Cantos* can be seen as taking the form of an experimental poetic autobiography, in which Pound often speaks in his own voice rather than those of his personae, and in which the poet becomes the protagonist of his own work. Pound's aim, as James Laughlin and Delmore Schwartz wrote in a 1940 essay on *The Cantos*, was nothing less than that of "painting, in vast detail, the mind-body-soul of Twentieth Century man."[2]

The first Canto begins in dramatic fashion, with a descent to the underworld, the *nekyia* of Western epic. Most of the Canto is a translation of Book XI of Homer's *Odyssey*, which tells the story of how Odysseus leaves Circe's island and travels to Hades, where he asks the prophet Tiresias how to return to his home in Ithaca. The use of the Homeric scene functions in several ways: it establishes the motif of a voyage – in time (to the beginnings of Western literature) as well as in space (to the underworld); it declares Pound's poem as a modern epic in dialogue with Homer's poem; it introduces the figure of Odysseus as one of several *personae*, or masks, Pound will adopt in the course of *The Cantos*; it describes a ritual involving animal sacrifice and prophecy that invokes the magical or prophetic powers of poetry; and it highlights its own status as translation, the actual text Pound translates being a previous translation into Renaissance Latin. The story of Odysseus is one of the many stories, or myths, that will make up *The Cantos*, like fragments in a mosaic or collage. Within the first sixteen Cantos (published together in 1925) Pound would use pieces of many other stories, including Helen's beauty as a cause of the Trojan War, the metamorphoses of Dionysus, troubadour and Italian parallels to Ovid's metamorphoses, the heroic activities of Malatesta during the Italian Renaissance, the life of Confucius, and the sordid activities of modern monopolists, war profiteers, and userers. The fragment from the *Odyssey* is both the first and the oldest piece of the mosaic Pound is constructing. The *Odyssey* is perhaps the ideal model for Pound's poem, providing the figure of the heroic, self-reliant explorer in search of knowledge and experience as he attempts to find his way home to Penelope.

The complexity of *The Cantos* is not only on the level of stories and themes, but also on the level of language, form, and style. The linguistic layering of the first Canto is itself striking, since the text not only contains the three levels of Homer, the Latin translation, and Pound's twentieth-century English rendering, but also echoes in its style the alliterative "Seafarer" verse of Old English. In the final lines of the Canto, Pound introduces yet another text: a Latin translation of the second Homeric Hymn to Aphrodite. Thus the first Canto not only serves as the introduction to the entire work, but encapsulates the allusiveness and linguistic layering of *The Cantos* as a whole. This epic will not be simply a "tale of the tribe," as Pound described it, but a history book, an encyclopedia of Western (and at times non-Western) civilization, and an archive of previous texts.

The poem begins *in medias res*, drawing the reader immediately into the action:

> And then went down to the ship,
> Set keel to breakers, forth on the godly sea, and
> We set up mast and sail on that swart ship,
> Bore sheep aboard her, and our bodies also
> Heavy with weeping, and winds from sternward
> Bore us out onward with bellying canvas,
> Circe's this craft, the trim-coifed goddess.

The form of *The Cantos* is to be an "open" form, imitative of the flux and variety of life itself and the restless energy of Pound's own mind. Thus the first Canto begins with "And then . . ." and ends with "So that:.." The reader is immediately brought into the scene, propelled forward both by the "and" which initiates the poem and by the blunt force of the language itself. It is a language of origins, of beginnings, capturing a sense of the archaic or primitive quality in Homer's text. The first and third lines are composed entirely of monosyllables, and virtually all the two-syllable words in the opening lines are accented on the first syllable; in this way, Pound establishes the strong trochaic beat that propels the poem forward, imitating the "sea-surge" that he hears in Homer's poetry. A list of these words gives us a sense of the almost archaic density of Pound's language: breakers, godly, bodies, heavy, weeping, sternward, onward, canvas, goddess. Also effective is the delay of the pronoun "We" until the third line, as if the action is suspended in time for a brief moment. It is not until line 7 that we are given a clue as to our surroundings, but the language is so evocative and so different from the poetic standard of Pound's era that it holds our attention nonetheless.

If the first Canto begins with the originary model for all Western poetry, the second begins with an evocation of Pound's more recent poetic predecessor, Robert Browning:

> Hang it all, Robert Browning,
> There can be but the one "Sordello."
> But Sordello, and my Sordello?
> Li Sordels si fo di Montovana.
> So-shu churned in the sea.
> Seal sports in the spray-whited circles of cliff-wash
> Sleak head, daughter of Lir,
>   eyes of Picasso

Pound's question here is fundamental to his conception of *The Cantos* as a whole. There are in fact three Sordellos: the historical figure, an Italian troubadour of the thirteenth century; the fictionalized version from

Browning's long poem *Sordello*, which Pound considered the "best long poem in English since Chaucer"; and Pound's own version of Sordello, which must be different from Browning's. Pound acknowledges that he cannot surpass Browning at the long historical poem, a form at which Browning excelled; but he can do something new, inventing the epic as "poem including history" rather than as fictionalized history. Pound immediately foregrounds the relationship of poetry to history by quoting from a Provençal biography of Sordello: "Li Sordels si fo di Montovana" ("Sordello comes from Mantua"). This introduction of a documentary fact about Sordello rejects the pseudo-historical fiction of Browning's poem, establishing Pound's claim to a Sordello who is closer to the original historical figure.

In the following lines, however, Pound shifts to an entirely different poetic register, evoking a series of metamorphoses that seem far removed from the story of Sordello. By embracing the fanciful and mythic resonances of Ovidian metaphorphosis, Pound distances himself from Browning's focus on history and historical figures. The "So-shu" who "churned in the sea" is based on a Chinese Taoist philosopher who, in Pound's version, churns the sea with a moonbeam. We have already seen the invocation of magic in the soothsaying ritual of Canto I (where Tiresias, the blind prophet, tells Odysseus' fortune); here, we have a further indication of the importance of magic, ritual, and transformation to the poetic process. Pound's use of this particular sea image is very deliberate: it echoes the use of the sea in Canto I and it introduces a series of sea images in Canto II that culminates with Proteus, the shape-changing sea god. Further, as Michael Alexander has noted, the image of churning the sea with a moonbeam more generally represents "the flux of perception, imagination, and memory which makes up experience"; the Canto as a whole will proclaim "both the flux of phenomena and the necessity of imagination as the source of primal knowledge."[3] The magical transformations that follow in the Canto are of various kinds: from a seal sporting in the water into the daughter of Lir, a Celtic sea-god, and then into the cubist face of a Picasso painting; from Eleanor of Aquitaine to Helen of Troy (based on a Greek pun linking Helen's name to the word *elenaus*, "ship-destroying"); from a ship into natural fauna; from a swimmer into underwater coral.

By the end of the second Canto, Pound has already established three models for the long poem he is writing: the classical epic, based primarily on narrative (Homer); the historical poem, based on character (Browning); and the metamorphic poem, based on the transformative power of the lyric imagination (Ovid). Canto II is written with an intensity of language that has rarely been matched in modern English or American poetry. The phantasmagorical changes evoked in the poem take place within a natural setting that is presented in sensuous detail:

Quiet sun-tawny sand-stretch,
The gulls broad out their wings,
        nipping between the splay feathers
Snipe come for their bath,
        bend out their wing joints,
Spread wet wings to the sun-film . . .

Naviform rock overgrown,
        algae cling to its edge,
There is a wine-red glow in the shallows,
        a tin-flash in the sun-dazzle.

The importance of *The Cantos* as a twentieth-century long poem that seeks to redefine the epic in the modern world was first recognized by Eliot, and was later acknowledged by many other American poets. *The Cantos* cannot easily be compared to any other modern poem, for no other attempt at the modernist epic contains its scope, its complexity, and its universalizing power. *The Cantos* is by no means a work of consistent poetic achievement. In recent years, *The Cantos* has undergone a great deal of critical scrutiny – from political and ideological points of view as well as from more strictly literary perspectives – but it remains a puzzling text to most readers. Further, some of its ideas and statements are highly objectionable: this is particularly the case with Pound's support of the Fascist dictator Mussolini and his increasingly anti-semitic rhetoric. Nevertheless, *The Cantos* opened up American poetry to the inclusion of historical sources and documents and to a wider range of languages, cultures, and poetic styles, contributing to the move away from the more narrowly defined set of texts comprising the Anglo-American canon.

T. S. Eliot and the wasteland of modernity

Though Thomas Stearns Eliot was born in St. Louis, Missouri, both sides of his family were descended from old New England stock. Eliot's paternal grandfather was a Unitarian minister who had founded the first Unitarian church in St. Louis as well as its chief institution of higher learning, Washington University. Eliot attended Smith Academy in St. Louis and Milton Academy in Massachusetts before entering Harvard in 1906. A precocious literary talent, Eliot began writing poetry while still a school boy, and by the age of twenty-two he had published several quite accomplished poems.

In 1908, Eliot was to come across the book which was to be crucial to his poetic development: Arthur Symons' *The Symbolist Movement in Literature* (1899). In Symons' study, Eliot discovered the work of French symbolists such as Arthur Rimbaud, Paul Verlaine, Tristan Corbière, and especially

Jules Laforgue. Laforgue's rejection of Romantic style was a revelation to Eliot: the French poet's use of slang and colloquialism, his ironic wit, and his construction of the poem as a short dramatic scene rather than a lyric utterance all contributed to Eliot's sense of the direction his own poetry should take. Eliot later claimed in an essay entitled "Reflections on Contemporary Poetry" (1919) that reading Laforgue taught him "the poetic possibilities of my own idiom of speech" and changed him "from a bundle of second-hand sentiments into a person."

Perhaps the chief lesson Eliot learned from Laforgue and other French symbolists was that poems could be made out of materials – such as the modern urban experience – that had previously been considered anathema to poetry. In giving poetic treatment to "the more sordid aspects of the modern metropolis," as he put it in an essay entitled "What Dante Means to Me" (1950), Eliot discovered that the source of new poetry might be found in what had previously been regarded as "the impossible, the sterile, the intractably unpoetic." Eliot's new understanding of poetry was apparent in his most important early poem, "The Love Song of J. Alfred Prufrock," which he wrote in 1910–11.

It was Pound who convinced Harriet Monroe, the editor of *Poetry* magazine, to publish "Prufrock," and in June 1915 the poem finally appeared in print. Eliot's first volume, *Prufrock and Other Observations*, was published in 1917, and it included "Portrait of a Lady," "Preludes," "La Figlia Che Piange" and other poems along with the title work. The publication of *Prufrock* was greeted with cries of outrage by many readers in both the United States and England, and the first edition of 500 copies took four years to sell out. The book's lack of popular appeal is not surprising, since Eliot's poetry was highly intellectual as well as strikingly modern.

Eliot completed his PhD dissertation on the philosophy of F. H. Bradley – having pursued his academic studies at the Sorbonne, Harvard, and Oxford – but he never returned to Harvard to defend the thesis and receive his degree. Like Pound, Eliot felt the urge to live and write in Europe, and after 1914 he decided to settle permanently in England. While still in college he had written of the "failure of American life," concluding that while educated Americans may stay in America out of a sense of duty or for business reasons, "their hearts are always in Europe." As for poetry, the situation in America was disastrous: as Eliot commented, "there was not one older poet writing in America whose writing a younger man could take seriously."

"The Love Song of J. Alfred Prufrock" was a total departure from the genteel tradition of American poetry. It was certainly the most "modern" poem to have been written by an American, and in many ways it was the most obviously original American poem since the works of Walt Whitman and Emily Dickinson. When Ezra Pound first read "Prufrock" in 1914, he was impressed enough to declare, in a letter to Harriet Montoe, that Eliot was the only American poet to have "made adequate preparation for writing" and to have "trained himself and modernized himself on his own." The poem was difficult for its contemporary readers in several ways: it had no plot (at least no discernable beginning, middle, and end), no real action apart from the internalized movement of a loose psychological narrative, and no real characters, presenting instead a speaker ("I"), an unnamed addressee ("you") and an unidentified woman ("one"). While the poem purports to be a "love song," it does not conform to that genre in any conventional way. Finally, the poem has no clearly definable setting (it could take place in any modern city).

"Prufrock" puts the sort of demands on its readers that later modernist poems like *The Waste Land* and *The Cantos* would greatly intensify. In order to fully grasp the poem, the reader must recognize and place in a new context a number of literary and Biblical allusions, including Dante's *Inferno*, Shakespeare's *Hamlet*, Marvell's "To His Coy Mistress," Hesiod's *Works and Days*, and the stories of Lazarus and John the Baptist. Further, Eliot's use of imagery, diction, and figurative language contribute to a style utterly different from that of any previous American poem.

The reader is drawn into the speaker's world by the opening lines, which are among the most famous in American poetry:

> Let us go then, you and I,
> When the evening is spread out against the sky
> Like a patient etherized upon a table;
> Let us go, through certain half-deserted steets,
> The muttering retreats
> Of restless nights in one-night cheap hotels
> And sawdust restaurants with oyster-shells;
> Streets that follow like a tedious argument
> Of insidious intent
> To lead you to an overwhelming question . . .
> Oh, do not ask, "What is it?"
> Let us go and make our visit.

Eliot's poem is, as Piers Gray puts it, "elegantly unsettling," opening up "several layers of uncertainty."[4] First of all, the use of pronouns creates an uncertainty about exactly who is speaking and who is being addressed. The first line contains three pronouns – "us," "you," and "I" – all referring to people as yet unidentified; aside from allusions to Michelangelo, Hamlet, and Lazarus, no proper nouns appear in the poem at all. The speaker is clearly "J. Alfred Prufrock," and the poem is his "love song," but who is this Prufrock, and what relation does he bear to Eliot himself? In contrast to Robert Browning's dramatic monologues, which are uttered by historical characters who reveal telling details about their lives, this poem is in the voice of an invented persona about whom we learn relatively little.

What we do learn about Prufrock in the course of the poem is presented in mostly negative terms: he is neither a prophet (Lazarus) nor a tragic hero (Prince Hamlet); he feels that his best years are past him, if they ever existed ("I have seen the moment of my greatness flicker"); he appears to have an existential and almost crippling fear of life ("Do I dare / Disturb the universe?"); he seems unable to communicate with a woman at a late-afternoon tea party; and he is extremely fastidious and sensitive to the possibility of social humiliation ("Shall I part my hair behind? Do I dare to eat a peach?"). According to Eliot, Prufrock was in part himself and in part a man of about forty: a timid middle-aged lover, he worries about being past his prime and about missing out on life ("I grow old . . . I grow old / I shall wear the bottoms of my trousers rolled"), and he fears death, "the eternal Footman." This confusion of identities is carried out on the level of the poem's language as well: we are constantly reminded by the use of rhyme, meter, and figurative language that the voice of the poem is Eliot's as much as the fictional Prufrock's. The "you" of the opening line is also vaguely disconcerting: while on one level it is clearly the reader, on another level it is a fictional interlocutor, presumably male, whom Prufrock invites to join him on his "visit" through the city streets as he confesses his various problems. Yet the "you" is also prohibited from asking questions, from prying too deeply into the speaker's consciousness: "Oh, do not ask, 'What is it?' / Let us go and make our visit."

The poem's setting is disturbingly anti-conventional. The physical environment of "Prufrock" is modern, urban, and nocturnal; the poem evokes a world very different from that which most of Eliot's middle-class readers would have experienced. The "half-deserted streets," "one-night cheap hotels," and "sawdust restaurants" suggest a descent into a Dantean Hell, a voyage that will constitute the first part of the "visit" to which the speaker invites the reader in the opening lines. This reading is suggested by the epigraph, which is taken from a speech in Dante's *Inferno* by Guido da Montefeltro, one of the "False Counselors" of the eighth level of Hell. Guido tells Dante and Virgil that he can speak with them only because "never from this abyss has anyone ever returned alive." The "abyss" is presumably the city itself, as well as the psychological torment Prufrock experiences within his social circle. While the city here may not yet be the "waste land" depicted in Eliot's poem of ten years later, it is already a sordid, depressing, and nightmarish place. In a section originally intended to be included in "Prufrock" but removed before the publication of the poem ("Prufrock's Pervigilium"), Eliot's vision of the nightmarish city and its effect on Prufrock is even more pronounced: here he refers to another nighttime walk "through narrow streets" in which Prufrock encounters prostitutes ("Women, spilling out of corsets, stood in entries") and sees "evil houses leaning all together / Point[ing] a ribald finger at me in the darkness."

We are also unsettled by the *language* of the poem, and in particular by Eliot's figures of speech. There are two similes in the opening lines, both of which would have seemed highly unusual, even shocking, to post-Victorian readers. The first simile compares the evening, "spread out against the sky," to a "patient etherized upon a table." In Romantic and post-Romantic poetry the evening was generally treated as a moment of sublime rapture, as in Wordsworth's famous lines,

> It is a beauteous evening, calm and free,
> The holy time is quiet as a Nun
> Breathless with adoration; the broad sun
> Is sinking down in its tranquility.

Eliot is clearly working against this kind of Romantic image, forcing the reader to accept a very different register of diction in place of Romantic idealization. To say that the evening is "spread out against the sky" suggests something mechanical or artificial, rather than natural. In a literal sense, the evening cannot be separated from the sky which provides its physical manifestation; yet here the sky is treated as a kind of backdrop – a stage or screen, perhaps – against which the evening is projected. (An echo of this same image occurs later in the poem when Prufrock feels "as if a magic lantern threw the nerves in patterns on the screen.") The reader has little time to fully appreciate the novelty of Eliot's visual image, however, since the completion of the simile is even more striking: the evening is depicted as being "like a patient etherized upon a table." Where Wordsworth used the image of an adoring "Nun" to suggest the holiness and sanctity of the sunset, Eliot works against such a Romantic impulse in comparing the evening to a patient undergoing a medical procedure. Not only does the use of medical jargon ("etherized") clash with the conventional poetic treatment of the evening sky (as if to announce to the reader that this will be a thoroughly "modern" poem), but the idea of evening as an etherized patient suggests a number of possible meanings, none of them positive. Is the evening sick, requiring some kind of operation? If so, the evening may serve as an analogy of Prufrock's own psychically damaged condition. Is the evening drugged, put out of its pain just as Prufrock himself desires to be anaesthetized against a hostile and uncomfortable world? Is "etherized" a pun on "ethereal," capturing the discrepancy between the spiritual or heavenly realm and the hellish world, devoid of spiritual grace, to which Prufrock's nightly visit will lead? Or is the image of the etherized patient meant to suggest Prufrock's crippling passivity, which we will see again later in the poem in his fear of being "formulated, sprawling on a pin . . . pinned and wriggling on the wall"?

As these alternatives suggest, Prufrock himself feels etherized in more ways than one: he may be carefully groomed, with his "collar mounting firmly to the chin," but he is paralyzed with indecision and figuratively if not literally impotent. Prufrock's physical weakness is suggested by his thinning hair and spindly limbs, and he fears that when he is alone with a woman, he will not have the physical or emotional strength "to force the moment to its crisis." He is overpowered by the eyes, arms, and perfume of the women who surround him, yet because of age, physical weakness, and a crippling fear of rejection, he cannot act on his desires. Even the fantasy of the mermaids riding the ocean waves at the end of the poem does not allow Prufrock any real contact with female sexuality: "I do not think they will sing to me," he laments.

With the poem's second simile – "Streets that follow like a tedious argument / Of insidious intent" – Eliot seems more concerned with the associative meanings of the words he uses than with the precision of the comparison itself. Eliot moves from the more concrete visual image of the first simile to the more abstract comparison of the second, as if to encapsulate the poem's alternation between an external world of sensory particulars and an internal world of personal associations. Though we may not be able to say in exactly what way the city streets resemble a "tedious argument" – beyond the general sense of sameness or monotony the simile conveys – the rhyme of "tedious" and "insidious" emphasizes the unpleasant connotations of both adjectives. Both words apply more generally to Prufrock's situation: if Prufrock's existence is "tedious" – tedium being the most apparent fact of this world of afternoon teas and monotonous discussions of Michelangelo's paintings – the intent of the streets is "insidious" in its corrupting influence on the speaker's moral and sexual behavior. Eliot fully exploits the aural and connotative power of a word like "insidious" to create a tonality for the poem as a whole: the streets lie in wait for Prufrock, ready to entrap him in an act beneath the propriety demanded by the stuffy upper-class world he inhabits.

The "tedious argument" of the streets also leads the speaker to "an overwhelming question." This question, though never made explicit, introduces a series of questions which Prufrock asks in the course of the poem. In fact, the mode of address in the poem, despite its title, is less that of the "love song" (typically a declaration of love for the object of the speaker's affection) than that of the endlessly repeating question. The single "overwhelming question" mentioned in the first stanza is later broken down into a series of smaller questions – "Do I dare?" . . . "How should I begin?" . . . "How should I presume?" – all of which emphasize Prufrock's inability either to arrive at a decision ("In a minute there is time / For decisions and revisions which a minute will reverse"), or to make any declaration of his feelings. The "overwhelming question" is repeated in line 93 in the context of Prufrock's desire to speak to a woman and perhaps open his heart to her:

> And would it have been worth it, after all,
> After the cups, the marmalade, the tea,
> Among the porcelain, among some talk of you and me,
> Would it have been worth while,
> To have bitten off the matter with a smile,
> To have squeezed the universe into a ball
> To roll it toward some overwhelming question,
> To say, "I am Lazarus, come from the dead,
> Come back to tell you all, I shall tell you all" –
> If one, settling a pillow by her head,
>> Should say: "That is not what I meant at all.
>> That is not it, at all."

This crucial stanza juxtaposes references to Marvell's "To His Coy Mistress" ("Let us roll all our strength and all / Our sweetness up into one ball") and the story of Lazarus being raised from the dead, setting the two allusions in ironic counterpoint to each other. The "overwhelming question" here concerns both sexual desire – unfulfilled but constantly on Prufrock's mind – and death, as suggested by the appearance of the "eternal Footman" in the previous stanza. The story of Lazarus is the crowning miracle revealing Jesus as the giver of life. Yet Prufrock's allusion to a miraculous return to life is ironized by the banal details of the afternoon tea and by the blasé response of the "one" – the woman to whom he wishes to express himself. The changing tone of the stanza can be charted in the progression of the word "all": from the tired banality of "after all" to the prophetic power of "I shall tell you all," and then back to the deflating impact of the woman's dismissive response, "That is not it at all."

The reference to Marvell's poem further ironizes Prufrock's position: unlike Marvell's speaker, who attempts to use his powers of rhetorical persuasion to convince his "coy mistress" to sleep with him, Prufrock fails to persuade the woman of anything. Indeed, he can only wonder whether it would have been "worth while" to "squeeze the universe into a ball" and "roll it toward some overwhelming question." The absurdly hyperbolic nature of Prufrock's attempt to speak to the woman (also echoing the Greek myth of Sisyphus, condemned to roll a rock endlessly up a mountain and have it fall back down again) highlights the futility of his efforts. Eliot's curious use of prepositions – "*After* the cups, the marmalade, the tea, / *Among* the porcelain, *among* some talk of you and me" – emphasizes the triviality of Prufrock's conversation, which never transcends the social and physical environment in which he is trapped. Prufrock does not blame the woman for not understanding him; in fact, as he says in the following stanza, "It is impossible to say just what I mean!" In reducing himself to "a pair of ragged claws / Scuttling across the floors of silent seas," Prufrock expresses a sense of isolated despair about his inability to engage in meaningful communion with another person.

The impossibility of human communication would also be a central theme of *The Waste Land*, written in 1921, heavily edited by Pound, and first published in *The Criterion* in October 1922. In fact, as A. Walton Litz suggests, the poem's "essential psychology" is "that of someone who can perceive but cannot act, who can understand but cannot communicate."[5] Such a pessimistic vision of life is not surprising, since Eliot was recuperating from a nervous breakdown during the period in which he wrote the poem.

Eliot had suffered greatly from a disastrous marriage to Vivien Haigh-Wood in 1916. The other important context for the poem was World War I and its aftermath, which clearly took its toll on Eliot as it did on every writer or artist of his time. It is no mere coincidence that the opening section of *The Waste Land* is entitled "The Burial of the Dead": the poem is obsessed with death, and with the hoped-for possibility of a psychological and spiritual rebirth.

Perhaps no modern poem has received as much critical attention as *The Waste Land*: as a result, interpretations of the poem are extremely varied. The poem has been read as a critique of contemporary civilization, as a kind of modern-day dejection ode, as a Dantean descent into hell, as an experiment in stream-of-consciousness technique, as a pastoral elegy, as an attempt to create a new mythic structure, as a poem of the modern city, and as a poem of imperial apocalypse. In the first years after its publication, *The Waste Land* represented a kind of dividing point between those who admired it – accepting its revolutionary form, its highly allusive style, and even its fifty-two explanatory footnotes – and those who detested it. Louis Untermeyer, for example, felt that the poem was a kind of literary hoax, as he put it in his essay "Disillusion vs. Dogma" (1923), "a set of separate poems, a piece of literary carpentry, a scholarly joiner's work, the flotsam and jetsam of dessicated culture . . . a pompous parade of erudition." Of course, in a literal sense, Untermeyer was correct about the construction of the poem, if not necessarily about its aesthetic result. The poem was assembled from various pieces Eliot had written over a period of several years, and it was heavily cut and revised based on suggestions from Pound. Pound persuaded Eliot to delete a number of sections from the poem, including 72 lines in rhymed couplets from the beginning of "The Fire Sermon" and another 82 lines from the beginning of "Death by Water." He also convinced Eliot to cut three short lyrics he intended to use as interludes, and to eliminate conventional poetic diction and nonessential verbiage. The final product is, as Eliot himself tells us at the end of the poem, a loosely connected patchwork of "fragments." The poem has no single speaker, no single rhetorical mode or style (it is in turns narrative, conversational, descriptive, lyric, colloquial, hallucinatory, and allusive), and no single action or setting: although the poem is focused on London, it begins in Bavaria and ends in India.

The Waste Land is certainly difficult, though it no longer seems as impenetrable as it did to its first readers. The difficulties are of at least four kinds: its disjunctive and discontinuous form, its quotations in foreign languages (Latin, German, French, Italian, and Sanskrit), its multiple allusions, and its mythic structure. It is Eliot's allusions that will probably cause the most problems for the average reader: references to at least thirty-seven works of art, literature, history, and music can be found in the poem. Further, as Eliot's use of explanatory footnotes suggests, these allusions are not always obvious. Whereas the allusions in "Prufrock" were relatively familiar, the references in *The Waste Land* are often arcane, including not only the central texts of Western literature (the Bible, Virgil, Ovid, St. Augustine, Dante, Shakespeare, and Spenser) but also poems by Baudelaire, Verlaine, and Nerval, plays by Thomas Middleton, Ben Webster, Thomas Kyd and John Lyle, operas by Wagner, a book by Hermann Hesse, and Buddha's Fire Sermon. Like Pound's *Cantos*, Eliot's poem is conceived as a compendium or archive of Western civilization, a civilization that has fallen into disrepair and needs to be put back together. David Perkins explains the use of these allusive "fragments" in the poem:

> The individual mind and the civilization are on the edge of a crack-up . . .
> Yet the panoramic range and inclusiveness of the poem, which only Eliot's
> fragmentary and elliptical juxtapositions could have achieved so
> powerfully in a brief work, held in one vision not only contemporary
> London and Europe but also human life stretching far back into time.
> The condition of man seen in the poem was felt to be contemporaneous
> and perennial, modern yet essentially the same in all times and places.[6]

An understanding of Eliot's "mythic method" is also a key to reading *The Waste Land*. Eliot called attention to two sources which had provided much of the background for the poem: Jessie Weston's *From Ritual to Romance*, which argued that the Arthurian quest for the Holy Grail was based on pre-Christian fertility myths, and James Frazer's *The Golden Bough*, an anthropological study of myths including that of the Fisher King, the dying and reviving god who was regarded as the incarnation of the land's fertility. Though critics have differed as to how closely *The Waste Land* is based on these mythic structures, Eliot's poem loosely follows the narrative of a quest for renewed life. The king is dead, and the land lies in a state of infertile desert; only when the king is healed or resurrected can the spring return, bringing with it the rain needed to sustain life. The poem moves from the desire for death (represented by the Cumaean Sibyl in the epigraph) to the beginnings of new life at the end. Eliot had not yet embraced Christianity at this point, and although the poem contains elements of Christian symbology (the Grail itself, as well as allusions to the New Testament, Dante's *Purgatorio*, and St. Augustine's *Confessions*), its final turn is not toward a Christian resurrection but toward an alternative form of spirituality based on the teachings of the Hindu Upanishads.

The Waste Land is divided into five sections, some much longer than others. The title of section I, "The Burial of the Dead," is a phrase from the Anglican burial service that refers to the dead of World War I but also to the dead body of the Fisher King, and thus, symbolically, to the death of civilization itself. It begins with some of the most celebrated lines in all of modern poetry:

> April is the cruellest month, breeding
> Lilacs out of the dead land, mixing
> Memory and desire, stirring
> Dull roots with spring rain.
> Winter kept us warm, covering
> Earth in forgetful show, feeding
> A little life with dried tubers.

The first line clearly echoes the opening of another famous long poem, Chaucer's *Canterbury Tales*: "Whan that Aprille with his shoures soote / The droughte of March hath perced to the roote." Yet it is an ironic echo: where Chaucer's prologue celebrates the renewing and engendering powers of spring, Eliot's speaker points to the unresolved memories and desires the season brings to the surface. The two statements are based in paradox: while April is "the cruellest month," it is winter that "kept us warm." For the speaker, it is winter snow and not spring rain that proves comforting, sustaining the speaker's "little life" without forcing the painful encounter with the past that the rest of the poem represents. The speaker, whom we could call the poem's first protagonist, is an inhabitant of the waste land; he is also the poet himself, who declares himself through his perfect control of poetic language. The language here is highly lyrical in a poem where lyricism is not the dominant mode, as if to demonstrate the possibility of a traditional lyric mode in the twentieth century before calling that very mode into question through the discontinuous and allusive form of the poem.

The permutations of desire and memory are the thematic thread that holds the poem together. Desires are of various kinds: the desire for death expressed by the Cumaean Sibyl, the sexual desire of the house agent's clerk for the young typist, the brutal desire that causes King Tereus to rape Philomel, and Philomel's desire at the end of the poem to sing like the swallow. Clearly, in this poem, desire is a dangerous commodity: it can lead to disappointment, to frustration, to sordid affairs and unwanted children, and even to violence. The protagonist distrusts desire, preferring winter's dullness and forgetfulness to the "stirring," "mixing," and "breeding" of spring. Memory also takes various forms in the poem: there is the cultural memory of which the poem's many allusions are the emblems, the mythic memory of vegetation rituals and sacred quests, the historical memory of the war and the decay of Europe, the personal memories of Eliot himself (his unhappy marriage, mental breakdown, and recovery), and the memories of various characters including Marie and the "hyacinth girl" in "The Burial of the Dead."

It is perhaps the figure of the blind seer Tiresias, whom Eliot identifies in the footnotes as "the most important personage in the poem who unites all the rest" – who best encompasses both memory and desire. As the poem"s "spectator," Tiresias is fated to remember all the scenes he witnesses during his long life – "And I Tiresias have foresuffered all / Enacted on this same divan or bed." As an androgynous figure who has experienced being both a man and a woman – "throbbing between two lives, / Old man with wrinkled female breasts," he has a double acquaintance with desire. In one version of the Tiresias myth, he was blinded by Hera for judging that women enjoy sex more than men, yet the opposite is the case in the scene he witnesses between the typist and the office clerk in "The Fire Sermon." Here, the young man is clearly the aggressor in the sexual act, and the indifferent woman lets herself be seduced more out of boredom and exhaustion than out of any interest in her lover. For Eliot, this encounter is clearly emblematic of the modern waste land as it impacts the lives of both men and women. The pompousness and insensitivity of the clerk ("One of the low on whom assurance sits / As a silk hat on a Bradford millionaire"), the boring, routine, and tawdry existence of the woman, and the utter sterility of their relationship all point to a fallen modern world. Eliot ends the passage with an ironic commentary:

> When lovely woman stoops to folly and
> Paces about her room again, alone,
> She smoothes her hair with automatic hand,
> And puts a record on the gramophone.

The "automatic hand" here is a synecdoche for the generally automatized life of the woman: she works as a typist (itself a monotonous form of labor), and her movements of pacing the room, smoothing her hair, and putting a record on the gramophone suggest that she is caught in a groove from which she cannot escape. The typist can be compared with the other modern women who populate the poem, from Lil, a drained mother of five with rotting teeth, to the hysterical middle-class wife who declares to her husband, "My nerves are bad tonight. Yes, bad. Stay with me." The lines also contain an allusion to Oliver Goldsmith's eighteenth-century novel *The Vicar of Wakefield*, in which the seduced and deserted Olivia sings that when "lovely woman stoops to folly," the only solution to her shame and grief is to die. The modern woman in Eliot's poem – no Romantic heroine but a naturalistic inhabitant of the urban metropolis – has no intention of dying: instead, her complete emotional detachment from her own situation represents a kind of death in life.

If scenes of modern urban life dominate the first three sections of the poem, the final section, "What the Thunder Said," moves outside the city to a desert landscape, where "there is no water but only rock." Here the vision of London as an "Unreal City" expands to include the destruction of various civilizations: "Jerusalem Athens Alexandria / Vienna London / Unreal." The wandering protagonist finally reaches a chapel in the mountains, the "Chapel Perilous" that must be passed on the quest for the Grail. With the quest nearly at an end, the rains come and we shift landscapes again, this time arriving at the shores of the Indian Ganges (itself a more spiritual counterpart to London's Thames). The sound of the thunder is imagined as a heavenly voice which speaks the syllable "DA," the source of the three great disciplines of Hindu thought: "datta" (give), "dayadhvam" (sympathize), "damyata" (control). To give, in the sense of surrendering oneself to another, is the direct opposite of desire: it is an act that requires an "awful daring" in an "age of prudence." Sympathy or compassion for others will allow us to leave the "prison" of our own consciousness that has in part created the waste land. And finally, the control of our baser natures will allow us to achieve a kind of effortless harmony with the divine force. The new awareness that comes with these disciplines provides a means by which the protagonist, now figured explicitly as the Fisher King, can at last "set [his] lands in order."

The poem ends with an explosion of fragments in different languages, offering a kaleidoscopic vision of a fallen bridge, a ruined tower, and a refining fire. This apocalyptic moment is in turn followed by the thrice-repeated Sanskrit word *shantih* ("the peace which surpasseth understanding") with which the poem ends. An ending in which scraps of Western literature mingle with the ancient wisdom of the Upanishads is by any standard highly ambivalent – it must have appeared almost insurmountably so to most of

Eliot's first readers – yet it is an appropriate conclusion to such a fundamentally unstable poem. The ending of *The Waste Land* was the closest Eliot could come, at this stage of his life, to anything resembling formal or thematic closure. Eliot's readers would have to wait twenty more years, until the completion of *The Four Quartets* (see chapter 9), for an ending that affirmed an unambiguous spiritual doctrine.

Chapter 3

Lyric modernism: Wallace Stevens and Hart Crane

This chapter focuses on the work of two poets – Wallace Stevens and Hart Crane – who exemplify the mode of what I am calling "lyric modernism." The title of the chapter brings together two concepts that we might normally consider to be polar opposites: "lyricism" and "modernism." Both Stevens and Crane were centrally important figures in the development of American poetic modernism; yet at the same time they were poets working within the tradition of post-Romantic lyric poetry in a way that experimental modernists like Pound, Eliot, and William Carlos Williams were not. Stevens and Crane represent, in very different ways, the twentieth-century synthesis of post-Romantic lyricism and modernist innovation.

Modernist poetry, as we have seen in the work of Pound and Eliot, involved a rejection of the inherited models of traditional English poetry. The nineteenth-century lyric, the modernists felt, had too often relied on the beauty and melodiousness of its language rather than on the depth or complexity of its thought. With the Imagist movement of the 1910s, poets began to move away from a reliance on musicality and sonic richness and toward a greater precision and directness of language. Further, the Romantic and post-Romantic lyric was chiefly concerned with the expression of the poetic self, either celebrating that self (in relation to nature, a loved one, or some other aspect of the world), or questioning the isolation, victimization, or failure of that self. The language of late-nineteenth-century lyric was assumed to express in its intensest form the subjectivity and personality of the poet himself. This focus on the poem as a reflection of its author's personality or as an expression of his personal emotions was anathema to Pound and Eliot, who felt that such a focus would do nothing to advance poetry as art or technique. As Eliot put it in his influential essay "Tradition and the Individual Talent" (1921), poetry "is not a turning loose of emotion, but an escape from emotion; it is not the expression of personality, but an escape from personality." Eliot's statement may seem to exaggerate the modernist requirement that poets avoid emotionalism and sentimentality, but it was an important corrective to the excesses of the post-Romantic lyric. It was only through the process of "depersonalization," Eliot argued, that poetry could approach "the condition of science." The analogy with science was a telling one: the modernists believed that the practice of poetry could be improved only by continued and methodical experimentation. Just as the scientific method involved developing new techniques that in turn could lead to new kinds of knowledge, the experimental method of poetry could lead to new ways of using language and new ways of describing experience.

Wallace Stevens and the supreme fiction

If Stevens is a very different poet from Eliot, it is in part because of his different relationship to poetic lyricism. Walton Litz, who entitled his book on Stevens *Introspective Voyager*, characterizes Stevens' poetic project as a voyage in search for the "self": 'a 'self' dependent on the pure poetry of the physical world, a 'self' whose terrifying lack of belief is turned into a source of freedom."[1] This self is both solitary and interiorized (in dialogue with what he called "the Interior Paramour"); it is engaged in a meditative or whimsical communion with nature but rarely engaged in any form of interaction with the world of social or historical particulars. As opposed to the various "selves" operating within the multivoiced modernist poems of Eliot and Pound – each of which stands in a variety of historical and symbolic relationships with the poet himself – Stevens' self is defined through the manipulation of his own authorial voice. Stevens' primary concern is not with history, or civilization, or even nature, but with the "mythology of self" and with the self's relationship to both the world outside and the inner workings of the mind as it attempts to order and shape that world. The central philosophical theme which runs in various permutations throughout Stevens' poetry is that of the tension, opposition, or interplay between reality and the imagination. As Denis Donoghue remarks, Stevens was interested in reality "only when it [had] been refracted through the idiom of art," or, to be more precise, only when it had been refined and colored by the poet's imagination.[2]

Neither Pound nor Eliot would have considered Stevens' question about reality and the imagination to be particularly important to the writing of poetry. For Pound it was not possible to define the poetic imagination apart from the structures and insights contained in history, mythology and cultural tradition, all of which supplied the poet with both his inspiration and his primary subject. For Eliot, the defining feature of poetry was not how successfully it negotiated between reality and the imagination, but rather how fully it engaged literary tradition: the best poems, according to Eliot, were those in which the poet's predecessors "assert their immortality most vigororously." In the work of modernists like Pound and Eliot, we can speak of the imagination only in a particular sense – the auditory imagination at work in many of Pound's *Cantos*, for example, or the visual imagination behind Eliot's remarkable imagery in *The Waste Land* – but we cannot find an all-embracing theory of the imagination in its relationship to an external, objective reality.

The poetic mode typical of Stevens, on the other hand, is one in which he contemplates the workings of the imagination itself. Poems such as "Sea Surface Full of Clouds," in which he imagines the same seascape in five different ways, or "Thirteen Ways of Looking at a Blackbird," in which he presents a series of poetic statements about how the imagination works to structure reality, reveal a fundamentally different idea of poetry from that of Pound and Eliot. Poetry, Stevens claimed in a 1940 letter to Hi Simons, was the "Supreme Fiction" in a world in which "one no longer believes in God (as truth)." It is this belief in poetry as a Supreme Fiction that places Stevens in the Romantic tradition of Emerson and Whitman; Stevens can be seen as the major twentieth-century exemplar of what Harold Bloom has called "High American Romanticism."

But what exactly is the Supreme Fiction, and what is its significance for American poetry in the twentieth century? As Frank Kermode argued in his seminal study of Stevens, the Supreme Fiction is an alternative world, a world of the imagination which "weaves its always changing, always delightful, fictive covering" over the world of reality.[3] Stevens himself describes this fictive world in highly Romantic terms: the "imaginative man" (i.e. the poet) delights in the world of the imagination rather than in the "gaunt world of reason," creating "a truth that cannot be arrived at by the reason alone, a truth that the poet recognizes by sensation." The purpose of poetry, then, would be to give the reader a glimpse of such a world, to provide a sense of reality transformed by the poet's imaginative powers.

Stevens' life was relatively uneventful, at least when compared with the more momentous careers of expatriate writers like Pound and Eliot. Born and raised in Reading, Pennsylvania, where his father was a lawyer, Stevens attended high school in Reading and then entered Harvard. During his three years at Harvard, Stevens studied French and German, read philosophy, wrote poems, and became editor of the *Harvard Advocate*, the same magazine in which Eliot would later publish his early poems. He also met a number of aspiring poets, including Witter Bynner and Walter Arensberg, and became friendly with George Santayana, whose dual interest in poetry and philosophy resembled his own. After briefly taking a job as a journalist with the *New York Herald Tribune*, Stevens was convinced by his father to enter law school. He completed a law degree, was admitted to the New York Bar in 1904, and worked for several law firms over the next twelve years. In 1916 he joined the Hartford Accident and Indemnity Company, where he was employed for the rest of his career, working his way up to the position of vice president by 1934.

Stevens began publishing his poems in *Poetry* and other little magazines in 1914, but he did not complete his first volume of poetry, *Harmonium*, until 1923. Like Frost, Stevens was relatively late in reaching his poetic maturity: he was forty-four when *Harmonium* was published, and he took another twelve years to bring out a second volume, *Ideas of Order*. His reputation grew slowly, so that until the 1950s his work was less generally known than that of Frost, Eliot, or Pound: Stevens' status as a major American modernist was not clearly established until near the end of his life.

Many of Stevens' most famous lyrics were contained in *Harmonium*, certainly the most impressive first volume of any twentieth-century American poet. As in the case of Walt Whitman, whose 1855 first edition of *Leaves of Grass* was a similarly stunning achievement, there is little in the early poems and journals of Stevens to anticipate the appearance of such a strikingly original book. The poems Stevens had written at Harvard were Romantic exercises in the style of Keats and Shelley, but as the poems of *Harmonium* began appearing around 1915, the unusual combination of a diverse set of influences began to be felt. The most commonly cited influences on Stevens' poetry, aside from the Romantics, are the American transcendentalist tradition of Whitman and Emerson, the French symbolist tradition of Baudelaire, Valéry, and Mallarmé, and the Imagist practices of modernists like Pound and Williams. Given the eclecticism of Stevens' influences and his lack of a fully articulated agenda for poetry such as that of the Imagists, it is not surprising that the style of *Harmonium* varies considerably from poem to poem. The book was at once traditional and experimental, conforming neither to the programmatic experimentalism of the Imagists nor to the traditional notion of poetry as formal and high-minded.

Stevens' guardedly irreverent stance is summed up by the poem "A High-Toned Old Christian Woman," where he argues that poetry should not only be written according to the "moral law" and the "conscience," but also be animated by a "bawdiness / Unpurged by epitaph." While the poem's speaker may "agree in principle" with the traditional view of poetry as a lofty and serious affair (a view in concert with Stevens' own Lutheran upbringing), he prefers to imagine poets as "disaffected flagellants" who will "whip from themselves / A jovial hullaballoo among the spheres." Here, too, we find Stevens' characteristic mixing of diction for comic effect: the formal latinate diction of "disaffected flagellants" is thrown into comic relief by the lines that follow (the "whipping" here less a penance than a celebration), just as the poetic sublime of "haunted heaven" is reduced to the "tink and tank and tunk-a-tunk-tunk" of poetic exuberance.

I will focus my discussion on *Harmonium*, not only because it contains many of his most celebrated and frequently anthologized poems, but also because it introduced the major preoccupations which would continue to occupy Stevens throughout his poetic career. If Stevens' later volumes are more meditative and elegiac in style and less prone to humorous wordplay, they continue to develop and refine the two central ideas first addressed in *Harmonium*: the relationship of reality and the imagination, and the search for order and meaning in a world without religious belief.

The poems of *Harmonium* fall into several generic categories. There are meditative blank-verse poems such as "Sunday Morning," "Le Monocle de Mon Oncle," and "To the One of Fictive Music"; there are short, imagistic poems such as "Bantams in Pine-Woods," "Ploughing on Sunday," "Earthy Anecdote," "Disillusionment at Ten O'Clock," and "Domination of Black"; there are poems organized as variations on a theme, such as "Thirteen Ways of Looking at a Blackbird," "Sea Surface Full of Clouds," "The Plot Against the Giant," "Six Significant Landscapes," and "Peter Quince at the Clavier"; there are shorter blank-verse poems such as "A High-Toned Old Christian Woman" and "On the Manner of Addressing Clouds"; there are parable-like free-verse poems like "Anecdote of the Jar" and "The Snow Man"; and, finally, there is the long narrative poem "The Comedian as the Letter C."

As many critics have remarked, Stevens' early poetry is clearly marked by the influence of Imagism, yet at the same time the poems depart from Imagist practice in their far greater tendency to abstraction and philosophical argument. Joseph Riddel argues that while Stevens' early poetry has affinities with Imagism, it is marked by an opposite strategy: "relating himself to his world by ingesting its flow of appearances and transforming sensation into the rhythms and forms of his own sensibility."[4] While Pound's notion of the image was largely governed by the analogy of painting or sculpture (in other words, forms involving a fixed visual representation in a moment of time), Stevens allows his images to flow into the motions and forms of continuing and changing experience. Throughout *Harmonium*, Stevens is more interested in describing movement and flux than in representing static forms or in objectifying the world through a presentation of its images. In a poem like "Domination of Black" (1916), for example, Stevens is far more focused on the whirling movement of the fallen leaves and on the use of repetition as a formal device than on the objects themselves as images. Stevens differs from poets like William Carlos Williams and Marianne Moore – both of whom were more closely allied with Imagist practice – in being primarily a lyric poet and only secondarily a descriptive or objective poet. As Stevens put it in a rhetorical oversimplification of the Imagist aesthetic: "Not all objects are equal. The vice of imagism was that it did not recognize this."[5] While Stevens was clearly interested in relating the self to the natural or physical world, he was more concerned, as Riddel suggests, with the question of "how far the imagination could or should remake the world."[6] In other words, he was less attracted by "the discovery of 'things as they are,'" and more by "the discovery of himself in the act of discovery."

It is surely significant that Stevens chose to begin *Harmonium* with a poem, "Earthy Anecdote" (1918), that can be read as anti-Imagist:

> Every time the bucks went clattering
> Over Oklahoma
> A firecat bristled in the way.
>
> Wherever they went,
> They went clattering,
> Until they swerved
>
> In a swift, circular line
> To the right,
> Because of the firecat.
>
> Or until they swerved
> In a swift, circular line
> To the left,
> Because of the firecat.
>
> The bucks clattered.
> The firecat went leaping.
> To the right, to the left,
> And
> Bristled in the way.
>
> Later, the firecat closed his bright eyes
> And slept.

Here, Stevens is less interested in describing the objects presented – "the bucks" and "the firecat" – than in the imaginative dance or drama played out between them. No descriptive terms are given for either bucks or firecat until the final stanza, and there is no attempt to make either the bucks or the firecat visually present to the reader. Stevens appears to find in the complementary motions of the bucks and the firecat an abstract principle of order rather than a concrete or realist description of reality: the bucks clatter and swerve "in swift, circular lines" to left and right; the firecat bristles and leaps to right and left. The poem is structured as a narrative, teasing the reader with hints of both physical locatedness ("the bucks went clattering / Over Oklahoma") and temporal progression ("Every time . . . Until . . . Or until . . . Later"). But the minimalist and anti-referential language of the poem ultimately frustrate any attempt at entering its world of particulars.

Let us consider a more famous poem, "The Snow Man" (1922):

> One must have a mind of winter
> To regard the frost and the boughs
> Of the pine-trees crusted with snow;
>
> And have been cold a long time
> To behold the junipers shagged with ice,
> The spruces rough in the distant glitter
>
> Of the January sun; and not to think
> Of any misery in the sound of the wind,
> In the sound of a few leaves,
>
> Which is the sound of the land
> Full of the same wind
> That is blowing in the same bare place
>
> For the listener, who listens in the snow,
> And, nothing himself, beholds
> Nothing that is not there and the nothing that is.

Here again, Stevens departs from an image-based poetic. Though he presents such concrete images as "the pine-trees crusted with snow," "the junipers shagged with ice," and "the spruces rough in the distant glitter," this cluster of images is framed by the more abstract proposition of the poem as a whole. The poem's opening line – "One must have a mind of winter" – suggests a level of abstraction that Pound and the Imagists had sought to avoid. Stevens appears to be posing questions of a philosophical nature, questions that the poem will attempt to address: what exactly is a "mind of winter"? Why must one have it? The poem's syntax, too, differs dramatically from that of the typical Imagist poem: the entire poem is composed as one long sentence, a sentence prominently displaying the complexity of its own syntax. The argument of the poem moves through a series of syntactic turns that reproduce the movement of a mind accustomed to thinking in logical or philosophical terms. The syntactic complexity culminates in the final stanza, where both the syntax and the abstraction of the language (the word "nothing" appears three times in the last two lines) propose a conundrum for the reader: what does it mean to behold "nothing that is not there and the nothing that is"? The shift from vision to sound in the final stanzas is itself symptomatic of Stevens' own movement away from Imagist representation toward more abstract modes of poetic thinking and writing.

Similarly, in "Thirteen Ways of Looking at a Blackbird" (1917), a brief section like the following can be read as an Imagist poem:

> The blackbird whirled in the autumn winds.
> It was a small part of the pantomime.

Superficially, the lines seem to resemble a poem like Pound's "In a Station of the Metro." When the lines are read in the larger context of the poem's thirteen sections, however, their meaning changes. The blackbird is "part of the pantomime" not simply in the sense that it mimics the movement of autumn leaves or even in the metaphorical sense that it mimics the turning of the seasons. It is also part of the larger cosmic "pantomime" represented by the poem as a whole, of which this section presents only one view. The section can be read on its own – as a discrete Imagist lyric – but it should more properly be read in relationship to the other sections, creating a far more complex poetic text.

A final example of Stevens' relation to Imagist practice can be found in the opening stanza of "Sunday Morning" (1915):

> Complacencies of the peignoir, and late
> Coffee and oranges in a sunny chair,
> And the green freedom of a cockatoo
> Upon a rug mingle to dissipate
> The holy hush of ancient sacrifice.
> She dreams a little, and she feels the dark
> Encroachment of that old catastrophe,
> As a calm darkens among water-lights.
> The pungent oranges and bright, green wings
> Seem things in some procession of the dead,
> Winding across wide water, without sound,
> Stilled for the passing of her dreaming feet
> Over the seas, to silent Palestine,
> Dominion of the blood and sepulchre.

While Stevens presents a rich array of visual images here, the scene is not presented in the directly visual terms one might find in an Imagist poem. Instead, Stevens adopts a technique of combining abstract words with concrete images to form phrases such as "complacencies of the peignoir," "green freedom of a cockatoo," and "late coffee and oranges in a sunny chair." In each case, the place normally held by a descriptive adjective is filled by a word that expresses some abstract concept involving either temporality ("late"), behavior ("complacencies"), or a state of experience ("freedom"). Thus in a phrase like "complacencies of the peignoir," we find not a visual description of the woman's peignoir (a loose-fitting dressing gown) such as we might in a poem by Pound or Eliot, but a plural noun, "complacencies," placed in apposition to it. Both "complacencies" (a plural form of a word normally used as a singular noun) and "peignoir" (a French borrowing) are unusual usages, calling attention to the poem's typically Stevensian diction but providing little in the way of a concrete image.

Instead, the reader is forced to create a composite meaning out of the various denotations and connotations of the two words. The plural form of "complacencies" suggests that this Sunday morning is not unique, but instead one in a series of Sundays enjoyed by the woman in this same way. The fact that she has not gone to church, and that she is still dressed in her "peignoir" while taking her "late" coffee and oranges, reflects an attitude of complacency, whether in the more positive sense of contentment and satisfaction with the secular life she has chosen, or in the more negative sense of passivity and attachment to habit. In either case, the composite image suggests a sense of sensual comfort that, along with the coffee and oranges (foods of exotic origin that have strong visual, olfactory, and gustatory associations), the sunny chair, and the green cockatoo woven into the rug, is able to "dissipate" the religious impulse she might otherwise be expected to feel at this church-going hour. Nevertheless, the complacent sensuality of the woman's morning ritual cannot completely dispel the "holy hush" of the hour, and in her dreamy state she turns to thoughts of Christ's sacrifice and his crucifixion ("that old catastrophe"). The oranges and cockatoo's wings that had previously been the signs of her "freedom" from religious sensibility are now transformed into "things in some procession of the dead" that take her across the "wide water" of time and space to "Palestine," the site of Christ's agony.

Already, Stevens has taken the reader far beyond a strictly Imagist perception of the scene: he has presented a central character, established the basis of a narrative, supplied the crux of a philosophical argument (between the nostalgia for religious belief and the acceptance of our existence in a secular world), and introduced the three central symbolic motifs of the poem: fruit, birds, and water. The tension between visual and non-visual elements is a major structuring principle of the stanza. The visual scene of the woman taking her breakfast was suggested by a Matisse painting, and the first part of the stanza maintains a painterly quality despite the abstractness of its diction. In the second half of the stanza, however, as religious thoughts begin to encroach upon the secular setting, visual imagery is replaced by aural imagery, albeit an aural imagery of negation: "without sound . . . without sound . . . silent Palestine." We could say that while the beginning of the stanza is visually noisy, the end is auditorally silent, representing the shift from the bright and "pungent" world of the senses to both the reverential "hush" of religious devotion and the woman's dreamlike state as she contemplates Christ's sacrifice.

Stevens' use of sound in the poem intensifies our sense of this change. The repetition of the bright, forward vowels on the three accented syllables of the first line ("Compláceñcies of the péignoir, and láte"), along with the internal rhyme of "green freedom," suggests the woman's plenitude and her self-sufficiency in a world without religious belief, both ideas repeated more explicitly in the second stanza: "Why should she give her bounty to the dead? . . . Divinity must live within herself." The energy of the opening description is further propelled by the repetition of certain consonants: the percussive "c" of "complacencies," "coffee," and "cockatoo" and the plosives of "complacencies" and "peignoir." In contrast, the repeated "w" sound of lines 11 and 12 emphasizes the dreamlike and unworldly quality of the woman's reverie. Stevens is masterful in representing through sound the argument the poem will make: Christianity is a religion of the dead with little value in the modern world, while true divinity lies in the human and its relation to nature and natural process.

"Sunday Morning" is a crucial poem of early modernism: it serves as a paradigm for the kind of meditative or philosophical poem that would constitute a central part of Stevens' opus. The form and rhetoric of the poem are relatively traditional: as Harold Bloom suggests, the poem is heavily indebted to the tradition of the Romantic Sublime as practiced by Keats, Wordsworth, Tennyson, and Whitman. Yet at the same time the persuasiveness of the poem is largely dependent on the ways in which Stevens breaks with or manipulates traditional form and language. For example, the poem begins with a line that is essentially free verse (containing only three accented syllables) and it is not until line 5 that the iambic pentameter rhythm of Stevens' blank verse is fully established. The varied number of accents per line and the frequent use of caesura and enjambment suggest that Stevens wished to carry some of the flexibility of his free verse poems into his blank verse.

"Sunday Morning" is also the first fully realized example of what we can call Stevens' "poetry of thought," a mode that is intensified in "Le Monocle de Mon Oncle" (1918) and "The Comedian as the Letter C" (1922), as well as in later poems such as "The Man with the Blue Guitar," "Notes toward a Supreme Fiction," and "An Ordinary Evening in New Haven." Stevens himself believed that "the poetry of thought should be the supreme poetry," and that the "poem in which the poet has chosen for his subject a philosophical theme should result in the poem of poems."[7] Since the philosophical argument of "Sunday Morning" has been frequently summarized and its themes and rhetorical structures have been analyzed in a number of critical studies, I will refrain from a stanza-by-stanza explication of the poem. Instead, let me suggest two of its more important structural features: its use of the dialogue form, and its repetition of symbolic motifs.

The poem takes the form of a dialogue between his fictionalized speaker – the woman whose thoughts serve as the basis for Stevens' philosophical inquiry – and the poet himself, who attempts to answer her questions. In the first three stanzas, the poet establishes the desirability of belief in an earthly paradise that can replace the Christian idea of a division between earth and heaven: "The sky will be much friendlier than now . . . Not this dividing and indifferent blue." But in stanza IV, the woman asks about the transitory nature of an earthly paradise: "when the birds are gone, and their warm fields / Return no more, where, then, is paradise?" The poet answers that no imagined paradise endures any longer than the repetitions of nature's seasons. In stanza V, the woman follows up on her previous question, suggesting that her contentment is always troubled by "the need of some imperishable bliss." This time the reply is longer, taking us through an explanation of mortality and concluding that an unchanging paradise would be worse than our constantly renewing world: it is only in death, the "mother of beauty," that new life is created.

The second important structuring principle of the poem is the repetition of symbolic motifs which occur in slightly different form throughout the poem. This structure of repetition with change lends a sense of harmony and internal cohesion to the poem, and at the same time it emphasizes Stevens' theme of the importance of change in an earthly paradise. The oranges in the second line become the "pungent oranges" later in the stanza, the "pungent fruit" of stanza II, and later the "new plums and pears / On disregarded plate" (V), the "ripe fruit" of paradise that never falls (VI), the pears and plum on the river-bank (VI), and the "sweet berries" that "ripen in the wilderness" (VIII). Similarly, the cockatoo in the rug is echoed by the "wakened birds" of stanza II, the swallows' wings of stanza IV, the serafin (winged angels) of stanza VII, and the whistling quail and "casual flocks of pigeons" in stanza VIII; the "wide water without sound" of the first stanza becomes the "wet roads on autumn nights" (II), the rivers of paradise (VI), the "windy lake" (VII), and the "wide water, inescapable" (VIII). Even the mythic "hinds" of Jove in stanza III are refigured at the end of the poem as the naturalized "deer [who] walk upon our mountains."

In this way, Stevens is able to use a more limited range of images, but to recycle them in such a way as to give them more resonance with each use. By the time the pigeons make their famous descent in the poem's final lines, they can be linked symbolically with all the other images of birds and flight in the poem.

> Deer walk upon our mountains, and the quail
> Whistle about us their spontaneous cries;
> Sweet berries ripen in the wilderness;
> And, in the isolation of the sky,
> At evening, casual flocks of pigeons make
> Ambiguous undulations as they sink,
> Downward to darkness, on extended wings.

The pigeons' "extended wings" are the wings of imaginative freedom, a freedom from the constraints of religious belief, and yet they remain more "ambiguous" than the green wings of the cockatoo in the opening stanza: their "ambiguous undulations" represent the need to choose the more unknown destiny of the constantly changing physical world rather than the supernatural order of a heavenly paradise. The poem ends with a movement into stillness and darkness rather than with the orgiastic celebration of stanza VII, but the sustained appreciation of the sensual details of nature makes a fitting complement to the woman's final realization that Christ's tomb in Palestine is no "porch of spirits lingering." We live, Stevens concludes, in "an old chaos of the sun," a world "unsponsored" and "free" of supernatural intervention. It is, as Joseph Riddel suggests, an "ironic paradise of impermanence" where "nature's casual harmonies enact the only permanence," but it is nonetheless preferable to a world forever divided from its transcendental source of meaning by an "indifferent blue."[8]

In his later work, Stevens turned from the more lyric mode of *Harmonium* to a style that was more philosophical and meditative in nature. In the poems collected in *Parts of a World* (1942), *Transport to Summer* (1947), and *The Auroras of Autumn* (1950), Stevens' primary concern can be said to be the search for a "supreme fiction." Stevens did not believe that any system of belief could be more than a "fiction," a set of imaginary constructions that can help us to understand and enjoy the world. As he put it in a notebook entry, "The final belief is to believe in a fiction, which you know to be a fiction, there being nothing else." In entitling his most important philosophical poem "Notes Toward a Supreme Fiction" (1942), he acknowledges the fact that any poem claiming to discover an absolute truth is an act of hubris: we can make only notes *toward* such a poem.

Stevens' "Notes" is a long poem divided into three parts of ten cantos each; each canto contains seven three-line stanzas. The section titles – "It Must Be Abstract," "It Must Change," and "It Must Give Pleasure" – refer to the "supreme fiction" of the title. The "supreme fiction" is abstract in the sense that it can never be entirely grasped by the human observer (Stevens called the poem "a struggle with the inaccessibility of the abstract"); it must change in order not to become a static or repetitive system of belief (neither a religious doctrine nor a Platonic idealism); finally, it must give pleasure, since "the purpose of poetry is to contribute to man's happiness." The poem ends, like "Sunday Morning," with a celebration of the natural and sensual world: in the penultimate canto, the songs of the wren and the robin, like the "notes" of the poet, can only go in circles, "merely going round / And round and round, the merely going round, / Until merely going round is a final good." In the final stanzas, Stevens evokes "the fiction that results from feeling" as the highest good:

They will get it straight one day at the Sorbonne.
We shall return at twilight from the lecture
Pleased that the irrational is rational,

Until flicked by feeling, in a gildered street,
I call you by name, my green, my fluent mundo.
You will have stopped revolving except in crystal.

Here the world ("my fluent mundo") becomes the poet's lover during a twilight walk following a lecture at the Sorbonne. Stevens chooses the "irrational" or sensual moment of his encounter with the world over systems of rational or philosophical discourse.

Hart Crane and the logic of metaphor

Crane's development as a poet owed a good deal to the work of first-generation modernists such as Eliot, Pound, Stevens, and W. B. Yeats, under whose collective shadow he began his career. Of these, it was Eliot who had the most important influence on Crane's work. Crane's relationship to Eliot's poetry could be described as obsessive: he claimed to have read "Prufrock" at least twenty-five times, and after an initial disappointment with *The Waste Land* he went on to read it, too, over and over again. Both Crane's long poem "For the Marriage of Faustus and Helen" (1923) and his verse epic *The Bridge* were written at least in part as a response to *The Waste Land*.

While Crane was impressed by Eliot's undeniable poetic genius, he rejected what he considered the spirit of "pessimism" underlying the older poet's work. As he wrote in a 1923 letter to Gorham Munson:

> There is no one writing in English who can command so much respect, in my mind, as Eliot. However, I take Eliot as a point of departure toward an almost complete reversal of direction . . . I would apply as much of his erudition and technique as I can absorb and assemble toward a more positive, or (if I must put is so in a skeptical age) ecstatic goal.

Whether or not Crane succeeded in realizing this "ecstatic" goal is a matter of some dispute. Not all readers respond affirmatively to Crane's poetry, and while poets such as Allen Tate and Robert Lowell have praised Crane's accomplishments, a number of distinguished critics – including Yvor Winters and R. P. Blackmur – have found fault with one or more aspects of Crane's writing. There is no doubt that Crane was among the most naturally gifted of American poets: lacking the education and erudition of a Pound or an Eliot, he was to become the most purely Romantic poet of the modernist era, a visionary American poet in the tradition of Emerson and Whitman. Crane's "ecstatic goal" of achieving a "mystical synthesis of 'America'" is unrivalled in twentieth-century American poetry.

Crane was born in 1899, and spent most of his early years living in his grandparents' home in Cleveland, Ohio. He moved to New York City after high school and held a series of menial jobs before returning to Ohio to work in his father's candy store. After a violent quarrel with his father, Crane returned to New York, where he worked for several advertising firms while pursuing his career as a poet. It was during this period that Crane had the first of many homosexual love affairs. Some of these relationships were to take on a mystical dimension in Crane's mind, and they would serve as an inspiration for much of his poetic writing.

Crane also began a serious study of poetry in the late 1910s and early 1920s. In addition to American writers such as Whitman, Melville, Eliot, Pound, and Williams, Crane read deeply into the work of Elizabethan dramatists and poets – Christopher Marlowe, John Webster, Ben Jonson, and Shakespeare, among others – as well as the French symbolists. From the eclectic mixture of these influences, Crane fashioned his densely packed lyric poems, the best of which would be published in the 1926 volume *White Buildings*. In the spring of 1924, Crane moved to an apartment building in Brooklyn which overlooked the Brooklyn Bridge: the sight of the bridge helped inspire the creation of *The Bridge*, which occupied most of his time and energy for the next six years. After the publication of the poem in 1930, Crane was awarded a Guggenheim Fellowship; he used the money to travel to Mexico, where he hoped to begin a new epic. On the return voyage in 1932, however, Crane jumped from the ship on which he was traveling and committed suicide.

Crane's poetic style depends heavily on what David Perkins calls his "alogical language of packed associations," a highly symbolic and often almost impenetrable language depending more on connotation and allusion than on rational meaning. As Crane himself put it in his essay "General Aims and Theories," the construction of his poems is guided by a "logic of metaphor," such that the "terms and expressions employed are often selected less for their logical (literal) significance than for their associational meanings." Crane gives as an example of this kind of writing the expression "adagios of islands" from the poem "Voyages." Rather than using a more literal phrase like "coasting slowly through the islands," Crane employs the associational term "adagios" to suggest a musical cadence (an adagio being a slow tempo in musical composition), thus capturing both the rhythm of the boat's motion and the aesthetic beauty of the islands themselves. At the same time, Crane exploits both the sound and the foreign derivation of the word "adagio," using its long vowels and soft consonants to suggest a fluid motion and a peaceful exoticism.

Crane's complex, enigmatic poems proved difficult for editors as well as general readers. In 1925, Marianne Moore accepted "The Wine Menagerie" for publication in *The Dial* only with the stipulation that she be allowed to rewrite the poem in the interests of clarity. The "clarified" result, however, was so different from the original that Crane "almost wept." When Crane submitted "At Melville's Tomb" to *Poetry* the following year, Harriet Monroe wrote back asking for an explanation of the poem's more elusive lines. Crane provided some clarification but refused to give a prose paraphrase, which he felt would be a "poor substitute for . . . the more essentialized form of the poem itself." As he went on to explain, he was more interested in "the so-called illogical impingements of the connotations of words on the consciousness," as well as their "combinations and interplay in metaphor," than in "the preservation of their logically rigid significations."

"At Melville's Tomb" is one of Crane's most famous lyrics, its tightly wound stanzas exhibiting both his penchant for linguistic density and his characteristic allusiveness. The poem begins with a reference to Melville, the author of *Moby-Dick*, whose "tomb" is imagined to be resting on the ocean floor:

> Often beneath the wave, wide from this ledge
> The dice of drowned men's bones he saw bequeath
> An embassy. Their numbers as he watched,
> Beat on the dusty shore and were obscured.

Crane explained the central image of the "dice of drowned men's bones" as the small pieces formed from sailors' bones by the repeated action of the sea and then washed up on shore, where they are mixed in with shells and sand. In a general sense, the dice symbolize "chance and circumstance" (the element of risk taken on a sea voyage, and more generally in life itself), but they can at the same time be seen as illegible records of the sailors, erased or hidden messages about their lives and uncompleted voyages. The drowned men's bones "bequeath an embassy" in the metaphorical sense that they pass on or communicate messages from one person or one life to another; yet at the same time these messages are "obscured," rendered impossible to read. Crane also alludes to *Moby-Dick*, in which men's lives are viewed as a game played with an unpitying fate and the sea is a destructive force beyond human control or understanding.

The poem continues with a more direct reference to ship-wrecks such as the one with which Melville's novel dramatically ends:

> And wrecks passed without sound of bells,
> The calyx of death's bounty giving back
> A scattered chapter, livid hieroglyph,
> The portent wound in corridors of shells.

Here Crane's arcane vocabulary contributes to the stanza's extreme difficulty, as does his often cryptically associative logic. But the difficulty of deriving sense from the poem's language is not intended merely to frustrate the reader; it is meant to suggest the virtual impossibility of our hearing the drowned men's messages, their "portents." There is no sound of bells to mark the sinking of the ship, no recognition by those still living of the sailors' deaths; all that remains is a "calyx," the whirlpool or funnel caused by the disappearing vessel. As the ship sinks, the rising wreckage gives back a "scattered chapter," an incomplete record of the ship and her crew. This "chapter" (also a reference to the chapters in Melville's novel) is identified in two other ways: as a "livid hieroglyph" and as some kind of "portent" or omen. The "hieroglyph" – a written marking used to convey a coded message – is described as "livid," suggesting its discoloration by the ocean, but also conveying a sense of the anger or rage associated with the wreck. The portent – like Melville's enigmatic masterwork and now Crane's poem – is inaccessible, "wound in the corridors of shells." As Crane explained in his 1926 letter to Monroe, "about as much definite knowledge might come from all this as anyone might gain from the roar of one's own veins, which is easily heard . . . by holding a shell close to one's ear."

Despite the fundamental difficulty of the poem's language – which at times renders its meaning nearly impenetrable – "At Melville's Tomb" remains a strongly evocative poem, in large part because of Crane's careful use of sound and rhythm. The sound patterning includes alliteration (wave / wide; dice / drowned; bones / bequeath; bounty / back), assonance and consonance, and both internal and end rhyme. Crane's use of caesuras and enjambment is also highly effective in varying the basic pentameter rhythm.

It is the third stanza that constitutes the poem's climax in both narrative and lyric terms. Here Crane uses a more sustained rhythm, in keeping with the stanza's elevated rhetoric:

> Then in the circuit calm of one vast coil,
> Its lashings charmed and malice reconciled,
> Frosted eyes there were that lifted altars;
> And silent answers crept across the stars.

The calyx of the previous stanza has expanded into a "vast coil" as the poem moves from the immediate event of the shipwreck to a more cosmic perspective. In death, the drowned men are finally calm – all "malice reconciled" as their "frosted eyes" look toward the heavens – and they achieve at least the possibility of contact with the divine. The very action of lifting their eyes in search of some greater meaning (the "altars" of gods if not gods themselves) elicits the only "answers" mentioned in the poem: those "silent answers" which creep silently "across the stars." In the final stanza, Crane makes explicit the futility of man's attempt to find answers to his questions about the universe:

> The compass, quadrant and sextant contrive
> No farther tides . . . High in the azure steeps
> Monody shall not wake the mariner.
> This fabulous shadow only the sea keeps.

The instruments we have invented to measure space – the compass, quadrant, and sextant – cannot measure such eternities as death. Similarly, the poet himself cannot wake the mariners with his "monody" – the elegiac lament for their passing. All that remains of the shipwreck and its drowned sailors is a "fabulous shadow": they become a legend, myth, or fable whose truth is closely guarded by the sea. Crane's use of repeated sibyllants, especially in the final line, evokes the sea's ultimate withdrawal from the realm of human understanding.

Crane's *magnum opus*, the work on which he was to stake his final reputation as a poet, was clearly *The Bridge*. Before writing *The Bridge*, however, Crane had experimented twice before with longer forms. "For the Marriage of Faustus and Helen" (1922–23) is a poem in three parts, an attempt to update the Faust myth in a contemporary setting. Crane's use of the imagery of the modern city in a highly symbolic and intellectual poem – the poem's "fusion of our time with the past," as he put it – was clearly indebted to Eliot, but the Romantic tendency to seek a transcendent reality beyond the chaos of the city departs from Eliot's more skeptically modernist vision. The figures of Faustus and Helen represent the artist and his quest for unchanging beauty; the modern world is represented by stenographers, baseball scores, stock quotations, the subway, a jazz dance, and warplanes. The poem ends with an affirmation of both past and present, as the poet attains "the height / The imagination spans beyond despair."

"Voyages" (completed in 1925) is a six-part poem about the journeys of a seagoing lover, and it contains some of Crane's most lyrically evocative writing. These sea poems, which are also love poems, represent a step beyond "The Marriage of Faustus and Helen" in Crane's poetic maturity. As Warner Berthoff suggests, each lyric within the sequence constitutes its own "imaginative-expressive voyage": linking "private experience" with the "grandeur and immensity of the created world," the lyrics enact "a venturing out into the seaswell of conscious existence and above all into the turbulence of love."[9] In "Voyages I," written three years before the other sections, we find the speaker observing a group of children playing on the seashore. The section ends with a warning: the line that separates the sea from its shore is also that which divides childhood innocence from the erotic "caresses" of adult relationships. "The bottom of the sea is cruel," the speaker concludes.

In the famous opening of "Voyages II," Crane qualifies this last statement, suggesting that while "cruel," the sea is also sublimely beautiful and a source of inspiration for both poets and lovers:

> – And yet this great wink of eternity,
> Of rimless floods, unfettered leewardings,
> Samite sheeted and processioned where
> Her undinal vast belly moonward bends,
> Laughing the wrapt inflections of our love;
>
> Take this Sea, whose diapason knells
> On scrolls of silver snowy sentences,
> The sceptred terror of whose sessions rends
> As her demeanors motion well or ill,
> All but the pieties of lovers' hands.

The almost grandiose exuberance of the language is proclaimed by its imperative constructions – "Take the sea," "Mark how her turning shoulders . . . ," "hasten while her penniless rich palms" – its exaggerated use of alliteration (lines 7 and 8), and its elongated syntactic structures. The sea is a "great wink of eternity," both "rimless" (extending out beyond the horizon) and "unfettered" (free of all bonds). As Lee Edelman notes in his careful reading of the poem, Crane abandons normal syntax in order to "proclaim the triumph of imagination over reality."[10] A single sentence extends across the first two stanzas, which are both connected to and cut off from "Voyages I" by the syntactically broken "– And yet" with which "Voyages II" begins.

Similarly, the language of the poem suggests a break from normative speech or writing. The metaphoric "wink of eternity" which first describes the sea is an oxymoron: how can the eternal be expressed by a wink, a transitory motion of the eye? Is the wink meant to represent the sea as an eye, with the upper and lower lids meeting at the water's surface? Or is the "wink" some kind of private communication from eternity to the speaker?

Crane hardly allows us the time to ponder these questions before moving on to other images: the sea is "samite sheeted" and an "undinal belly" bending to the moon. The first of these images is fairly straightforward, once we know that "samite" is a heavy silk interwoven with gold or silver (anticipating the "silver snowy sentences" of stanza two). The second image operates on both a literal and a figurative level: the sea does "bend" moonward – toward the heavenly body that governs its tides – yet at the same time the image suggests the underlying erotic narrative of the poem, the joining of wave to moon figuring the meeting of the speaker and his lover. In the second stanza, the erotic subtext becomes clearer with the mention of "lovers' hands" and the call to his imaginary companion to "Take the sea."

In an earlier version of the poem, Crane had written that the sea "is our bed" and "enlist(s) us / to her body endlessly." Here the forbidden act of a sexual encounter with the sea is figured as a dangerous "voyage," the poet and his companion protected from the "sceptred terror" of the sea only by "the pieties of lovers' hands."

In the final three stanzas of the poem, Crane shifts to a softer register in describing the sea: the personified sea is no longer a terrifying monarch, but a nurturing muse who enables the speaker and his companion to experience beauty, love, and poetry. The dominant imagery of flowers signals this change: the lovers drift under "crocus lustres of the stars," they pass through "poinsettia meadows" of the sea's tides, and they finally reach a moment of ecstatic union – "sleep, death, desire, / Close round one instant in one floating flower." Having consummated their relationship with the sea in a moment where sleep, death, and sexual desire are joined, the lovers require no return to the "earthly shore" until they have experienced a total unification with natural forces. As in "At Melville's Tomb," where the sailors were pulled under by the "calyx of death's bounty," here the lovers will be dragged down to their deaths in a whirling vortex which will give them a final view of heaven: "The seal's wide spindrift gaze toward paradise."

The Bridge is a far longer and more complex poem than either "The Marriage of Faustus and Helen" or "Voyages," and we can only touch on its structure and major themes here. That Crane considered the poem to be an important modern epic is made evident in a 1927 letter to his benefactor Otto Kahn which compares *The Bridge* to Virgil's *Aeneid*: "I feel justified in comparing the historic and cultural scope of *The Bridge* to this great work. It is at least a symphony with an epic theme, and a work of considerable profundity and inspiration." The poem has eight numbered sections and contains a total of fifteen connected lyrics, including a "proem" dedicated to the bridge itself ("To Brooklyn Bridge"). *The Bridge* encompasses a number of places, historical moments, and characters. The poem also moves through an astonishing array of literary styles, from free verse to blank verse to rhymed quatrains, from montage sequences to rhythms based on ballads, blues, and jazz. The unifying symbol of the poem is that of the bridge, which represents a connection of the present moment both to the past and to the future.

The bridge also evokes other themes that run as important motifs through the poem. In a letter, Crane described the bridge as "a ship, a world, a woman, a tremendous harp." The comparison to a ship suggests the theme of spatial movement, a recurrent motif first established by the seagull's flight in "To Brooklyn Bridge," and found in the sea voyages of Columbus in "Ave Maria," the clipper ships in "Cutty Sark," the westward-moving pioneers of "Indiana," the trains of "The River," the spreading streets of "Van Winkle," the airplanes of "Cape Hatteras," and the subway of "The Tunnel." The bridge can also be seen as "a world" in the sense that it figuratively connects

North America both to Europe (through Columbus) and to other places reached by clipper ship: Cape Horn, Melbourne, Japan. The curving shape of the bridge suggests a feminine figure, later envisioned as Pocahontas in "The Dance" (who also stands for the "physical body of the continent"), as the pioneer widow in "Indiana," as a burlesque dancer in "National Winter Garden," as "blue-eyed Mary with the claret scarf" in "Virginia," as the unnamed "woman with us in the dawn," and as the various archtypal women named in "Southern Cross": Eve, Mary Magdalene, Venus, and the Holy Virgin.

Finally, the metaphor of the bridge as a harp is suggested by the visual presence of the long cables supporting its span. Music and dance are of central importance to the poem, and Crane himself indicated that certain sections corresponded to different musical forms: a "water-swell rhythm" for "Ave Maria," a "largo" for "The River," and a "fugue" for "Cutty Sark." Other kinds of music are contained in "The Dance," with its pounded tribal rhythms, "Three Songs" (the popular song and tom-tom music of the burlesque hall), and "Indiana," with its folksong or ballad structure. And throughout the poem, the presence of music and sound function as a kind of orchestra for Crane's "symphonic" form. We hear the "nasal whine" of the modern industrial world; the gongs, sirens, and fog horns of the harbor; the ambient sounds of the hurdy-gurdy, pianola, radio, and phonograph; and the songs of hoboes, road gangs, gypsies, and steamboat men. In "Quaker Hill," we hear the whippoorwill song ("That triple-noted clause of moonlight"), and in "Cape Hatteras" we hear the bird note "a long time falling." The airplanes in "Cape Hatteras" are "choristers of their own speeding," and the bridge itself is a giant wind-harp, whose "choiring strings" accompany all the activities of the modern city.

As the proliferation of musical figures suggests, Crane's gifts were above all those of a lyric poet, and his desire to construct an American epic out of what were essentially lyric materials was, as he himself feared, "too impossible an ambition." Crane's goal was never that of Pound in *The Cantos*: to engage in a poetic project that would last a lifetime. In fact, Crane was not well suited – either poetically or temperamentally – to writing the kind of long and complex poem *The Bridge* would become in its seven-year gestation. If *The Bridge* is to be judged primarily as a modern epic celebrating the mythic and historical sweep of America ("a synthesis of America and its structural identity," as Crane himself put it), then it must be considered a failure, since the project of presenting a coherent rendering of the American experience from its origins to the present day is never accomplished. If, however, we read the poem less for its epic structure and more for the intensity of its vision and the accumulating power of its often brilliant lyric sections, the poem can be seen as at least a qualified success.

Some critics have seen the poem as Crane's private psychodrama, a work more concerned with his own search for personal and artistic fulfillment than with its overt subject. As Crane himself suggested in a 1923 letter to Louis Untermeyer about *The Bridge*, the challenge of such a poem would be in how to transform "history and fact, location, etc . . . into abstract form that would almost function independently of its subject matter." Four years later, Crane expressed the tension between "the logical progression" of *The Bridge* and the need for an imaginative "temperature" or "fusion" that might disrupt its unity or logical coherence. *The Bridge* is a precarious attempt to balance the intensely personal and highly metaphorical style Crane had mastered in his shorter poems with the more expansive and "symphonic" form appropriate to his communal and historical subject.

This balancing act was more successful in some parts of the poem than in others, and at times we feel Crane's effort to finish the poem and "get the 5-year load of *The Bridge* off my shoulders." Much of "Cape Hatteras," a lengthy section originally conceived as "a kind of ode to [Walt] Whitman," seems both trite in its sentiment and forced in its language. "Quaker Hill" is another of the weaker sections. Composed of rhymed octaves, it attempts a satiric mode, contrasting the new suburban world of golf courses, antique auctions, and real estate deals with the vanished world of Quakers and Iroquois; but Crane clearly lacked Eliot's gift for satire, and his portraits do little to develop his overall themes. The most compelling parts of *The Bridge* are those in which the lyric voice and the presentation of contemporary or historical details form an imaginative synthesis that provides a new way of viewing the world. Clearly, the much-celebrated opening hymn "To Brooklyn Bridge" falls into this category, as does "The River" – with its concentrated voyage through both time and space – and "The Tunnel," with its gritty snapshots of a nightmarish urban environment.

At his very best, as in the final stanzas of "To Brooklyn Bridge," Crane is unparalleled in his ability to combine a precision of language with a unique sense of lyric rapture:

> O harp and altar, of the fury fused,
> (How could mere toil align thy choiring strings!)
> Terrific threshold of the prophet's pledge,
> Prayer of pariah, and the lover's cry, –
>
> Again the traffic lights that skim thy swift
> Unfractioned idiom, immaculate sigh of stars,
> Beading thy path – condense eternity:
> And we have seen night lifted in thine arms.
>
> Under thy shadow by the piers I waited;
> Only in darkness is thy shadow clear.

The City's fiery parcels all undone,
Already snow submerges an iron year . . .

O Sleepless as the river under thee,
Vaulting the sea, the prairies' dreaming sod,
Unto us lowliest sometime sweep, descend
And of the curveship lend a myth to God.

To analyze these stanzas in any kind of detail would require more space
than we have here, but I will suggest a few directions such an analysis could
take. In the previous seven stanzas, Crane has introduced the two major
symbols of the proem: the seagull flying "with inviolate curve" over the
New York harbor and the bridge itself, standing high above the river. The
gull and the bridge are opposites – one a part of nature and the other a human
creation – and yet they are closely associated in visual and symbolic terms:
the shape of the bridge reproduces the curve of the seagull's flight, and like
the bird the bridge serves as a mediating link between the mundane world
of the city and the transcendent realm of artistic or imaginative freedom.

In the eighth stanza, the bridge is figured as both "harp" and "altar," and
thus related both to music and to religious worship. These two functions are
fused by a "fury": the fury of creative process which will bring the poem
into being. The bridge, transformed into a sacred musical instrument (the
"choiring strings" suggesting the choirs of heaven), becomes the "threshold"
of a new era, one in which the poet is to play a central role. The poet is
seen in his three guises: as prophet, pariah, and lover.

Much of the imagery Crane uses suggests the religious dimension he
assigns to the bridge: in addition to the images of light and darkness, Crane
uses the word "immaculate" – usually applied to the Virgin Mary – and
describes the bridge as lifting the night in its arms, an allusion to Mary lifting
Jesus from the cross. Like the bridge under whose shadows he waits, the poet
remains "sleepless" – filled with creative expectation – as he hyperbolically
figures the bridge as connecting everything from the Atlantic Ocean to "the
prairies' dreaming sod." The bridge is "vaulting the sea" in two senses: it is
building a protective vault, or arched ceiling, over the sea (also suggesting the
vaulted architecture of a church or cathedral), and it is more actively vaulting,
or jumping, across both space and time. In the final and most dramatic
formulation of the poem, Crane proposes that the bridge "Unto us lowliest
sometime sweep, descend / And of the curveship lend a myth to God."
Crane's invocation to the bridge – at once his muse and his primary symbol –
has reached its climax. The word "curveship," Crane's own coinage, contains
within it the shape of the bridge, building on the "inviolate curve" of the
seagull and forming part of the circle ("white rings of tumult") delineated
by the gull's wings. At the same time, the suffix "-ship" suggests both the

majesty of the bridge ("lordship") and its sacredness ("worship"). The bridge becomes a kind of saviour, sweeping down to move among the "lowliest" of his folk but ultimately rising to the point of divinity.

The ambiguity created by the locution of the final line cannot be entirely resolved: how can a "curveship lend a myth to God"? In the most literal sense, myth gives a shape (a "curve") to God: it makes God visible through narrative. At the same time, the "curveship" of the bridge is its most sublime attribute, that which marks it as a work of art and an analogue for what Crane hopes to accomplish in his poem. As Lee Edelman suggests, the "godhead that Crane would fortify with myth" is less that of Christianity than "that of poetry itself."[11] Like the poem, the bridge is a modern creation, a work constructed by a combination of inspiration and "mere toil" that can "condense eternity."

The proem also stands as Crane's response to Eliot, who at the end of *The Waste Land* uses London Bridge as a symbol for the decay of Western civilization: "London Bridge is falling down falling down falling down." Crane's bridge, on the other hand, stands tall, vaults through space, and even, at the end of its curve, ascends to the sky, taking "the arching path / Upward" ("Atlantis"). While the depiction of urban alienation in the first stanzas of "To Brooklyn Bridge" echoes Eliot's "Unreal City" – the views of Wall Street, the bedlamite's suicide, and the cinemas where "multitudes" are "bent toward some flashing scene / Never disclosed, but hastened to again" all serving as analogues to Eliot's London – the ending of the proem shifts to a very different register of language. Here, Crane's concentrated lyricism moves toward an ecstatic expression of the Romantic sublime, one that becomes even more extreme in the "Atlantis" section which ends *The Bridge*.

Yet if *The Bridge* looks back to Whitman and the Romantics, it also looks forward to the poetry of the generation that followed Crane. Admired by such postwar poets as Charles Olson and Allen Ginsberg, Crane became a hero for the counterculture of the 1950s, and his hobos and sailors served as prototypes for the "angelheaded hipsters" of Ginberg's *Howl*. Crane's prophetic stance, his stylistic compression, and his surreal depictions of urban life all left their mark on the poetic language of thirty years later. Crane's agonized and heroic speaker, "Searching, thumbing the midnight on the piers . . . Tossed from the coil of ticking towers," is reborn in Ginsberg's Beats, "dragging themselves through the negro streets at dawn looking for an angry fix . . . burning for the ancient heavenly connection to the starry dynamo in the machinery of night."

Chapter 4

Gendered modernism

With the exceptions of Marianne Moore and H. D. (Hilda Doolittle), women poets of the modernist era have not fared especially well in accounts of American literary history. Not only has the importance of women modernists often been overlooked by male poets and critics, but it was at times deliberately suppressed by male writers who were threatened by the entry of women into the world of literary high culture. When women poets made a concerted attempt to compete in the literary marketplace, they risked being dismissed as "poetesses" or "sweet singers" rather than treated as serious artists. As feminist critics have argued, the invention of modernist form by male authors was in part an attempt to "rescue" literary writing from what they saw as the "effeminacy" of late-nineteenth-century literature. The effort to distance modernism from the "feminizing" influence of women writers can be seen in Pound's dismissal of Amy Lowell's Imagist poetry as "Amygism" and in Eliot's 1922 claim that "there are only a half dozen men of letters (and no women) worth printing."

In recent years, however, women poets of the 1910s and 1920s have begun to receive a more appropriate share of critical attention. Both Moore and H. D. have been canonized as major poetic modernists, and each has been the subject of numerous critical studies. Gertrude Stein's writing has been recognized as a crucial contribution to experimental modernism as well as an important influence on the postmodern writing of the Language poets and others. The work of women poets such as Louise Bogan, Amy Lowell, Edna St. Vincent Millay, Laura Riding Jackson, Sara Teasdale, and Elinor Wylie – often neglected by anthologists and critics in the past – has been rediscovered by readers and critics less under the sway of high modernist tastes. The writing of African American women poets such as Alice Dunbar-Nelson, Georgia Douglas Johnson, Angelina Grimké, and Anne Spencer is now beginning to be explored (see chapter 6). And the work of populist women poets such as Genevieve Taggard and Lola Ridge is at last beginning to attract a greater amount of critical attention.

In this chapter I focus on two main groupings of women poets: the traditionalists, here represented by Millay, and the experimental modernists (Lowell, H. D., and Moore). While the experimentalists engaged in formal and linguistic innovation rivalling and at times exceeding that of their male counterparts, the traditionalists made use of more conventional forms such as the sonnet, within which they could explore their personal experiences as well as their gendered position in society. Alicia Ostriker has contrasted these two distinct styles, arguing that the first group wrote a "formally innovative and intellectually assertive" poetry that avoids direct forms of autobiography, while the second group wrote in a manner that is an "extension and refinement of the traditional lyric style," concentrating their poems on states of "intense personal feeling."[1]

While this distinction is for the most part a valid one, it should not be seen as marking an irreconcilable opposition between two kinds of poetic writing by women of the period. In fact, the concerns of the two groups were by no means mutually exclusive, and there was significant overlap between them. Both groups were clearly concerned with the issue of gender and its implication for the production of literary texts. As Sandra Gilbert and Susan Gubar make clear in their comparative study of two such apparently opposite poets as Moore and Millay, even women from very different poetic camps were connected in their attempts to "translate the 'handicap' of 'femininity' into an aesthetic advantage."[2] Poets from both groups also struggled to find precursors at a time when few women poets provided usable models. H. D., Millay, and Teasdale all looked to Sappho for inspiration, and it was largely women poets like Lowell and Taggard who made possible the critical revival of Emily Dickinson in the 1920s. Further, women modernists of both groups sought to reimagine from female perspectives the kind of mythic structures used by male poets like Pound and Eliot: mythic figures such as Cassandra, Medusa, Artemis, Penelope, Helen, and Eurydice became important poetic personae for modernist women poets.

Another unifying trait in the poetry by women of the period was a deep ambivalence about traditional constructions of gender. Women poets turned to various forms of androgyny as a way of negotiating between the narrowly defined cultural space traditionally available to women writers and the desire to be taken seriously as poets in a male-dominated literary world. At various points in their careers, Lowell, H. D., and Wylie all adopted masculinized or androgynous personae as a way of expressing their frustrations with their cultural positioning as women poets in the early twentieth century, and in texts like "Patriarchal Poetry" (1927), Stein exposed the gendered biases built into the very structures of language and thought.

Edna St. Vincent Millay and the feminist lyric

Edna St. Vincent Millay is often read – perhaps unfairly – as the poetic counterexample to more experimental work by women modernists. Millay not only wrote in what was generally considered to be a typically "feminine" manner, but she also publicized her own status as a woman writer in a way Lowell, H. D., and Moore never did. It was no doubt Millay's unique prominence as a literary figure – her gender-identified "star" status within the world of American poetry – that made her the target for sexist critiques such as that of John Crowe Ransom. In a 1937 article entitled "The Poet as Woman," Ransom used Millay to stand for what he saw as a more general tendency of women poets to be "undeveloped intellectually" and to "conceive poetry as a sentimental or feminine exercise." Ransom's attack was unfair: while it is true that Millay remained relatively traditional in her poetic style and wrote in an idiom that was more emotionally expressive than it was intellectually challenging, she was an extremely talented poet and a centrally important literary and cultural figure of the 1920s. Not only was Millay the example to her generation of the hugely successful woman poet – a literary "flapper" whose candle "burned at both ends" – but the popularity of her poems helped to bring the sonnet and other traditional lyric forms into modern American literature.

Millay was born in Rockville, Maine, in 1893. After her parents divorced in 1900, her mother encouraged Millay and her sisters to pursue both reading and music. Millay was extremely precocious, publishing her first poem in 1906; her 1912 poem "Renascence," submitted to a literary contest, was praised by such prominent writers as Louis Untermeyer and Witter Bynner. Millay attended Vassar College, where she studied literature and acted in plays. It was her training in both music and drama (she at one point considered a career as a professional actress) that no doubt accounted for the uniquely lyrical and dramatic sense of her poetry.

In 1917, Millay moved to Greenwich Village, where she participated in the revolutionary mix of politics, modernism, and sexual experimentation that typified that community at the time. Millay was extremely productive during the next half decade: she published her first book of poems, *Renascence*, in 1917; she wrote and directed a play for the Provincetown Players in 1919; and she published several more volumes of poetry in the early 1920s, culminating with the Pulitzer Prize-winning *The Ballad of the Harp Weaver* (1923).

Millay's early poem "First Fig" (1918) remains her most famous work, and it contains one of the most memorable first lines in all of twentieth-century poetry:

> My candle burns at both ends;
>> It will not last the night;
> But ah, my foes, and oh, my friends –
>> It gives a lovely light!

The poem may be dismissed by some readers as sentimental, and it is certainly not a work of modernist sensibility, but it managed better than any other poem of the time to capture the exhilarating sense of freedom characterizing the new era. When the poem first appeared, there was hardly a literate young person who did not have it memorized. To "burn the candle at both ends" is to live life to its fullest potential, a potential only made possible for a young woman like Millay by a new social, sexual, and artistic freedom.

The poem is constructed around a single image, the candle, which clearly serves as a metaphor for the female body. Not only does the conceit of the burning candle refer to the traditional idea of "burning with desire," but the idea of the body as a candle suggests a site of pleasure that can be also consumed by its own flame. The image of the candle can cut in different ways, depending on how affirmatively we choose to read the poem. It can represent Millay's social role as a female poet who packages her body for consumption by a large and enthusiastic public, but it also corresponds to her vision of herself as depleted, brutalized, or objectified at the cost of some genuine sense of self-worth.

Despite the popularity of "First Fig," the poetic form for which Millay is best known is the sonnet; in fact, it was Millay's skillful use of the sonnet that helped restore it to respectability. "Sonnets from an Ungrafted Tree" (1923) is a sequence of seventeen poems in which a New England farm woman returns to the home of her dying husband, whom she no longer loves. The sonnets are unsentimental and antiromantic, as Millay uses precise imagery to convey the experience of her protagonist with a devastating realism. In the course of the sequence, we learn the history of the woman, who had been betrayed by loneliness and desire into an unfortunate marriage. In style and tone, the sonnets are probably closer to the work of Frost than to that of any other American poet; like Frost, Millay shows an impressive rhetorical dexterity in working with traditional forms and a profound understanding of human relationships. At the same time, we find in these poems a reversal of conventional gendered roles: it is the woman rather than the man who functions without sentimentality, and it is she who is ultimately empowered rather than saddened by her husband's death.

Millay provides a description of a relationship which – far from romanticized – is shown in its most destructive aspect. Though the woman is now an "ungrafted tree" – a subject free from her husband and from her former self – she has developed various neuroses that prevent her from living a happy life.

She is deeply disillusioned with her husband, her marriage and herself, and her days are reduced to a "wan dream." The sequence works through suggestion rather than through explicit explanation: we are never told why the woman left her husband or why she has decided to return to care for him. The reader witnesses her engaging in domestic tasks in a masochistic and seemingly pointless pattern. In poem VII, for example, she fanatically cleans the kitchen until it is "bright as a new pin, / An advertisement, far too fine to cook supper in." The closed sound of the end-rhyme pin/in is a sonic expression of her constricted life. In poem X, we are given a hint as to her ill-fated decision to marry her husband: "And if the man were not her spirit's mate, / Why was her body sluggish with desire?" When the husband dies, towards the end of the sequence, she feels only irritation at having to deal with his dead body: "The stiff disorder of a funeral / Everywhere, and the hideous industry, / And crowds of people calling her by name / And questioning her" (XVI).

In the final poem, she gazes dispassionately at his body laid out on the marriage bed, where "his desirous body" with its "great heat" had once held her:

> Gazing upon him now, severe and dead,
> It seemed a curious thing that she had lain
> Beside him many a night in that cold bed,
> And that had been which would not be again.

Millay's reticent style in these lines – with its monosyllabic iambic pentameter and simple, unadorned diction – captures eloquently the deadened feelings of the woman, who feels no sadness or wifely piety, but only a sense of relief that her husband is "for once, not hers, unclassified." The rhyme of "dead" and "bed" accentuates the changes that have taken place in her attitude toward love and marriage, as she first outgrew her husband's passion and then outlived him.

Amy Lowell and Imagism

The career of Amy Lowell is in many ways representative of the position of women poets during this period. Born in 1874 to an upper-class New England family, Lowell did not begin writing poetry until 1902 and did not publish her first volume until 1912. Lowell's first book, *A Dome of Many-Colored Glass*, was relatively conventional, recalling the style and attitudes of the Romantics and suggesting nothing in the way of an experimental or radically innovative style. Lowell's poetic development was rapid, however,

and by the publication of her 1914 volume *Sword Blades and Poppy Seed* she
had begun to deploy more modern techniques. The major cause of Lowell's
transformation was the discovery of Imagism. In a poem like "Aubade," we
see the influence of the new Imagist style:

> As I would free the white almond from the green husk
> So would I strip your trappings off,
> Beloved.
> And fingering the smooth and polished kernel
> I should see that in my hands glittered a gem beyond counting.

While the poem lacks the concision Pound called for in his Imagist manifestoes or the austerity H. D. had already achieved in her most perfected
lyrics, it makes effective use of the single image of the unsheathed almond
to suggest the naked body of a lover. Such forthright eroticism had rarely
been seen in American poetry since Whitman, and it announced Lowell as
a poet willing to take aesthetic and moral risks.

In the summer of 1913 Lowell went to visit Pound, the leader of the
Imagist movement, in England. At first, their association was productive:
Pound introduced her to the important writers in London, initiated her into
the Imagist group, and invited her to become editor of *The Egoist*. Soon,
however, Pound decided to move on, abandoning Imagism for Vorticism.
Lowell, lacking Pound's desire to remain on the cutting edge of literary
vanguardism at all costs, decided to remain in the Imagist camp and soon
became its chief proponent, organizer, and fund-raiser. After throwing a
party to celebrate Pound's *Des Imagistes* anthology, Lowell proceeded in
1914 to publish her own anthology, *Some Imagist Poets*, including several of
the same poets Pound had published. Pound accused Lowell of stealing the
movement from him and of watering down the term "Imagist" by including
poets whose work failed to adhere to the movement's principles.

From that point on, Pound and Lowell were to remain literary enemies.
While Pound scornfully derided Lowell's brand of poetry as "Amygism,"
Lowell refused to support either the journals with which Pound was involved
or the writers with whom he was associated, including such important
modernists as James Joyce and Eliot. Although Lowell remained a significant
force in American poetry until her death in 1925, she effectively isolated
herself from many of the most important developments in the literature
of her time. Nevertheless, Lowell achieved more literary fame than that of
any other woman poet of the early 1920s. The publicity generated by her
reading tours, lectures, and reviews – as well as her prolific production of
poems and other writings (including a two-volume biography of Keats) –
had made her one of the most celebrated poets in America.

In her poem "The Sisters" (1925), Lowell summarized the sense of marginality shared by all women poets of her generation:

> Taking us by and large, we're a queer lot
> We women who write poetry. And when you think
> How few of us there've been, it's queerer still.

Lowell posits three "older sisters" – Sappho, Dickinson, and Elizabeth Barrett Browning – as important predecessors, but she ultimately decides that none of them provides a workable model for a female poet in the modern era. Lowell recognized the double bind in which women writers are placed, between "masculine" ambitions and "feminine" selves:

> I wonder what makes us do it,
> Singles us out to scribble down, man-wise,
> The fragments of ourselves. Why are we
> Already mother-creatures, double-bearing,
> With matrices in body and in brain?

As Cheryl Walker suggests, "The Sisters" was a "major breakthrough," the first "grand attempt by a woman poet in America to situate herself within a feminine literary tradition."[3] Lowell's most famous poem, however, is "Patterns," a work that first appeared in *Poetry* in August 1915. Here Lowell moves beyond the imagistic register of a poem like "Aubade" to a longer narrative form and a fictionalized persona. Like Eliot's "Prufrock," the poem adapts the form of the dramatic monologue, but its setting is historical rather than contemporary. Spoken by an aristocratic woman during the Queen Anne period, "Patterns" uses the female perspective to critique the masculine world of war. The poem's speaker has just been informed that the man she was to marry has been killed in battle, and Lowell's poem reflects the state of shock into which she is thrown:

> I walk down the garden paths,
> And all the daffodils
> Are blowing, and the bright blue squills,
> I walk down the patterned garden-paths
> In my stiff, brocaded gown.
> With my powdered hair and jewelled fan,
> I too am a rare
> Pattern. As I wander down
> The garden path.
> My dress is richly figured,
> And the train
> Makes a pink and silver stain
> On the gravel, and the thrift
> Of the borders.

"Patterns" is an outstanding example of Lowell's skill in the manipulation of free-verse rhythms, and it displays her effective use of image and color to convey emotion. The variable meters and line lengths, combined with the frequent enjambment and irregular rhymes, communicate the despair felt by the woman, who feels that she is herself little more than a "pattern," a "plate of current fashion." By the end of the poem we realize that this walk through her garden, always in her "stiff, brocaded gown," is all she can expect from life. The emotional intensity of the woman's feelings is kept in check until the final lines, where Lowell allows a single exclamation to represent the powerful emotions trapped below the woman's finely decorated surface:

> And the softness of my body will be guarded from embrace
> By each button, hook, and lace.
> For the man who should loose me is dead,
> Fighting with the Duke in Flanders,
> In a pattern called a war.
> Christ! What are patterns for?

The poem expresses very effectively the tragic fate facing women in wartime; the woman is incapable of breaking the "pattern" of her life, and she realizes that the war, and the structure of society that makes war possible, are also patterns that cannot be broken.

Lowell's imagery and symbolism are central to the poem: the stiff brocaded gown, the garden paths, the changing seasons, and the war itself are all part of the larger social pattern of life that makes women the victims of men's folly. In her gender-marked use of imagery, Lowell conveys the idea of patterns as particularly tied to the circumstances of women's domestic lives; patterns may be beautiful to look at, but they can also function as repressive structures that hold women "rigid." The technique of "Patterns" can be seen as halfway between symbolism and Imagism. Lowell makes use of concrete, vivid images that give the poem a visual precision unlike that found in most symbolist poems; however, like both Frost and Eliot, she moves away from the limits of Imagist doctrine towards a symbolic register that allows for more flexibility in her approach to her subject.

Aside from "Patterns," Lowell's most enduring work as a poet can be found in her love lyrics addressed to Ada Dwyer Russell, a divorced actress who became Lowell's partner in 1912 and who served as the primary inspiration for her poetry until her death. Russell appears as a figure in many of Lowell's poems, which include some of the most original love poems of the period: "Two Speak Together," "Wheat-in-the-Ear," "The Weather-Cock Points South," "Madonna of the Evening Flowers," "Opal," and "Venus Transiens."

In "Venus Transiens" (1919), Lowell imagines her lover as Venus, the Greek goddess of love, and compares herself as artist–figure to the Italian Renaissance painter Botticelli, whose famous painting *Birth of Venus* depicts the goddess rising from the ocean astride a large scalloped seashell. For a woman poet in the early twentieth century to compare her lesbian love poem to one of the great masterpieces of Western art was in itself an audacious move. Here, Lowell refers to the tradition of male artists representing women subjects, declaring her own ability as a woman to describe her female lover, and then proceeding to do so in concise yet highly evocative terms:

> Was Botticelli's vision
> Fairer than mine;
> And were the painted rosebuds
> He tossed his lady,
> Of better worth
> Than the words I blow about you
> To cover your too great loveliness
> As with a gauze
> Of misted silver?
> For me,
> You stand poised
> In the blue and buoyant air,
> Cinctured by bright winds,
> Treading the sunlight.
> And the waves which precede you
> Ripple and stir
> The sands at my feet.

Here we find an economy and precision of language that recalls the original tenets of Imagism. In a final twist, Lowell enacts a play of perspective in the final lines by which the poet is suddenly made to appear in the scene with her lover. The waves rippling and stirring the sands at the poet's feet suggests a sexual encounter between the two lovers, a level of intimacy Botticelli never achieves in his painting.

H. D.'s revisionist mythmaking

Where Lowell's brand of Imagism tended to produce poems that were more overtly personal and less rigorously crafted, it was H. D. who perfected the form of lyric Pound recognized as the ideal Imagist poem: a poem at once emotionally austere and highly concentrated in its use of language. H. D. and Lowell first met in 1914, and their literary paths were to cross on several other occasions: Lowell's *Tendencies in Modern Poetry* (1917) contained one of the first critical assessments of H. D.'s poetry, and H. D.'s companion Bryher (Winifred Ellerman) wrote an early critical study of Lowell's work. But as opposed to Lowell, whose literary sphere became increasingly American, H. D. was to become truly international in her life and contacts. Beginning in 1911, when she first sailed to London, H. D. spent most of her life in Europe. She gained her pen-name in a London tea-shop in 1912 (where Pound famously signed her poems "H. D., Imagiste"), she became a British citizen through her marriage to the poet Richard Aldington, and she had friendships at various points with such literary figures as Pound, Lawrence, Stein, Djuna Barnes, Sylvia Beach, Nancy Cunard, Dorothy Richardson, and Edith Sitwell in Europe, as well as Lowell, Moore, and Williams in the United States. She was psychoanalyzed by Sigmund Freud in Vienna (in 1933–34), and she died in Switzerland in 1961.

Though much of the critical attention that has been paid to H. D. has focused on her late long poems *Trilogy* (1944–46) and *Helen in Egypt* (1961), I will focus my discussion on her early poetry, especially that collected in her first volume, *Sea Garden* (1916). The poems of *Sea Garden* exemplify the Imagist mode at its most successful. For the Imagists it is the visual image that is privileged above all other modes of representation. Despite Pound's various directives about rhythm, word choice and subject matter, the main focus of the Imagists was on finding the closest possible connection between the words used and the objects being described. If poetic language was ever to become capable of a concrete description of the world, the Imagists believed, it would need to show the world to the reader in terms that are free of all abstraction, banality, or sentimentality, and the most effective way of doing this was to present clear, unadorned visual images. H. D. grasped more clearly than any other Imagist (and perhaps more than any other modernist poet) the possibilities of the visual imagination, the faculty Pound called "phanopoeia." In the images of sand, bark, roots, wild flowers, leaves, and twigs that we find throughout the volume, H. D. conveys an "almost hallucinatory specificity"; in each natural fact she finds "the trace of a spiritual force."[4]

This suggestion of a spiritual force behind natural objects indicates the second level on which the reader can approach the poems in *Sea Garden*. The poems are evocations not simply of natural landscapes, but of a classical world inhabited by the gods, goddesses, and other human and mythological characters of ancient Greece. Like Pound, H. D. was strongly attracted to the Greek myths; but for her, it was the lesbian lyrics of Sappho, rather than the epics of Homer, that served as the central source of inspiration. As has often been noted, H. D. evokes Sappho as a mythic presence within the poems, adopting the Greek poetess as the authorizing muse whose example empowers her to write her own lyrics. The "sea garden" itself can be read as the island of Lesbos, Sappho's native land and a place from which H. D. feels freer to engage in what Alicia Ostriker has called "revisionist mythmaking."[5]

Revisionist mythmaking has been one of the primary strategies used by twentieth-century women writers to challenge patriarchal traditions and cultural standards. As Elizabeth Dodd puts it, revisionist mythmaking offered H. D. a method "whereby she could both rely on the cultural, literary foundations provided by mythology, and also provide a new – her own, female – view of those very foundations."[6] Unlike the male modernists, women modernists like H. D. had no sense of nostalgia about the past as a repository of truth or of ideal social structures. The very myths that might connote heroism and moral strength to a male poet could be seen by women poets in light of their patriarchal narratives and their victimization of women.

The poems in *Sea Garden* can be read as early examples of the feminist strain that would be found throughout the writing of women modernists. In "Sheltered Garden," for example, H. D. uses the extended image of the garden to suggest two very different aesthetic choices for the woman artist. On the one hand, the "sheltered garden" of traditional femininity ("border-pinks, clove-pinks, wax-lilies") supplies "beauty without strength" and "chokes out life," while on the other hand the wild garden of "some terrible / wind-tortured place" can serve as the basis for a newer, more innovative, and more daring aesthetic. As Susan Stanford Friedman notes, H. D.'s "distaste for the 'sheltered garden' and her celebration of the wild, scraggly, stunted sea rose were images of escape into a modernist green world beyond the confines of Victorian respectability and femininity."[7] H. D.'s persona "gasp[s] for breath" in the sheltered garden, which is also figured as a kind of hothouse enclosure for growing "fruit under cover." Instead, she chooses the more active, even violent world of the wild garden, where flowers are broken and borders are transgressed. Here, we move from a traditionally feminine ideal of beauty (sheltered, contained) to a more androgynous aesthetic in which categories are confused in the jumble of natural objects:

> I want wind to break,
> scatter these pink-stalks,
> snap off their spiced heads,
> fling them about with dead leaves –
> spread the paths with twigs,
> limbs broken off,
> trail great pine branches,
> hurled from some far wood
> right across the melon-patch,
> break pear and quince –
> leave half-trees, torn, twisted . . .

The upheaval of nature in these lines suggests the turmoil in the poet's own psyche as she seeks a poetic vision less dependent on inherited models of femininity.

The poem "Garden" is a good example of this more challenging aesthetic. Here, H. D. uses the image of the rose – a traditional symbol of beauty – in order to subvert the flower's usual associations.

> You are clear
> O Rose, cut in rock,
> hard as the descent of hail.
>
> I could scrape the colour
> from the petals
> like spilt dye from a rock.
>
> If I could break you
> I could break a tree.
>
> If I could stir
> I could break a tree –
> I could break you.

H. D.'s rose is an object that is at once inaccessible to the speaker ("cut into rock") and ambiguous in its physical properties. This ambiguity is conveyed by the very unusual similes used to describe the rose: it is described both in terms of an extreme event in nature ("hard as the descent of hail") and in comparison to an artifact of human production ("like spilt dye"). The speaker (here a thinly veiled version of the poet herself) wants to seize or possess the image, but is unable to do so. The attempts to capture the image or in some way control it become increasingly conditional and ineffectual. The speaker first imagines that she could "scrape the colour from the petals," but to do so would be to destroy the rose itself, to take only one part of the image – its "spilt dye" – rather than its entirety. She then realizes – using the conditional form of "If I could" – that breaking the rose would require superhuman strength ("I could break a tree"), and this realization in turn brings her to the point of admitting that she cannot stir herself enough to attempt such a powerful act of appropriation.

It is in this sense of powerlessness before the image that we see H. D.'s particular version of the Imagist aesthetic. As Eileen Gregory puts it, "poetry is the evocation and reenactment of the experienced power of the image," yet poetry cannot completely capture the desired object, which remains "beautiful but unyielding."[8] The second half of the poem emphasizes once again the almost unbearable nature of the creative process: here the speaker implores the wind to "rend open the heat" which oppresses her. Yet it is the visceral force of the heat itself, and not the wind, that produces the most exquisite lines of the poem:

> Fruit cannot drop
> through this thick air –
> fruit cannot fall into heat
> that presses up and blunts
> the points of pears
> and rounds the grapes.

In opposition to the cold, clear image of the rock-rose, we find here an image of the overheated garden where the air is so thick that the fruit cannot fall. Yet at the same time that the heat makes the world insufferable for the protagonist, it also gives form to the objects which become the poem's images: the blunted pears and the rounded grapes. The poetic process can only result from the intense pressures represented by such oppressive forces as the rock in the first half of the poem and the heat in the second half.

In the two volumes H. D. published in the early 1920s, *Hymen* (1921) and *Heliodora and Other Poems* (1923), she stretched her highly controlled Imagist idiom into longer narrative poems, many of them based on mythic female figures. In these volumes, H. D. revisits the lives and myths of such personae as Leda, Phaedra, Evadne, Demeter, Helen, Circe, Calypso, and Cassandra. These heroines – creators of life, consorts of mythic heroes, legendary beauties, sorceresses, and visionaries – are often transformed into works of art in H. D.'s poems and thus deprived of their power as living women. Helen, for example, in the poem "Helen," is imagined not as the mythic symbol of sexual beauty and illicit love, but as a wan, white, and static figure.

> All Greece hates
> the still eyes in the white face,
> the lustre as of olives
> where she stands
> and the white hands.
>
> all Greece reviles
> the wan face when she smiles,
> hating it deeper still
> when it grows wan and white,
> remembering past enchantments
> and past ills.
>
> Greece sees, unmoved,
> God's daughter, born of love,
> the beauty of cool feet
> and slenderest knees,
> could love indeed the maid
> only if she were laid,
> white ash amid funereal cypresses.

The lines "Greece sees, unmoved, / God's daughter" function to present both a voyeuristic Greek populace, unmoved by Helen's fate, and the fetishized mask of a woman who can only be loved in a state of virginal death. H. D.'s poem rewrites the myth of Helen, rejecting the adoring gaze projected onto the figure of Helen by male poetic tradition. In Edgar Allan Poe's famous poem "To Helen," for example, Helen is presented as a "statue-like" figure who can be contemplated almost voyeuristically by the poet, who praises her "hyacinth hair" and "classic face." Poe begins with a simile comparing Helen's beauty to ships carrying a voyager home to his native land, thus inserting Helen's myth into a more general structure of literary and cultural tradition. H. D.'s poem offers no such metaphorical construct, immediately challenging the reader with the powerfully direct assertion of the first two lines: "All Greece hates / the still eyes in the white face." That Helen is hated and reviled by "all Greece" (repeated twice) suggests that Helen's fate is also a more universal one: just as she was blamed as the cause of the Trojan War, all beautiful women are seen as threatening to a male-dominated society which fears that their beauty may bring about "enchantments" and "ills." Helen can be safely contained only in the form of "white ash" strewn on a graveyard. The progression of the poem's three stanzas enacts a movement from life to death: in the first stanza, Helen is surrounded by the "lustre of olives," an image of vibrant life; in the second, her smile is replaced by a "wan and white" countenance, symbolic of an absence of vitality; and in the final stanza she is reduced first to her separate body parts ("cool feet / and slenderest knees") and then to "white ash."

Just as Lowell's "Venus Transiens" was a challenge to the male tradition of depicting women in art, "Helen" is is an implicit attack on the masculine literary tradition of using women as symbols. Helen is silenced in this poem just as she is in Poe's, but here she is silenced by the hatred of society rather than by the poet's controlling male gaze. The female poet is powerless to invest the figure of Helen with any kind of redemptive significance, since she herself shares Helen's fate as a woman.

Marianne Moore and the poetics of gendered modernism

Of all the women modernists, only Marianne Moore was able to occupy a secure position within the male-dominated literary world. Moore exerted an important influence on the development of modern poetry through her poems, her extensive correspondence with other writers, and her position from 1925 to 1929 as editor of *The Dial*. She was also able to establish and maintain significant literary relationships with most of the important male modernists of her day (Pound, Eliot, Stevens, and Cummings, for example), as well as with women poets such as H. D., Bogan, Sitwell, and Elizabeth Bishop.

Moore was born in 1887 and grew up with her mother and brother, first in Missouri and later in Carlisle, Pennsylvania. She attended Bryn Mawr College (where H. D. was also a student) and graduated with a bachelor of arts degree in 1909. By the time of her graduation, Moore had decided to attempt a career as a writer, but it was several years before she was able to begin placing her poems in little magazines. In 1918, she moved with her mother to New York City, where she worked as a tutor before taking a job as an assistant librarian at the New York Public Library. During these years, Moore continued to develop her tastes in literature and the visual arts: by 1916, she was reading the work of Pound, Eliot, H. D., Stevens, and Williams, while also paying attention to current trends in painting and sculpture. The publication of her poems during the late 1910s and early 1920s in magazines like *Poetry*, *The Egoist*, *The Little Review*, *Others*, and *The Dial* placed Moore squarely in the center of the burgeoning poetic avant-garde. Her first volume *Poems* (1921) was published in England by The Egoist Press, and her second book, *Observations*, was published by The Dial Press in 1924, winning the press's second Dial Award for achievement in poetry (the first having gone to Eliot in 1922). Moore also wrote a number of influential reviews of modernist works, including Williams' *Kora in Hell*, H. D.'s *Hymen*, and Stevens' *Harmonium*. In July 1925 she was appointed acting editor of *The Dial*, and she became the permanent editor the following year, holding that position until the magazine closed in the summer of 1929.

Despite her close ties to Imagist poets such as Pound and H. D., Moore was not herself an Imagist. Her poetic style was highly idiosyncratic, and owed little to the influence of any particular poet or movement. What Moore shared with the Imagists was a clarity and precision of language, a highly evocative use of visual imagery, and a desire to make a strong break from post-Romantic conventions of poetic style. Moore may have been more closely allied with Imagism than with the symbolist strain in modernist poetry, but her use of stanzaic forms, end rhyme, and syllabically regular lines marked her style as distinct from Imagist practice. Moore felt "oversolitary" at times in "not being able to be called an 'Imagist.'" Yet it was this very freedom from the constraints of a given poetic school that allowed Moore to establish her unique poetic style, one that was almost universally appreciated by the major poets of her generation.

According to Cristanne Miller, it was Moore's poetic response to the three modes of poetry available to her – the post-Romantic, the male modernist, and the sentimental – that created her "anti-poetic mode of expression." Moore rejected the mode of Romantic and post-Romantic poetry during her college years; she also rejected early in her career the "voice of female experience" characteristic of many women poets of her generation, seeking instead a poetic voice "divorced from openly personal experience." Finally, she rejected the impersonal and culturally hierarchical poetic of male modernism, forging in its place a poetry that was "distinctly gender-conscious and distinctly new."[9]

Moore was less interested than either Lowell or H. D. in finding a female poetic tradition in which to ground her own work. Though clearly a feminist in the most general sense – as a woman determined to express herself as an individual within a male-dominated literary world – Moore preferred not to identify herself overtly as a "woman poet." As Miller puts it, Moore spoke "for herself, as woman, rather than for [all] women": instead of writing poems that were overtly feminist or female-identified, she attempted to write poems "in which the female writer may assertively articulate diverse feelings and beliefs, appealing to and invoking a strong sense of (largely female) community."[10] While Moore does not deal explicitly with questions of gender or gender-relations (with the notable exception of her 1923 poem "Marriage," which I discuss below), Moore conveys messages about gender through the style, structure, and voice of her poems.

One way in which Moore's poems differ strikingly from those of her male modernist counterparts is in her use of a first-person speaker to establish a voice that is neither ironically distanced from his subject (in the manner of Pound or Eliot) nor lyrically expressive (in the manner of Crane or Millay). We see this characteristic voice in one of her earliest anthologized poems, "Critics and Connoisseurs" (1916):

> There is a great amount of poetry in unconscious
>   fastidiousness. Certain Ming
>   products, imperial floor-coverings of coach
>   wheel yellow, are well enough in their way but I have seen
>   something
>   that I like better – a
>   mere childish attempt to make an imperfectly ballasted
>   animal stand up,
>   similar determination to make a pup
>   eat his meat from the plate.

This first stanza exemplifies several aspects of Moore's poetic style. First, we see the highly prosaic quality of her poetry: Moore's language here, if taken out of its form as poetic lines, could easily be that of a prose essay. The first sentence, for example, is in the form of a declarative statement: "There is a great amount of poetry in unconscious / fastidiousness." Even here, however, Moore plays with language in interesting ways. The relatively straightforward syntax and simple diction of the first part of the sentence play against the more unusual and somewhat ambiguous expression "unconscious fastidiousness" with which the sentence ends.

Moore's wide-ranging diction is one way in which she expresses her non-hierarchical approach to poetic language: in many of her poems, she moves freely from an erudite and precise vocabulary to a style that is either journalistic or conversational. Similarly, her syntax ranges from the very simple to the highly complex, making it difficult for the reader to find any sense of a traditional lyric elegance in her poetry. Moore also uses sound (alliteration, assonance, and rhyme) as well as the rhythms created by lines and line-breaks to disrupt normal reading strategies. Here the breaking of the line between "unconscious" and "fastidiousness" emphasizes the syntactic relationship between the two words (one is the modifier of the other) as well as their sonic resemblance. The line break also introduces a level of humor or irony into the poem: just as the image of making "a pup eat its meat from a plate" undermines the aesthetic dignity of "Certain Ming products" later in the stanza, the splitting of "unconscious" from "fastidiousness" helps undercut the dignity of such an epithet. Moore's catalogue of examples of "unconscious fastidiousness" further emphasizes her playfully ironic intent: beginning with "Ming products" (Chinese porcelain tiles appreciated by the "connoisseurs" of the title), she moves to several humorous examples the observant viewer might find in everyday life: a children's game of trying to make a toy animal stand up; the attempt to make a puppy eat from his plate; and an ant's repetitive activity of carrying a stick back and forth on the lawn.

If the ant becomes Moore's emblem for "unconscious fastidiousness," it is a swan that represents its alternative, "conscious fastidiousness":

> I remember a swan under the willows in Oxford,
>   with flamingo-colored, maple-
>   leaflike feet. It reconnoitered like a battle-
> ship. Disbelief and conscious fastidiousness were
>   ingredients in its
>   disinclination to move. Finally its hardihood was
>   not proof against its
>   proclivity to more fully appraise such bits
>   of food as the stream
>
>   bore counter to it; it made away with what I gave it
>   to eat.

When describing the swan, Moore elevates her diction – relying heavily on latinate words (reconnoitered, ingredients, disinclination, proclivity) and compound words (flamingo-colored, maple-leaflike, battleship) – and she heightens the musicality of the language through the use of assonance and repeated vowels ("leaflike feet"). But as the description progresses, both the sound and the diction reveal the swan to be a stubborn, greedy, and somewhat unpleasant creature: the close-lipped vowel sounds of "its . . . proclivity . . . bits . . . it" emphasize the swan's artificially stiff demeanor, while the term "made away with" suggests an almost guilty bearing. What begins as a magnifying appraisal of the swan ends as a diminishing one: the modulation of tone from nostalgic reminisence to suspicion reflects the mind's changing view of reality, and sets up the analogy Moore wishes to draw.

> I have seen this swan and
> I have seen you; I have seen ambition without
> understanding in a variety of forms.

If the "unconscious fastidiousness" was that of the connoisseur, the "conscious fastidiousness" is that of the critic, who exhibits "ambition without understanding." Moore plays with the two distinct meanings of "fastidious": on the one hand the more positive sense of careful, exacting, or meticulous (the connoisseur and the ant), and on the other hand the more negative sense of overcritical and difficult to please (the swan and the critic).

The ant – Moore's example of "unconscious fastidiousness" – is introduced very differently from the swan:

> Happening to stand
> by an ant-hill, I have
> seen a fastidious ant carrying a stick north, south,
> east, west, till it turned on
> itself, struck out from the flower-bed into the lawn,
> and returned to the point
>
> from which it had started.

Moore makes a skillful use of the stanzaic form to reenact the visual movement of the ant, turning back on itself and then returning – across the stanza break – to where it started. At the same time she uses a far less pretentious diction than she did in describing the swan, employing everyday language to create a tone that is sympathetic rather than ironic. The language used to describe the actions of the ant is straightforward – it "turned," "struck out," and "returned," rather than "reconnoitered" or "appraised" – and the entire event is presented as a casual observation ("Happening to stand . . .) rather than as a self-consciously remembered scene ("I remember a swan under the willows in Oxford"). While there is no elegance about the ant, there is also no falseness or hypocrisy: it simply does its job, carrying the stick until it proves useless, and then abandoning it to try "a particle of whitewash" instead.

"Critics and Connoisseurs" can also be read as a poem about writing poetry – an *ars poetica*. Like the ant, Moore suggests, the poet simply tries different materials — different ideas, themes, or combinations of words — until she finds the right one. The form of the poem itself plays with its own fastidiousness: on the one hand, it is exacting and meticulous in its rhythmical pattern — the lines of each stanza conforming to the same syllabic count — yet on the other hand it breaks formal rules about rhyme, line endings, and even the coherence of stanzas. The poem is constructed rather like the "imperfectly ballasted" animal of the first stanza: it stands, but its imperfections are allowed to show and become part of its charm.

Moore ends the poem by returning to the examples of the swan and the ant, using a rhetorical question to challenge the attitude of (male) critics more interested in "dominating" the literary world and "proving" their worth than in the kind of unselfconscious experimentation necessary for real poetry:

> What is
> there in being able
> to say that one has dominated the stream in an attitude of
> self-defense;
> in proving that one has had the experience
> of carrying a stick?

Moore's attack expresses her distrust of the world of male power, a world in which she was forced to struggle to find acceptance in the early part of her career. Moore's speaker in the poem is not strongly identified with the poet herself and is not explicitly identified as female; instead, the voice is that of a fictionalized speaker who is educated, witty, and intensely engaged with the physical world. Moore's poetic voice can be contrasted with the typical post-Romantic speaker who attempts to harmonize with some greater being or force, or who refers to intense moments of personal feeling or experience.

Moore's 1923 poem "Marriage" is a satire in which she calls into question the central institution of patriarchal culture. Though Moore insisted that the poem was not an expression of her views on the subject of marriage, this disclaimer is difficult to accept at face value. The poem is, as Miller suggests, "the climax of Moore's exploration of the relationships between poetry, gender and power" and a "tour de force of the various poetic strategies that Moore has been perfecting for the last ten or more years."[11] Moore may have written the poem in response to the difficult marriages of couples she knew, or she may have been speculating about the possible effect marriage would have on her own work. "Marriage" presents an extended portrait of relationships between the sexes, using the mythical couple of Adam and Eve to represent the typical man and woman. A collage-poem which draws on various sources — from articles in *Scientific American* and *The English Review* to books by Anthony Trollope, William Hazlitt and Anatole France — "Marriage" is Moore's longest poetic work, and given its date and ambitious length it can be read at least in part as a response to the production of such poems as *The Waste Land* and *The Cantos*.

Moore does not idealize either sex in the poem, but criticizes both sexes for their failure to see beyond their own vanity and selfishness. While the man "loves himself so much, / he can permit himself / no rival in that love," the woman "loves herself so much, / she cannot see herself enough– / a statuette of ivory on ivory." Still, Moore is somewhat more sympathetic to her female protagonist, and she analyzes the relationship in ways that can be read as feminist. Moore overturns the biblical story by having Eve come first in the poem and by giving her a linguistic ability that is at least the equal to Adam's. Eve is presented as a polyglot who is able to "write simultaneously in three languages . . . and talk in the meantime." Adam is also highly verbal ("alive with words"), but his speech is stiff and uninspired: he "goes on speaking / in a formal, customary strain" of "everything convenient / to promote one's joy." In the modern world, Moore suggests, the woman's position is more difficult than the man's. For women, marriage is an institution "requiring all one's criminal ingenuity / to avoid." As a woman in conventional society, to refuse marriage is to be seen not simply as eccentric or marginal but as "criminal." When she does marry, the woman can only be "the central flaw / in that first crystal-fine experiment, / this amalgamation which can never be more / than an interesting impossibility." While the woman is objectified as a object of beauty who can never be perfect enough, the man is portrayed as hopelessly awkward in his approach to love and marriage: he "stumbles over marriage," a "trivial object" which has "destroyed the attitude / in which he stood– / the ease of the philosopher / unfathered by a woman." Marriage is a constant reminder to the man that he cannot exist apart from the physical world of biological process.

The poem concludes with a quotation taken from a statue of Daniel Webster, one of the most famous American orators and statesmen of the nineteenth century, and a quintessential representative of the form of patriarchy Moore seeks to critique.

> the statesmanship
> of an archaic Daniel Webster
> persists to their simplicity of temper
> as the essence of the matter:
>
>> 'Liberty and union
>> now and forever'
>
> the Book on the writing-table;
> the hand in the breast-pocket.

Webster, a United States senator, attempted to preserve the Union at a time when some Southern states favored separation, but in order to do so he helped pass the Compromise of 1850 which allowed the spread of slavery to the Western territories. Webster's "Union" symbolizes the more private union represented by marriage in the poem, a union which is similarly believed to be permanent: "now and forever." Moore makes ironic use of the famous quote to suggest that if one must compromise one's most deeply held values in order to remain in any union, such a union may not ultimately be desirable. The poem voices a deep cynicism about marriage as both a public and private enterprise. The radically juxtaposed statements that make up most of the poem suggest that Moore will not take the kind of settled stand represented by Webster. Her stance is not that of the orator, more interested in appearing statesmanlike than in upholding moral or personal principles. Instead of expressing a fixed or authoritative position ("the Book on the writing-table / the hand in the best pocket"), the poem suggests the impossibility of achieving positive knowledge about human relationships. Love is both a "mystery" and a "science," worthy of careful scrutiny but ultimately beyond the reach of human understanding.

In the late 1920s, Moore's work at *The Dial* left her little energy for her own writing, and she published no new poems between 1925 and 1932. Moore's poems of the 1930s and 1940s are often considered to be less strikingly original than those of the 1910s and early 1920s, but they continue to display her unique poetic talents. Her most famous and most commonly anthologized poems are those which take as their ostensible subject different creatures from the animal world: in poems like "The Monkeys," "The Frigate Pelican," "The Plumed Basilisk," "The Pangolin," and "Elephants," Moore displays her keen powers of observation, giving emblematic and moral significance to the animals she describes. Moore's predilection for the form of the fable is clear in her verse translation of the complete *Fables of La Fontaine* (1954).

Moore's voice is unique among the women poets of her generation. Her characteristic speaker is neither the intensely personal "I" of a poet like Millay, nor the dramatized persona adopted by Lowell or H. D. Instead, we find a speaker who is able to express opinions and ideas while remaining somewhat abstracted from them: the speaker adopts political, aesthetic, and intellectual positions without conforming to what we normally think of as a "personality." Moore is a decidedly didactic poet, but she illustrates her points through example rather than simply by making statements. Most often, she reveals the play of her own mind around the complexities of a subject and then leaves it to the reader to put the pieces into a coherent whole. Even when the primary argument is relatively clear, the complexity lies in the poem's wealth of detailed observation and description.

Chapter 5

William Carlos Williams and the modernist American scene

William Carlos Williams was a unique figure in American poetry. A practicing family doctor who continued to care for his patients throughout his poetic career, Williams grounded his poems in a direct engagement both with the object world and with the contemporary social environment of the region where he lived and worked: the area around Rutherford and Paterson, New Jersey. As he continued to refine his craft throughout the first half of the century and into the beginning of the second half, Williams produced a body of poetry as impressive as that of any other American writer of his time. It is a poetry that celebrates the local American scene while remaining determinedly experimental in its form and language.

Williams was not alone in attempting to find a poetic language appropriate to the experience of modern America. During the period from 1910 to 1925 American poetry experienced a resurgence that was unprecedented in its breadth and intensity, as a steady stream of emerging new talent transformed the literary landscape. In addition to Frost, Eliot, Stevens, Lowell, H. D., and Moore, the list of important poets publishing their first volumes during these years included Robinson Jeffers, Vachel Lindsay, Conrad Aiken, Stephen Vincent Benét, Carl Sandburg, Alfred Kreymborg, Witter Bynner, Archibald MacLeish, Charles Reznikoff, John Crowe Ransom, E. E. Cummings, Yvor Winters, and Jean Toomer. The careers of many of these poets were propelled by the so-called "little magazines" that published their work, such as Harriet Monroe's *Poetry*, Kreymborg's *Others*, and Margaret Anderson's *The Little Review*. These magazines made possible the publication of poetry that was considered too experimental for the larger magazines and that lacked the popular appeal of more mainstream writing. Though their readership was small in comparison with publications like *Harper's* and *The Atlantic*, the little magazines were instrumental in the creation of communities of like-minded writers and intellectuals who saw themselves as provocateurs challenging the prevailing literary culture.

At the same time, the latest developments in European culture were reaching America's shores more quickly than ever before, and poets like Williams and Cummings were profoundly stimulated by the European avant-garde in the visual arts, literature, and music. New York could not yet equal Paris as a center of cultural activity, but it was making rapid strides in that direction. The Armory Show of 1913 introduced American poets to painters like Paul Cézanne, Vassily Kandinsky, Henri Matisse, Pablo Picasso, Georges Braque, and Marcel Duchamp, while Alfred Steiglitz's "291 Gallery" held shows of work by such artists as Francis Picabia and Constantin Brancusi. The Armory Show, a massive exhibit of two thousand paintings and sculptures, was a defining moment for the arts in America, a cultural "vortex" in which the most advanced European artists were displayed alongside young American painters like Charles Sheeler and George Bellows. For Williams, the paintings of the late impressionists, the cubists, the fauvists and the expressionists was a revelation, suggesting that exciting new directions were possible in all the arts, including poetry. When Cummings graduated from Harvard in 1915, he delivered his commencement address on "The New Art," commenting on a range of avant-garde expression that included Amy Lowell's Imagist poetry and Gertrude Stein's *Tender Buttons* as well as art-works by Brancusi and Duchamp, music by Igor Stravinsky, Arnold Schonberg, and Erik Satie, and dance performances by Anna Pavlova and Nijinsky.

It was a time when poetry was developing in close contact with the other arts, and when poets ardently believed themselves to be participating in the creation of revolutionary new forms. This desire for novelty was expressed most clearly by Williams in *Kora in Hell* (1920):

> Nothing is good save the new. If a thing have novelty it stands intrinsically beside every other work of artistic excellence. If it have not that, no loveliness or heroic proportion or grand manner will save it.

William Carlos Williams

Williams was born in 1883 in Rutherford, New Jersey, and spent most of his life living and working in the same vicinity. His father was of British birth and was raised in the West Indies; his mother was born in Puerto Rico and spoke mostly Spanish in the home. As a teenager, Williams lived for two years in Europe – attending schools in Switzerland and France – before returning to finish his education in the United States. He entered the University of Pennsylvania medical school, and while at Penn met both Pound and H. D. Williams was fascinated and somewhat awed by Pound, who though younger was already more accomplished and committed as a poet. After receiving his medical degree in 1906, Williams decided that he would attempt one of the most difficult dual careers imaginable, working both as a doctor and a poet.

Williams' first volume of poetry, published at his own expense, was by no means a success: even his friend Pound dismissed it as derivative and unoriginal. Williams was not deterred, however, continuing to write even as he set up his medical practice, married, and began a family. His second volume, *The Tempers* (1913), was published in London with Pound's assistance. The poems in *The Tempers*, though generally stronger than those of his first volume, still relied heavily on styles inherited from poets such as Browning, Yeats, and Pound. "I should have written about things around me," Williams later commented, "but I just didn't know how . . . I knew nothing of language except what I'd heard in Keats and the pre-Raphaelite Brotherhood."

It was over the next few years that Williams made his most important strides toward discovering his original poetic voice. In large part, this discovery was made possible by Williams' decision to reject the "old world spirit" and its "old forms" and embrace the "New World spirit" of "things around me." Williams was receptive to the ideas of the Imagist movement, and he was inspired by his contacts with the literary and artistic avant-garde in New York. He saw the paintings in the Armory Show, met artists such as Duchamp, Man Ray, and Steiglitz, and became a member of the group surrounding the magazine *Others*. Williams also began to question the influence of Pound's poetics on his work: "I can now put the Poundesque aside," he proclaimed in 1915, just as he began writing the first of his important early lyrics.

The poems of Williams' three pivotal volumes – *Al Que Quiere* (1917), *Sour Grapes* (1921), and *Spring and All* (1923) – were marked by a new intensity of vision and a greater subtlety in language and form. In his characteristic poems of the late 1910s and early 1920s, Williams sought to capture a sense of lived reality and of the particularity of the physical world. In aesthetic terms, Williams' poems depart from the model of the typical Imagist lyric: his subject was often the urban or semi-urban industrial landscape, and he portrayed scenes, objects, and human figures that would traditionally be viewed as ordinary, unattractive, or antipoetic. Further, Williams' move towards the use of a more authentic and spontaneous language – a language as close as possible to typical American speech – distances his poetry from the more self-consciously literary styles of Pound and Eliot.

Perhaps the most immediately striking aspect of Williams' poems is their appeal to the visual imagination. In a 1929 survey, Williams responded that his strongest characteristic was his "sight," and went on to affirm his "ability to be drunk with a sudden realization of things others never notice." We can see this attention to physical detail in many of his poems: a poem like "Young Sycamore" (1927), for example, is almost entirely composed of physical details presented in sparse, hard-edged language. Parts of the physical world that might appear inconsequential to another poet are often what Williams chooses to highlight. Here, for example, Williams delights in the "young tree / whose round and firm trunk / between the wet // pavement and the gutter / (where water / is trickling)" and the "young branches on / all sides — / hung with cocoons — ." As J. Hillis Miller has suggested, the sycamore is treated "as an object in space, separated from other objects in space, with its own sharp edges, its own innate particularity."[1]

If "Young Sycamore" represents Williams' visual poetic at its most fully developed, we see the beginnings of his aesthetic as early as the mid-1910s. Two poems written in 1916 — "The Young Housewife" and "Pastoral" — display Williams' search for an appropriate language, style, and form during this period. In "The Young Housewife," we find a clear expression of Williams' developing voice.

> At ten A.M. the young housewife
> moves about in negligee behind
> the wooden walls of her husband's house.
> I pass solitary in my car.
>
> Then again she comes to the curb
> to call the ice-man, fish-man, and stands
> shy, uncorseted, tucking in
> stray ends of hair, and I compare her
> to a fallen leaf.
>
> The noiseless wheels of my car
> rush with a crackling sound over
> dried leaves as I bow and pass smiling.

As James Breslin suggests, such traditional elements as rhyme, conventional meter, figurative language, and literary associations have been to a great extent purged from Williams' "matter-of-fact verse."[2] The poem's language is relatively straightforward — though words like "uncorseted" and "noiseless" move closer to a register of literary diction — and its tone is, for a poem of 1916, highly restrained. Nevertheless, Williams by no means rejects traditional literary devices in the poem. We find examples of both onomatopoeia (as the car's wheels "rush with a crackling sound") and alliteration ("wooden walls of her husband''s house,' "comes to the curb / to call"). The use of symbolism is also more overt than it will be in Williams' later poetry. The poem's imagery moves toward a larger social significance through the connotations of words ("walls," "solitary," "fallen"), the explicit comparison of the woman to a fallen leaf, and the extension of this image into a symbol of the leaves crushed by the speaker's car.

Williams also uses syntax to underline the woman's situation as part of her husband's property. In the first stanza, the prepositions suggest her imprisonment ("behind / the wooden walls") and her status as property ("of her husband's house"). In the second stanza, the more active verbs emphasize the woman's movement and the language suggests her freedom from restraint ("uncorseted"): her desires, now freed from the confines of the house, are suggested by the strong trochaic rhythms and the frequent use of both caesura and enjambment. Finally, in the third stanza, the more controlled syntax and smoother rhythms evoke the social isolation of the doctor as he passes noiselessly by the woman's house.

To the speaker (a version of the poet himself) the woman seems like a fallen leaf, but Williams' ambiguous construction ("I compare her to a fallen leaf") suggests the possibility that his simile is inaccurate. Williams' self-consciousness about the use of such metaphorical constructions indicates his modernist awareness of the potential for falsity created by poetic discourse. The speaker can only "compare" her to something in a futile attempt to make sense of her existence: he has no access to her emotional life or even to the details of her life within the house.

Another early poem in which Williams declares his developing aesthetic is "Pastoral" (1917):

> When I was younger
> it was plain to me
> I must make something of myself.
> Older now
> I walk back streets
> admiring the houses
> of the very poor:
> roof out of line with sides
> the yards cluttered
> with old chicken wire, ashes,
> furniture gone wrong;
> the fences and outhouses
> built of barrel staves
> and parts of boxes, all,
> if I am fortunate,
> smeared a bluish green
> that properly weathered
> pleases me best
> of all colors.

Even more clearly than in "The Young Housewife," Williams displays a hard-edged, clean, and accurate modern style. The poem is a kind of *ars poetica* in which Williams rejects his earlier attempt to "make something of myself" and embraces a poetics of engagement with the flux of life. His diction is even plainer than in "The Young Housewife," and the form of the poem seems as simple and unpretentious as the "houses of the very poor" he admires. What Williams finds most important in his observation of a poor, semi-urban neighborhood is not any explicit social significance; instead, he focuses on the neighborhood's visual appearance – its lines and colors. The poem's title is at least partly ironic: this "pastoral" is not an idealization of rural life, but a no-nonsense description of a scene that most poets would find distastefully mired in the real world, with its "cluttered" yards and "furniture gone wrong."

Spring and All (1923) was the volume that established Williams not just as an important force in American poetry, but as the leader of a new American avant-garde. The book consists of twenty-seven untitled but numbered poems, introduced and accompanied throughout by sections of prose that attempt to define Williams' poetics. *Spring and All* represents an advance from Williams' previous poetic work in several respects. As Breslin suggests, it is the first of Williams' volumes to illustrate "the poem as a field of action." For the most part, the poems in the volume are not organized according to any fixed narrative or thematic consideration; instead, they proceed from the experimental impulse to create fluid and multifaceted relations between objects, ideas, and emotions. Secondly, Williams' manipulation of poetic form has moved beyond that of the earlier lyrics. Williams commented that *Spring and All* "was written when all the world was going crazy about ty-pographical form," and although the experiments with typographical form in *Spring and All* seem relatively modest when compared with the more radical experimentation of Guillaume Apollinaire's *Calligrammes* (1918) and Cummings' *Tulips and Chimneys* (1923), the poems constitute a continu-ing experiment in free-verse form, ranging from the perfectly symmetrical stanzas of "The Red Wheelbarrow" (poem XXII) to the asymmetrical ty-pography of poem IV ("Flight to the City"), poem IX ("Young Love") or poem XXV ("Rapid Transit"). Williams' use of the page as a space for visual and typographical experimentation is even clearer when the poems are read in the context of the prose sections with which they are interspersed.

Finally, the poems in *Spring and All* can be read as illustrations or ex-amples of the argument Williams makes in the prose sections. The most important word in the prose of *Spring and All* is certainly "imagination": Williams attempts at several points in the book to define the poetic or artistic imagination. Toward the close of the volume, Williams provides his most coherent account of the imagination:

> Imagination is not to avoid reality, nor is it description nor an evocation of
> objects or situations . . . It affirms reality most powerfully and therefore,
> since reality needs no personal support but exists free from human
> action . . . it creates a new object[.]

We might paraphrase Williams' rather cryptic comment by suggesting that for him the imagination was the faculty that allows the poet to take the most ordinary materials and free them from their their conventional associations: the imagination "attacks, stirs, animates, is radio-active in all that can be touched by action." Rather than "a removal from reality" in the Stevensian sense, the imagination is a means of discovering a new notion of reality; it is a "dance," a "dynamization" by which the writer can "free the world of fact from the impositions of 'art.'" Williams adopts an effective simile to describe the effect of the imagination: "As birds' wings beat the solid air without which none could fly so words freed by the imagination affirm reality by their flight." The imagination cannot function without reality as its base, yet it constantly transforms our understanding of the object world.

Williams' polemic about the imagination is in part an argument with Stevens that goes back to his prologue to *Kora in Hell* of three years earlier. In that book, Williams had criticized Stevens' idea of a central imagination as one which creates a poetry of "associational or sentimental value" rather than a poetry of true imagination. He accused Stevens of an "easy lateral sliding" in his poetry: that is, an overreliance on metaphor to relate seemingly disparate objects. As Joseph Riddel suggests, the difference between Stevens' and Williams' ideas of metaphor is something like the difference between metaphor and metonymy: where metaphor seeks to find a fundamental resemblance between things (and ultimately to discover a perfected order in aesthetic or epistemological terms), metonymy "reveals a center which is everywhere and nowhere, in which imagination is a force and not a focus."[3] It is Williams' more contingent and more spontaneous sense of the imaginative act (the results of which Stevens called his poetry of "incessant new beginnings") that is displayed in the poems of *Spring and All*.

"The Red Wheelbarrow" is undoubtedly Williams' most famous poem, partly because it is highly accessible (the vocabulary and syntax are comprehensible to any fifth grader), and partly because it is such a vivid example of the poem adopting Imagist techniques within a highly controlled form. The poem's efficiency of language and its clarity in both verbal and visual presentation have often been pointed out. What makes the poem memorable is its use of syllabic patterning (each line counterbalancing a three-word first line with a single two-syllable word in the second line), its play with rhythm and syntax (splitting a word from its syntactic partner at the end of each first line, and splitting a compound word in the case of stanzas II and III), and its presentation of three discrete images which are linked by the poem's syntax into a single image cluster.

> so much depends
> upon
>
> a red wheel
> barrow
>
> glazed with rain
> water
>
> beside the white
> chickens

The visual and tactile quality of the poem is more painterly than conventionally literary. The word "glazed" is particularly effective in drawing the reader's attention, since it is the only word in the poem that carries with it an ostensibly aesthetic connotation (suggesting a ceramic or painted surface). Williams, who praised Gertrude Stein for her "formal insistence on words in their literal, structural quality of being words," also treats words as things: what depends upon the red wheelbarrow is, most immediately, the poem itself, or the possibility of making poetry from even the most ordinary of materials. The poem also evokes a prototypical American iconography: not only does Williams describe a common scene of American rural life, but he uses the colors of the American flag (the red wheelbarrow, the white chickens, and the blue water). The "so much depends" of the first line renders the poem open-ended in its larger meaning: the significance of the red wheelbarrow can be seen in economic terms (it contributes to the livelihood of the farmer), in aesthetic terms (it adds beauty to its surroundings), in national terms (it represents the possibility of an American way of life), in personal terms (it brings a sense of satisfaction or balance to the poet/speaker), and in poetic terms (it generates the reader's pleasure at contemplating the scene). The slow movement of the poem forces us not only to concentrate on the scene, but to partake of the intensity of the poet's emotion and to discover beauty in commonplace objects.

Along with "The Red Wheelbarrow," the most commonly anthologized poem in *Spring and All* is the poem given the title "Spring and All."

> By the road to the contagious hospital
> under the surge of the blue
> mottled clouds driven from the
> northeast – a cold wind. Beyond, the
> waste of broad, muddy fields
> brown with dried weeds, standing and fallen
>
> patches of standing water
> the scattering of tall trees
>
> All along the road the reddish
> purplish, forked, upstanding, twiggy
> stuff of bushes and small trees
> with dead, brown leaves under them
> leafless vines –

It is already apparent from these first stanzas that this is no ordinary nature lyric celebrating the arrival of spring. We are placed in a setting usually associated with disease and death ("the contagious hospital"), and the season is not given the traditional trappings of spring: the clouds are driven by a "cold wind" and the bushes, trees, and vines are still in their brown, wintry state. Further, the imagery and diction emphasize the desolation of the scene: we find the "waste of broad, muddy fields," the "patches of standing water," and the "scattering" of trees. But in the latter part of the poem, we begin to witness signs of rebirth rising from the mud. The inclusive indefiniteness of the pronoun in the phrase "They enter the new world naked" allows us to view the process as a kind of birth as well. The prose context of the poem within the text of *Spring and All* – a book devoted to the renewal of the imagination – also suggests that Williams also had in mind the birth of new forms of poetry.

At first, the panoramic view offers nothing with which the imagination can connect itself, but Williams pushes through the apparent barrenness of the scene to uncover dormant life. Implicitly, the poem argues that Eliot's despair in *The Waste Land* derives from his cosmopolitanism and his detachment from any specific locality. The scene Williams presents is no waste land but a "new world." In fact, the imagery at the end of the poem strongly evokes Eliot's poem. Where Eliot asks "What are the roots that clutch, what branches grow / Out of this stony rubbish?" Williams presents a series of regenerative images.

> Now the grass, tomorrow
> the stiff curl of wildcarrot leaf
>
> One by one objects are defined –
> It quickens: clarity, outline of leaf
>
> But now the stark dignity of
> entrance – Still, the profound change
> has come upon them: rooted, they
> grip down and begin to awaken

The poem does not simply describe the physical qualities of a landscape; instead, it focuses on the act of perception, the slow penetration of a desolate landscape by an awakening observer. The poem's trajectory follows the thrust of the imagination downward to a new union with the physical environment.

E. E. Cummings and Robinson Jeffers in the 1920s

It might have seemed to a follower of American poetry in the mid-1920s that it was E. E. Cummings, rather than W. C. Williams, who was the rising star of the poetic avant-garde. Cummings published four volumes of verse between 1923 and 1926, his poems appeared in a wide range of periodicals – including the *Dial*, *Vanity Fair*, and *The Little Review* – and in 1925 he was the third poet to receive the coveted *Dial* award, following Eliot and Moore. While not all critics were favorably disposed toward Cummings' work, the reception of his poetry was generally positive and at times even adulatory. One reviewer argued that his first book, *Tulips and Chimneys* (1923), contained "as beautiful poems as have been written by any present-day poet in the English language," and Cummings' friend Slater Brown made the even more hyperbolic claim that the volume represented "the most important work of poetry yet published in America."

Yet despite the brilliant successes of his early career, Cummings does not figure prominently in most literary histories of the modernist period. Cummings' poems, while they have achieved more popularity among general readers than those of any twentieth-century American poet other than Frost, have gradually fallen out of the central canon of American modernism. Though poems such as "Buffalo Bill's," "O sweet spontaneous," "In Just-" and "anyone lived in a pretty how town" remain standard anthology pieces, it is increasingly rare to see Cummings cited as a primary force in twentieth-century poetry.

Born in 1894 in Cambridge, Massachusetts, where his father was a Congregationalist minister and a former Harvard professor, Cummings grew up in a securely middle-class environment and attended Harvard, where he studied classics and English literature and joined the editorial board of the *Harvard Monthly*. Though Cummings had been writing poems regularly since the age of eight, it was at Harvard that he began to write and publish in a more serious way, inspired by the exciting cultural environment of the mid-1910s and by the discovery of Keats and Dante Gabriel Rossetti. In 1917, he and several of his classmates published an anthology of their poems, *Eight Harvard Poets*. That same year, Cummings went to France to serve in the ambulance corps, and he was detained for three months at a prison camp in Normandy on suspicion of espionage. Out of this experience, he wrote one of the most important autobiographical novels of the modernist era, *The Enormous Room* (1922). Later publications included the experimental play *Him* (1927), a book of collected stories, epigrams, and puns (1930), and an experimental account of his trip to the Soviet Union, *Eimi* (1933). At the same time, Cummings maintained a successful career as a visual artist, exhibiting his paintings on many occasions.

Cummings' poems are immediately recognizable, with their eccentric use of typography, punctuation, syntax, and visual form. Cummings is best known as a lyric poet who wrote on themes of love and nature, but he was also one of the most effective poetic satirists of his age, often using his poems as skillful critiques of governmental policies and the ills of an overly consumeristic society. Cummings' failure to gain the stature of a major modernist poet is attributable to several factors. First, his poems often lack complexity on the level of ideas: they do not force the reader, as do the works of Stevens, Pound, Eliot or Williams, to think about the world in a profoundly different way. There is a great deal of sentimentality in Cummings' work, and he remains in large part a conventional lyric poet despite his experimental surfaces. Secondly, Cummings did not continue to grow as a poet in the way other modernists did: although some critics note a change between Cummings' early poems and his later work, many of the poems utilize the same typographical and linguistic devices, treat the same themes (love, spring, childhood), and use the same basic vocabulary.

Finally, while Cummings was an important innovator and experimentalist – especially in terms of the typographical and the visual aspects of his poems – his work was not guided by the kind of defining aesthetic, ideological, or philosophical project we find in the work of the major modernists: there is no central idea or group of ideas which lead to a whole that is greater than the sum of its parts. As a result, his typographical devices and playful distortions of language sometimes feel like mere mannerisms, stylistic tics with no function except that of displaying themselves to the reader. Frequently, there is a vagueness in Cummings' use of language that can lead to a superficiality of idea. Despite Cummings' frequent use of coinages – typically combinational words such as "unstrength," "almostness" and "flowerterrible" – much of his language remains on the level of banal poetism, attaining neither the sharp precision of the Imagist poem or the verbal complexity of the Stevensian or Cranian lyric.

Cummings' most successful poems are those in which the delightfully playful rush of words is balanced by the controlling discipline of formal craft. We find this balance most successfully achieved in Cummings' sonnets, such as "the Cambridge ladies who live in furnished souls," from *Tulips and Chimneys*:

> the Cambridge ladies who live in furnished souls
> are unbeautiful and have comfortable minds
> (also, with the church's protestant blessings
> daughters, unscented shapeless spirited)
> they believe in Christ and Longfellow, both dead,
> are invariably interested in so many things –
> at the present writing one still finds
> delighted fingers knitting for the is it Poles?
> perhaps. While permanent faces coyly bandy
> scandal of Mrs. N and Professor D
> . . . . the Cambridge ladies do not care, above
> Cambridge if sometimes in its box of
> sky lavender and cornerless, the
> moon rattles like a fragment of angry candy

The poem begins in striking fashion with a statement of its controlling metaphor or conceit. The "souls" of the "Cambridge ladies" (by which Cummings ironically indicates their minds, attitudes, and opinions) are compared to the decor of furnished rooms: like the rooms to which they are compared, the women's minds are "comfortable" but "unbeautiful," and they are filled with the furniture and bric-a-brac of inherited ideas that are never refurbished. These "ladies" still inhabit the nineteenth-century New England mindset represented by the church and the poetry of Longfellow (the epitome of comfortable literary conventionality); yet as the highly ironic fifth line suggests, they are not capable of making a distinction between their unthinking religious belief in Christ and their equally unthinking acceptance of inherited literary taste. Though they are "invariably interested in so many things" (the word "invariably" undercutting the seriousness of such interests), their lives consist primarily in gossiping about their fellow Cambridge residents ("the scandal of Mrs. N and Professor D") and in knitting sweaters for the current underprivileged group, whose ethnicity they no longer even remember.

Cummings' poem is certainly indebted to the mode of modernist social satire found in poems such as Pound's "Portrait d'une Femme" and Eliot's "The 'Boston Evening Transcript,' " yet Cummings keeps his social observations fresh through his novel use of sonnet form, his unusual punctuation and typography (ellipses, parentheses, lack of periods, use of lower-case letters), and his clever juxtapositions of language. The poem is a rejection of Cummings' protected and traditional upbringing: he himself grew up surrounded by the complacent small-mindedness described in the poem, and Longfellow was an important early model for his own poetry. Cummings skillfully manipulates different registers of discourse within the poem: the empty language of conventionality in describing the Cambridge ladies ("at the present writing one still finds") is contrasted with the almost surreal lyricism of the final lines.

Cummings displaces his own anger toward these women onto an exterior object, the moon, which appears in the poem's second metaphor as a "fragment of angry candy" rattling in its "box of sky / lavender and cornerless." The oxymoronic image of the sky as a cornerless candy box – along with the somewhat ambiguous syntax created by the line breaks – suggests the poet's final escape from social and literary convention into a world of imaginative freedom. Formally, the poem reenacts this struggle between conformity and liberation. The sonnet's envelope rhyme scheme (abcddcba efggfe) suggests confinement and rigid pattern (perhaps a verbal echo of the women's knitting), yet the rhymes themselves are playfully irreverent: Cummings rhymes the letter "D" with "the" and "of" with "above," as if pushing to the limit the possibilities of rhyme as a traditional structuring device.

At the opposite end of the literary and geographical spectrum from Cummings was Robinson Jeffers, a poet best known for his long narrative poems set on the Monterey peninsula of central California. Jeffers had little interest in the kind of poetic experimentalism represented by modernists like Pound, Eliot, Williams, and Cummings: he believed that the modernists had "turned off the road into a narrowing lane," moving toward a stylistic originality at the expense of "substance and sense, and physical and psychological reality." Jeffers resolved "not to become a 'modern'"; instead, he would seek a poetic mode that could sustain a serious philosophic inquiry and project a strong emotional intensity while remaining within the bounds of more traditional poetic expression. His thematic aims, however, seem paradoxical: resolving to "draw subjects from contemporary life," he also decided to exclude "much of the circumstance of modern life, especially in the cities," since he viewed the experience of modern urban life as less "permanent" and less suited to the kinds of universals he wished to express. Such beliefs would later lead to Jeffers' philosophy of "inhumanism," one based on the idea that we must abandon the "introverted" focus on the human and "uncenter the human mind from itself," identifying instead with the "transhuman" power of nature.

Born in 1887 in Pittsburgh, Pennsylvania, and introduced to classical languages and the Bible as a young boy, Jeffers was educated in a series of Swiss boarding schools. By the time he entered the University of Pittsburgh at age fifteen, he had a command of French, German, Latin, and Greek, as well as a keen interest in poetry. The family moved to Los Angeles, California, a year later, where Jeffers attended Occidental College and began publishing poems in magazines. After graduating from college, Jeffers studied in a series of academic programs: literature and languages at the University of Southern California and the University of Zurich, medicine at Southern California, and forestry at the University of Washington.

Though Jeffers never began a career in any of these fields, the latter two courses of study were important to his poetry, much of which focuses on details of the natural world. In 1913, Jeffers married and moved with his wife to Carmel, where they built Tor House, a granite cottage overlooking the ocean. It was not until about 1920 that Jeffers discovered his mature poetic voice, and he did not gain a wide readership for his poems until the 1924 publication of *Tamar and Other Poems*, which contained the long narrative poem "Tamar" as well as a number of shorter lyrics. Enthusiastic reviews helped make Jeffers a popular as well as a critical success throughout the late 1920s and early 1930s; by the late 1930s, however, he had dropped out of critical favor, in part because of his unpopular ideas, and in part because the dominant New Criticism of the period privileged a very different kind of poetry from that which Jeffers was writing.

The poem "Salmon Fishing," from *Tamar*, is one of Jeffers' most impressive shorter lyrics:

> The days shorten, the south blows wide for showers now,
> The south wind shouts to the rivers,
> The rivers open their mouths and the salt salmon
> Race up into the freshet.
> In Christmas month against the smoulder and menace
> Of a long angry sundown,
> Red ash of the dark solstice, you see the anglers,
> Pitiful, cruel, primeval,
> Like the priests of the people that built Stonehenge,
> Dark silent forms, performing
> Remote solemnities in the red shallows
> Of the river's mouth at the year's turn,
> Drawing landward their live bullion, the bloody mouths
> And scales full of the sunset
> Twitch on the rocks, no more to wander at will
> The wild Pacific pasture nor wanton and spawning
> Race up into fresh water.

The careful revisions Jeffers made on "Salmon Fishing" demonstrate that he was interested in something far more complex than simply painting a natural scene. Like Frost – whose poetry Jeffers admired – he often uses the depiction of a natural setting to develop larger ideas, though his use of nature does not generally take the form of a *paysage moralisé* in the way Frost's does. In Jeffers' poem, the natural world is not made to function as an analogy or symbol for human life or emotions; instead, human existence is subsumed to nature. The title "Salmon Fishing" may remind us of the titles of Frost poems such as "Mowing" or "After Apple-Picking," but Jeffers' poem enacts a far more violent tension between human activity and the natural world into which it is introduced. The opposition between man and nature is more muted than in the original typescript of the poem, in which the anglers were said to "torture" the fish, but it is still crucial to the poem's structure and meaning. Here the fishermen are seen from a distance, and only through the eyes of a second-person observer ("you see the anglers"). As Tim Hunt suggests, the humans are no longer in the foreground (as the human speakers or protagonist would be in a typical Frost poem), but are seen as "elements of landscape, of nature."[4] Significantly, the anglers are not introduced until nearly halfway through the poem, which begins with what appears to be a benign description of a natural scene.

Syntactically, the poem is divided into two sentences, the first much shorter, simpler, and emotionally contained than the second. In the first sentence we find a series of five statements, each an observation about the effects of the changing season. Nature appears to be in harmony, operating according to the cause and effect of cyclical process, and there is as yet no sign of human presence. With the beginning of second sentence, however, the poem's tone and imagery change abruptly. Here the imagery is associated with fire and ash rather than with wind and water. Jeffers plays with the irony of a ritualized slaughter of salmon taking place "in Christmas month." The highly evocative imagery of the central lines mixes pagan and Christian elements, while the men's presence is seen both as an anachronism (they are "primitive" and compared to the prehistoric priests of Stonehenge) and as an affront to nature, viewed against the backdrop of a "long angry sundown."

The use of figurative language is important throughout the poem. The dominant trope is personification, though the personification functions in a nontraditional way. When nature is personified (the wind "shouts to the rivers") or given human attributes (the "long angry sundown" and the fish who "wander at will") we do not have the sense that nature is domesticated or made to seem more human; on the contrary, such figures enhance the felt otherness of nature. Jeffers does not anthropomorphize nature in an attempt to understand or control it, but instead makes human actions and emotions appear to be simply part of a larger natural order. This refusal to let the human dominate nature is clear in Jeffers' use of perspective: Jeffers presents the fishermen as "dark silent forms" who perform their "remote solemnities" at a distance from the onlooker, yet when he describes the fish we see their mouths and scales in close-up detail. The men are removed from the reader/viewer in other ways as well. They are shrouded in darkness, their mysterious and "primeval" activity compared to that of the priests at Stonehenge, while the fish are described with words suggesting brightness, value, and plenitude: "live bullion," their scales "full of the sunset." While the men are "pitiful" and "cruel," the fish are full of heroic vitality, wandering at will, spawning, and racing up-river to meet their destiny.

Finally, the poem gains much of its power from its rhythms and the force of its sound. Jeffers did not consider his poems to be in free verse, but insisted that they had a rhythmic movement "as regular as meter, or as the tides." In the first four lines of "Salmon Fishing," the strongly accented meters contribute to the overall sense of vital activity. The trochaic and spondaic rhythms, along with the alternating long and short lines, capture the tidal movement and the accompanying surge of the fish from the sea to the rivers. At the same time, the repeated open vowel sounds of the beginning lines ("south," "showers," "now," "south," "shouts," and "mouths") contrast with the closed, nasalized vowels that dominate lines 5–7. The fishermen's disruptive influence on the harmonious world of nature is made clear through Jeffers' use of sound as well as his imagery.

Objectivism in the 1930s

In the spring of 1928, Williams met a twenty-three-year-old poet by the name of Louis Zukofsky, who was living in New York City. Williams was immediately impressed with the younger poet's work, and saw in him the possibility of "another wave of the [modernist] movement." Nearly twenty years younger than Williams, Zukofsky was soon to become the central figure in the short-lived but important "Objectivist" movement of the early 1930s. Objectivism was in some ways an extension of Imagism, though it sought a greater complexity of thought and emotion than Imagism had provided. In 1931, Zukofsky edited an Objectivist issue of *Poetry*, and the poems were reprinted, along with Zukofsky's explanatory essay "An Objective," in *An "Objectivists" Anthology* (1932). Although the work of twenty poets was included in the anthology, only four of them were of central importance to the original Objectivist group: Zukofsky, George Oppen, Charles Reznikoff, and Carl Rakosi.

While the immediate influence of Objectivism on the poetry of the early 1930s was nothing like as important as that of Imagism had been two decades before, the significance of Objectivism as a source of twentieth-century American poetics goes far beyond its contemporary impact. Since about 1970, the Objectivists have been embraced as important predecessors by a range of American poets, most notably those affiliated with the experimental "Language Poetry" (see chapter 10). The appeal of Objectivism comes from three principal aspects of its poetics: a rejection of symbolist and subjective (i.e. confessional) modes of poetry, a rigorously close attention to matters of poetic technique, and a high level of theoretical sophistication.

In a sense, Objectivism was an attempt to redefine the original goals of Imagism and put it back on the course from which it had strayed. According to Williams, Imagism had failed because it had lost a sense of "formal necessity";[5] the Objectivists sought to put a more rigorous structure back into the poem through the technique of what they called "sincerity." The idea of sincerity had both an aesthetic and an ethical or political dimension. In aesthetic terms, the poem's sincerity was manifested in the extent to which objects or details in the world were expressed through a particular "sound or structure, melody or form," as Zukofsky claimed in his essay "Sincerity and Objectification (1931). As the reference to "melody" suggests, the Objectivists were as concerned with the use of sound and aural structure as they were with the visual image. Where Pound's Imagist doctrine had suggested that poets avoid the "metronome" of iambic pentameter in order to achieve new rhythms, Zukofsky went even further, proposing that the poet must "look, so to speak, into his ear as he does at the same time his heart and intellect" in order to convey "the range of [sonic] differences and the subtleties of duration."

The Objectivists also used the idea of sincerity as an ethical or political directive. Most of the Objectivist poets were either members of the Communist Party or fellow travelers during the 1930s, and unlike the generation of modernists who had preceded them, they came from mostly urban, Jewish, working-class backgrounds. For them, sincerity connoted a commitment to their social and political situation. George Oppen argued that the Objectivist poetic of sincerity could be opposed to traditional post-Romantic poetics. The "sincere" poem should not be based on metaphors or images intended primarily for the "delectation of the reader," and the poem should convey nothing extraneous to "the poet's attempt to find his place in the world." It was the truthfulness of the poet's language that would be the ultimate test of his sincerity: "there is a moment, an actual time, when you believe something to be true, and you construct a meaning from these moments of conviction."[6]

The Objectivists' emphasis on the "moment," the "actual time," and the historical "situation" of their poetry, marks an important change from earlier phases of American poetic modernism (such as Imagism) that stressed the atemporality of the creative act. In general, as we have seen in the work of Pound, Lowell, and H. D., Imagist poems did not refer directly to their immediate social, historical, and political situation, nor did they depend on an awareness of such a context for their impact. The poetry of the Objectivists, on the other hand, was highly aware of its historical situatedness, and much of the Objectivist writing of the 1930s reflected a left-wing politics that was in direct response to the conditions of Depression-era America. In this respect, the goals of the Objectivists overlapped with those of politically radical poets of the 1930s such as Genevieve Taggard, Muriel Rukeyser, Lola Ridge, and John Wheelwright, though the Objectivists' heightened concern with matters of form and technique differentiated them from these other writers.

Paterson and Williams' later poetry

While Williams continued to write lyric poetry throughout the 1930s, 1940s and 1950s, his attention turned increasingly to a project that would be his answer to Eliot's *Waste Land* and Pound's *Cantos*. As early as 1926, he had written an eighty-five-line poem called "Paterson," which would be the seed for his attempt at an American epic, *Paterson*. *Paterson* was published in five books during the period from 1946 to 1958. Its setting is the New Jersey city from which it takes its title. Unlike Pound, who wanted to write an epic encompassing all of world history, Williams sought in the fairly ordinary town of Paterson "an image large enough to embody the whole knowable world about me." Williams' inspiration for *Paterson* came both from the geographical features of the city (with its river and waterfall as a central image) and from local histories of the region, some of which he would include directly in the collage-like text of the poem.

Both Pound's *Cantos* and Crane's *The Bridge* could serve as partial models for what Williams wanted to achieve in *Paterson*, but he would differentiate his own epic from both of these works. *The Cantos* were the "algebraic equivalent" for what he wished to accomplish, but Pound's poem remained "too perversely individual" and too removed from the possibility of "universal understanding." *The Bridge*, on the other hand, was too much of a "lyric-epic singsong." Williams' epic would be less tied to the forms of traditional lyric, and would move closer to the documentary style of the newspaper, which presented "the precise incentive to epic poetry, the poetry of events." Williams felt he needed to develop a "concise sharpshooting epic style" that would send out "bullets" of information.

Williams' comments about the origins of *Paterson* – written as a press release for the publication of Book IV in 1951 – are useful in our overall understanding of the poem's complex formal, narrative, and thematic structure. Williams claimed that his general theme was to be "the resemblance between the mind of modern man and the city," and that the language of the poem had to "speak for us in a language we can understand." The choice of Paterson as the city was based on several factors: it was a city he knew intimately, having worked there as a doctor; it was a place not too big to be understood in its totality yet varied and distinguished enough to provide thematic interest; it had a history "associated with the beginnings of the United States"; and it had a central geographical feature, the Passaic Falls, which could serve as an symbolic figure for the poem as a whole. As to the form of *Paterson*: Williams decided on four books which would roughly follow "the course of the river whose life seemed more and more to resemble my own life." The four books would delineate, in chronological and geographical sequence, "the river above the Falls, the catastrophe of the Falls itself, the river below the Falls, and the entrance into the great sea." These four segments would in turn correspond to four movements in the life of a man: "beginning, seeking, achieving, and concluding his life." Finally, and perhaps most importantly, *Paterson* would be a poem about the search for language, with the noise of the Falls serving as a metaphor for "a language which we were and are seeking."

Opinions about the success of *Paterson* as a twentieth-century long poem vary greatly: David Perkins is particularly harsh in his assessment of the poem, calling it "a botch."[7] Most of the criticisms of the poem have centered on its looseness of organization, its lack of a coherent structure, and the absence of a unifying voice such as is arguably present in *The Waste Land*, *The Four Quartets*, and (at least in parts) *The Cantos*. As Joseph Riddel points out, critics have sought in the poem "an organizing center, a controlling image, [or] a mythic predesign," and they have focused on such imagistic or symbolic centers as the river, the cycle of seasons, the quadrilateral structure of the first four books, the metaphor of the city, and the trope of marriage and divorce.[8] But according to Riddel's reading, the poem does not rely on any such symbolic or organizational center; instead, it is radically decentered, designed more on the model of the cubist painting, palimpsest, or helix than on the centralizing model of the traditional poem. *Paterson* is a poem containing "layers upon layers of interpretations"; it is "an unfolding sequence of words"[9] which never achieves thematic, narrative, or formal closure.

Though many of these same qualities can be attributed to *The Cantos* as well, Williams' stance toward the construction of *Paterson* was fundamentally different from that of either Pound or Eliot. Where Pound saw the artistic process as a matter of exerting vigorous control over his medium – "yanking and hauling" his materials out of the "indomitable chaos" and into "some sort of order" – Williams described the process of writing his long poem more as one of discovery. He sought to allow the composition to "assume a form" rather than forcibly imposing one. The formal organization of the poem resembles the flow of a river: just as the river moves forward in a direction and at a speed that is variable and subject to changes in the landscape, the poem is subject to the poet's discovery of new materials and new ideas. Such a form cannot be predetermined, and as a result Williams' general plan for what he called "the impossible poem *Paterson*" underwent numerous modifications on the way to its completion. As James Breslin puts it, the poem's form assumes openness and immediacy as primary values: "*Paterson* is by no means a finished work . . . instead, [it] is the act of its creation, recording the consciousness of its creator, whose dual fidelity to the *world* and to the *poem* constantly forces him to turn back and start all over again."[10]

This more open conception of *Paterson* appealed strongly to the generation of younger poets beginning to write in the late 1940s and early 1950s, who saw in the poem a necessary alternative to Pound's *Cantos*. As Charles Olson put it in a letter to Robert Creeley (1951), Williams' poem "gave us the lead on the local" and made possible "extensions and comprehensions" *The Cantos* did not. *Paterson* opened the way for such postmodern epics as Olson's *Maximus Poems* and Edward Dorn's *Gunslinger*.

A thorough reading of *Paterson* would require far more space than we can devote to it here. What I have tried to provide is a general sense of the poem which emphasizes Williams' own plan for its composition. The importance the poem held for Williams is indicated by his decision to add another book after the completion of the original four-book project. *Paterson V* appeared in 1958, when Williams was seventy-five years old. By this time he had suffered a series of strokes, another of which was to follow later in that year. Williams had written some of his most memorable poetry during the past decade, including the long narrative poem "The Desert Music" (1951), the meditative love poem "Of Asphodel, That Greeny Flower" (1953), and shorter lyrics such as "The Ivy Crown" and "The Sparrow."

Most of the lyric poetry Williams published in the 1950s was written in a triadic stanza pattern he called the "variable foot," which he had begun using in the second book of *Paterson*. In the triadic stanza, each group of three lines moves progressively toward the right margin as it steps down the page; each line is to be given equal weight, despite the difference in the number of syllables from one line to another. This form helps contribute to the measured, slow, almost halting, but highly evocative and meditative quality of the later poetry. We see this quality in the following passage from the ending of "Asphodel":

> As I think of it now,
>   after a lifetime,
>   it is as if
> a sweet-scented flower
>   were poised
>   and for me did open.
> Asphodel
>   has no odor
>   save to the imagination
> but it too
>   celebrates the light.
>   It is late
> but an odor
>   as from our wedding
>   has revived for me
> and begun again to penetrate
>   into all crevices
>   of my world.

In this moving love poem to his wife Flossie, the back-and-forth movement of the lines is suggestive of the alternation between past memories and the present act of writing the poem. At the same time, the variable line lengths allow Williams to place differing emphases on individual words and phrases while still maintaining an overall sense of formal structure. Within this loose "measure," Williams can choose to devote a line to a single word or an entire phrase. "Asphodel," the flower which serves as the central image of the poem, clearly merits a line to itself, but perhaps more surprising is the placement of a phrase like "it is as if." Lacking any of what are normally considered the most important words in poetry (nouns, pronouns, verbs, or adjectives), the line indicates the importance Williams assigns to the mental process itself, the turning of the mind toward a new idea or metaphor.

Williams uses the flexibility of the form to his advantage, stretching his thought back across the page from the end of one three-line unit to the beginning of the next: "it is as if // a sweet-scented flower / were poised." The circling movement suggested by the use of the triadic feet establishes the thematic and symbolic motion of the poem as a whole, which moves "through the recognition of the fact of death" to "an affirmation of the transcendent power of love."[11] The asphodel itself is the flower of the dead, which in classical mythology covers the Elysian Fields. Since the flower was also familiar to Williams from his childhood in modern-day New Jersey, its use here represents the "confluence of [poetic] tradition with his local world."[12] The flower links past and present, and its symbolic resonance moves between death and a rebirth through love and memory. Williams, who resisted overt symbolism throughout most of his career, now allows himself to indulge freely in the process of turning image into symbol: the asphodel is odorless and nearly colorless (signifying Williams' own sense of physical fading), yet this frail flower returns every year "after winter's harshness," and in the poet's imagination it takes on a potent physicality, penetrating the "crevices / of my world." In "Asphodel," the older Williams uses the latent power of the image to construct larger symbolic structures, thus celebrating the endless turning of the mind rather than the more static focus on the visual object.

Chapter 6

From the Harlem Renaissance to the Black Arts movement

The history of African American poetry in the twentieth century can be divided into three generational moments: the Harlem Renaissance of the 1920s and early 1930s, the post-Renaissance poetry of the 1940s and 1950s, and the Black Arts movement of the 1960s and 1970s. The Harlem Renaissance, part of a more general "New Negro" movement in the United States, was the first major flowering of creative activity by African American writers, artists, and musicians in the twentieth century. In the 1940s and 1950s, there was a revival of African American verse, led by Melvin Tolson, Gwendolyn Brooks, and Robert Hayden. Finally, a third wave of African American poetry emerged in the late 1960s with the Black Arts movement or Black Aesthetic. Infused with a newly defined racial and political consciousness, poets such as Amiri Baraka, June Jordan, Nikki Giovanni, Sonia Sanchez, Audre Lorde, Ishmael Reed, and Michael S. Harper produced poetry that was more clearly militant in its message and rawer in its language and form. This chapter will focus on the two most important cultural moments for African American poets in the twentieth century – the Harlem Renaissance and the Black Arts movement – with a brief discussion of the poets who constitute the middle generation.

The "New Negro" and African American poetry

Although we can locate the actual beginning of the Harlem Renaissance in about 1922, the literary and cultural roots of the Renaissance can be traced to the end of the previous century. The Harlem Renaissance was the literary and artistic expression of ideas that had been developing within African American culture since the end of the Civil War. Foremost among these ideas was the concept of the "New Negro," a term that was first used in 1895 to describe a new class of American blacks who for the first time had access to both money and education. The "New Negro" movement stressed racial pride and self-reliance, full rights for blacks as American citizens, and, in general, the desirability of assimilation into white middle-class culture. Another important element in the New Negro movement

114

was the interest in the African heritage of American blacks: this heritage was held up as a source of pride and the basis for a worldwide racial solidarity. The so-called "pan-Africanism" movement was embraced by a number of black intellectuals, including W. E. B. Du Bois and Marcus Garvey.

It was in the Harlem district of upper Manhattan that the promise of the "New Negro" was turned into a reality. By the mid-1920s, the vanguard of young black writers and painters had moved to Harlem, and it was there, as Alain Locke proclaimed in his 1925 book *The New Negro*, that "Negro life [was] seizing its first chances for group expression and self determination."[1] It was the involvement of black intellectuals like Locke as much as the production of writers and artists that shaped the Harlem New Negro movement. This black intelligentsia included Locke, a professor at Howard University, James Weldon Johnson, the general secretary of the NAACP (National Assoiation for the Advancement of Colored People), and Charles S. Johnson of the Urban League.

Another important source for the Harlem Renaissance was the literary tradition of African American writers. Two of the most celebrated black poets of the generation prior to that of the Renaissance writers were Paul Lawrence Dunbar and James Weldon Johnson. Dunbar, who was born in Dayton, Ohio, in 1872 to two former slaves, dedicated himself to becoming a writer in order to "interpret my own people through song and story." Dunbar's second volume of poems, *Majors and Minors* (1896), received a positive review in *Harper's Review* from William Dean Howells, then America's foremost literary critic. Howells went on to write the introduction to Dunbar's next collection, *Lyrics of the Lowly Life*, and Dunbar was launched on a successful literary career that allowed him to publish ten more books of poetry and fiction before his death in 1906. Dunbar wrote two basic types of poetry: poems in black dialect and poems in standard English. In the dialect category we find poems like "When Malindy Sings" and "A Negro Love Song," while among his finest non-dialect poems are "We Wear the Mask" and "Sympathy."

While editors and patrons encouraged Dunbar to submit more dialect poetry, these poems placed him in a double bind. Such poems could be seen as expressing more directly the thoughts and feelings of the black race, but they could also be read as reinforcing negative racial stereotypes and conforming to a nostalgic vision of antebellum plantation life. James Weldon Johnson, for example, criticized dialect poetry as a form typified by "exaggerated geniality, childish optimism, forced comicality, and mawkish sentiment."[2] While some of Dunbar's dialect poems suffered from these faults, others are redeemed by their skillful composition and their humor and irony. In "When Malindy Sings" (1895), Dunbar celebrates the "natural"

singing of the black Malindy as superior to that of the musically trained
white mistress:

> G'way an' quit dat noise, Miss Lucy –
> Put dat music book away;
> What's de use to keep on tryin'?
> Ef you practise twell you're gray,
> You cain't sta't no notes a-flyin'
> Lak de ones dat rants and rings
> F'om de kitchen to de big woods
> When Malindy sings.

Despite Miss Lucy's ability to read music, she lacks the "nachel o'gans" to
"make de soun' come right." Malindy, on the other hand, has an intuitive
gift that puts even the birds to shame: "Robins, la'ks, an all dem things, /
heish dey moufs an' hides dey faces / When Malindy sings." Dunbar not
only presents the "reality" of black life, but manipulates racial stereotypes;
as Shelly Eversly suggests, he uses "existing assumptions about the qualities
of a distinctly African American temperament to illustrate the depths of
Malindy's skill."[3]

The Harlem Renaissance

Harlem became the center of African American life only in the second
decade of the twentieth century, when the great migration of blacks from the
rural south to the industrialized north brought a large black population into
New York City. Between 1910 and 1930, the black population of New York
increased from under 100,000 to over 300,000. The mass exodus from the
south had several causes: a deteriorating racial climate (including an increase
in lynchings), an economic depression, and such natural catastrophes as
cotton boll weevils and floods. While other northern cities such as Chicago,
Detroit, and Cleveland also saw dramatic increases in their black populations,
none of them became centers for African American culture in the way New
York City did.

   By 1920, Harlem had become, as James Weldon Johnson put it, "the
greatest Negro city in the world."[4] A self-contained community of over
100,000 blacks, it was a "City of Refuge" from the racist attitudes of white
America and from the threat of racial violence which was a constant presence in the Southern states. Harlem was a locus of migration not only
for black Southerners, but also for foreign-born blacks, especially from the
Caribbean. Equally important was Harlem's status as a cultural center where

artists, writers, musicians, intellectuals, and various other individuals could feel free to meet, express themselves, and test their creative energies in an environment undisrupted by white America. There was for example A'Lelia Walker, an heiress who gave legendary parties in her Harlem mansion. There were other gatherings at the homes of such luminaries as James Weldon Johnson, the novelist and critic Jessie Fauset, and the painter Aaron Douglas. There were journals such as *Negro World*, *Crisis*, and *Opportunity*, as well as a wide range of black newspapers. There was the American Negro Press, founded in Harlem in 1919. And there was an active nightlife, with music and dancing at places like the Sugar Cane Club – which boasted performers like Bessie Smith, Duke Ellington, and Louis Armstrong – as well as a number of speakeasies, ginhouses, and jazz bars.

The centrality of Harlem as a symbolic site of African American life and culture is demonstrated by the extraordinary number of poems and books of the 1910s, 1920s, and 1930s that include the word in their titles: "Harlem," "Harlem Dancer," "Harlem: The Black City," "Harlem Street Walkers," "Harlem Life," "Harlem Wine," "Harlem Night Club," "Harlem Night Song," *Harlem Shadows*, *Home to Harlem*, and *Harlem: Negro Metropolis*. Langston Hughes arrived in New York in 1921, drawn to the city mainly by the allure of Harlem, and enrolled in the fall of that year at Columbia University. He soon met W. E. B. Du Bois, editor of *Crisis*, as well as Jessie Fauset, the journal's literary critic. A year later, Claude McKay was to publish *Harlem Shadows*, the first book of poems to display the new sensibility of the Harlem Renaissance.

McKay was born in Jamaica in 1889, and published two books of dialect poems, *Songs of Jamaica* and *Constab Ballads*, in 1912. His next volume, *Spring in New Hampshire and Other Poems*, was published in England in 1920, but by that time he had already led an eventful life, studying agriculture, opening a restaurant, working as a railroad dining-car waiter, and washing dishes in a boarding house. "The Harlem Dancer," first published in 1917, is arguably the earliest Harlem Renaissance poem. McKay focuses on an exotic dancer objectified by the "applauding youths" and "young prostitutes" who watch "her perfect, half-clothed body sway." For the poem's speaker, however, the prurient attitude of the audience which "devour[s] her shape with eager, passionate gaze" can never reach the essence of the dancer, whose deeper self is expressed in the more innocent comparison of her voice to "the sound of blended flutes / Blown by black players on a picnic day" and of her body to "a proudly swaying palm / Grown lovelier for passing through a storm." McKay concludes with lines that make reference to the disillusionment of his own immigrant experience: "But looking at her falsely-smiling face, / I knew her self was not in that strange place." While McKay's use of the sonnet form is traditional, his poem is one of the first to capture the pathos – as well as the gritty reality – of black life in the urban ghetto. In this respect at least, it is a significant step beyond the poetry of Dunbar and Johnson.

It was the publication of the poem "If We Must Die" in 1919 that established McKay as a leading figure of the Harlem Renaissance, and the poem was quickly to become a *cause célèbre* within the African American community. McKay's sonnet is a powerful declaration of racial anger, particularly given its historical context: that summer, deadly antiblack riots in Chicago and other cities had caused many to grow pessimistic about the place of African Americans in postwar society. In the poem, McKay describes urban blacks as "hogs / Hunted and penned in an inglorious spot," while whites are referred to as a pack of "mad and hungry dogs" who "mock at our accursed lot." The poem's speaker vows to avenge the brutality of the attacks on black citizens: "Like men we'll face the murderous, cowardly pack / Pressed to the wall, dying, but fighting back." Never before had the social antagonism between the races been expressed so directly in poetic form.

Despite its celebrity, "If We Must Die" is more effective as propaganda than as poetry, and its stilted diction and awkward phrasing ("Though far outnumbered let us show us brave") detract from its success as a poem. A more accomplished protest poem is "The White House":

> Your door is shut against my tightened face,
> And I am sharp as steel with discontent;
> But I possess the courage and the grace
> To bear my anger proudly and unbent.
> The pavement slabs burn loose beneath my feet,
> A chafing savage, down the decent street;
> And passion rends my vitals as I pass,
> Where boldly shines your shuttered door of glass.

Here the language is less stilted than in "If We Must Die," and the images more nuanced. McKay chooses his words carefully, creating ironic contrasts which comment on the situation of blacks excluded from full participation in the American dream. In line 6, for example, McKay contrasts the "chafing savage" with the "decent street," pointing to the racist attitudes of middle-class whites who view him as a "savage" merely because of the color of his skin. Later in the poem, he inserts another irony when he asks for the "superhuman power" to obey "the letter of your law." The laws created by the "White House" are "your law"; they serve white society while defending various forms of discrimination against blacks. The poem ends with a final irony, as the speaker must "keep my heart inviolate / Against the potent poison of your hate." The black man is allowed only to "bear [his] anger," while holding himself back from expressing the "hate" he feels toward his white oppressor.

McKay left the United States in 1922 and did not return until the 1930s. In his absence, Countee Cullen and Langston Hughes competed for the position as the "poet laureate" of Harlem. Cullen and Hughes were in many ways direct opposites as poets: where Cullen preferred to write in traditional forms like the sonnet, Hughes used free-verse forms inspired by blues and jazz; where Cullen's favorite poets were Keats, Shelley, and A. E. Housman, Hughes preferred the American tradition of Whitman and Sandburg; where Hughes was attracted to Africa and the Caribbean, Cullen preferred the classics and French culture; where Cullen had a strong religious background (his adoptive father was a Methodist pastor in Harlem), Hughes' spiritual roots lay in the history of African and African American folk culture.

Finally, Hughes and Cullen displayed very different attitudes toward their racial identity. Hughes celebrated his color, writing in his essay "The Negro Artist and the Racial Mountain" (1926) that black writers should express their "individual dark-skinned selves without fear or shame." In his famous early poem, "A Negro Speaks of Rivers" (1921), Hughes identifies with the Euphrates and the Congo as well as the Mississippi:

> I've known rivers ancient as the world and older
> than the flow of human blood in human veins

Cullen, on the other hand, was highly ambivalent about his race, either avoiding the racial theme altogether or expressing his racial identity as a purely negative factor. In "Yet Do I Marvel" (1925), for example, the speaker accepts various natural and mythical horrors, from the blinding of the mole to the torture of Tantalus and Sisyphus, but he remains puzzled by his situation as a black poet:

> Yet do I marvel at this curious thing:
> To make a poet black, and bid him sing!

Of the two poets, it was Hughes who was to become the leading voice of the Harlem Renaissance and the most important African American poet of the twentieth century. Hughes was born in Joplin, Missouri, in 1902, and grew up in Kansas and Illinois before attending high school in Cleveland, Ohio. By 1918, he was publishing poems and stories in his high school magazine. After graduation, Hughes went to live for a year with his father in Mexico before moving to New York City to enter Columbia University. He withdrew from Columbia after one year and worked a series of jobs before traveling on a steamship to the west coast of Africa, later traveling by another ship to Europe. In 1925, he won the first prize in a literary contest sponsored by *Opportunity* magazine for his poem "The Weary Blues," which the following year became the title poem of his first volume.

"The Weary Blues" remains one of Hughes' most frequently anthologized poems, in part because of the way it incorporates blues lyrics into its structure. The poem describes a nightclub blues performer who plays and sings "to the tune o' those Weary Blues." The incorporation of the blues song within the poem itself is a crucial innovation by Hughes, who saw the juxtaposition of blues forms with more traditional poetic forms as a kind of literary syncopation, much like the "drowsy syncopated tune" the bluesman himself plays. Significantly, this is no famous performer but an anonymous "Negro," who plays with such deep feeling that he transcends his surroundings, making the "poor piano moan with melody." The poem gradually moves from a more humorous vision of the man – a "musical fool" who plays a hopeful blues about putting his "troubles on the shelf" – to a darker vision of the man's weariness, his lack of satisfaction, and his desire to die. After his second blues, which conclude with the singer's wish to die, we move beyond the artificial confines of the club and the blues songs to a glimpse of the collective weary blues of blacks in America:

> And far into the night he crooned that tune.
> The stars went out and so did the moon.
> The singer stopped playing and went to bed
> While the Weary Blues echoed through his head.
> He slept like a rock or a man that's dead.

It is only the tradition of the blues that gives meaning to the singer's life; when he goes home to sleep he is associated with an inanimate object and a dead man. The last line brilliantly transfigures a common expression ("I slept like a log") into a more disturbing image. The triple rhyme of the ending (bed / head / dead) contributes further to the feeling of finality expressed in the final lines (also echoing the triple "thump, thump, thump" of his foot on the floor).

In the 1930s, Hughes' poetry became more explicitly political in content and more clearly ironic in tone as he emphasized the need for radical political and social action. Some of his most powerful denunciations of racism and racial violence are "Christ in Alabama" (1932), a bitterly ironic poem on the subject of race; "Let America Be America Again" (1935), an ironic anthem about racial and social divisions during the Great Depression; and "A Bitter River" (1942), a trenchant commentary on lynching in the Southern states. "Bitter River" concerns the lynching of two black youths in Mississippi. In contrast to the vision of the river as a source of spiritual solace in "A Negro Speaks of Rivers," the "bitter river" of this poem is a symbol of the practice of lynching that has "poisoned" the South:

There is a bitter river
Flowing through the South.
Too long has the taste of its water
Been in my mouth.
There is a bitter river
Dark with filth and mud.
Too long has its evil poison
Poisoned my blood.

The river speaks in the voice of a Southern white uttering platitudes about "patience" on the part of blacks, but such patience is useless in an environment where social conditions do not change:

"Work, education, patience
Will bring a better day."
The swirl of the bitter river
Carries your "patience" away.

In the poem's penultimate stanza, Hughes sums up the problem in a language that is forceful and immediate:

You have lynched my comrades
Where the iron bridge crosses the stream,
Underpaid me for my labor,
And spit in the face of my dream.
You forced me to the bitter river
With the hiss of its snake-like song –
Now your words no longer have meaning –
I have drunk at the river too long.

The parallelism between the lynching of the speaker's "comrades" (the two black youths murdered by whites) and the exploitation of his "labor" suggests that the speaker's "dream" involves economic equality and class solidarity as well as an end to racial violence. Hughes intensifies the power of his rhetoric by the use of concrete images: the "iron bridge" that looms as an uncrossable connection between black and white, and the river as a snake whose shape and "hiss" evoke the slaver's whip and foreman's lash as well as the "forked tongue" of those who seek to urge patience while exploiting and perpetrating violence on African Americans.

Two other poets – Jean Toomer and Sterling Brown – are often grouped with the Harlem Renaissance writers even though they did not live in Harlem and were not an active part of Harlem literary life. Toomer, who was born and raised in Washington, D.C., spent the summer of 1921 in rural Georgia. This trip to the South inspired his most important literary work, a collection of poems and stories that was published as *Cane* in 1923. *Cane* was not only a major contribution to African American literature, but it remains one of the most powerful and challenging works by any twentieth-century American writer.

The poems in *Cane* dramatize the conditions of life for blacks in the rural South rather than those living in the urban and industrial North. "Reapers," for example, places the actions of Southern agricultural workers in the larger context of nonhuman activity:

> Black reapers with the sound of steel on stones
> Are sharpening scythes. I see them place the hones
> In their hip-pockets as a thing that's done,
> And start their silent swinging, one by one.
> Black horses drive a mower through the weeds.
> And there, a field rat, startled, squealing bleeds.
> His belly close to ground, I see the blade,
> Blood-stained, continue cutting weeds and shade.

While the reapers prepare for the harvest by sharpening their scythes, a mower, driven by black horses, cuts through the weeds with indifferent violence, destroying a rat with its blades. The poem can be read both as a minutely detailed description of an agricultural scene, or as a densely symbolic poem about the contrast between the purposefulness of human beings and the automated disinterestedness of machines. The poem's latent symbolism is suggested by the association of these "black reapers" with the "grim reaper" traditionally signifying death. Yet at the same time the "field rat" – cut to death by the turning mower – might be associated with the black field hands who themselves are destroyed by the oppressiveness of the social and economic system operating in the Southern United States. Finally, the ominous and deadly progress of the mower may represent the change in the rural South from the simpler way of life represented by the reapers sharpening their scythes with "hones" (stones used for sharpening blades) to the more mechanical mower. Toomer's skillful use of sound (particularly the alliteration of the "s" sounds in lines lines 1, 2, and 6), his compact presentation of images, and his economical syntax ("squealing bleeds," "his belly close to ground"), all contribute to the eerie naturalism of the poem.

Like Toomer, Sterling Brown grew up in Washington, D.C., and wrote about the experience of black life in the "Cotton South." Brown attended Williams College and Harvard, where he was exposed to the modernist poetry of Frost and Carl Sandburg. In his college teaching jobs during the 1920s, he was also exposed to the dialect and black folk traditions of the Southern countryside. His first book, *Southern Road*, was not published until 1932, and as a result it did not receive the kind of attention paid to volumes published during the 1920s by McKay, Cullen, Toomer, and Hughes. Nevertheless, it is one of the most important volumes published during the period of the Harlem Renaissance. Unlike the other major Renaissance poets, Brown wrote primarily in dialect. Brown's use of dialect went beyond that of Dunbar: he was interested not only in capturing the black folk tradition, but also in using dialect as a way of pointing out cultural differences and in ironizing the conditions of racial and social oppression.

In "Old Lem," Brown chronicles the condition of life under the economy of the cotton crop, where whites maintain brutal domination over black workers. Apart from the first two lines, the poem is in the voice of a speaker named "Lem," an older black man who describes the severity of life and the relentless demands and brutality of whites.

> They weigh the cotton
> They store the corn
>> We only good enough
>> To work the rows;
> They keep the commissary
> They keep the books
>> We gotta be careful
>> For being cheated.

Brown establishes a contrapuntal play between two groups: "we" (the black cotton pickers) and "they" (the white clerks, lawyers, and store-keepers who seek to maintain their power through racist domination).

In the next stanza, Brown uses anaphora to reinforce the domination of "they":

> They got the judges
> They got the lawyers
> They got the jury-rolls
> They got the law
>> They don't come by ones
> They got the sheriff
> They got the deputies
>> They don't come by twos
> They got the shotguns
> They got the rope
>> We git the justice
>> In the end
>>> But they come by tens

The irony of the stanza's final lines is made clear in the anecdote Lem tells about his "buddy" who is killed by a gang of whites after he refuses to leave the county. Not only is there no "justice" for Southern blacks – who are forced "to slink around" like "hangtailed hounds" – but the whites are portrayed in the poem's refrain as cowardly men who can only exercise their domination through superior numbers: "They don't come by ones / They don't come by twos / But they come by tens."

Brown is perhaps most famous for his poems in the Slim Greer series, which were based on the adventures of a comic folk hero. In *Southern Road*, Brown presents the first three poems of the series – "Slim Greer," "Slim Lands a Job?" and "Slim in Atlanta." The poems present the trickster figure of African American folk culture, who can both circumvent social restrictions and use them for his own gain. Slim uses his rhetorical skills to diffuse oppressive or dangerous situations, thus satirizing the racist norms of white society. In "Slim Greer" he dupes a "nice white woman" into thinking he is white, but ironically reveals his racial identity when he plays the blues too well and has to escape from an angry white mob. In "Slim in Atlanta," Brown ridicules segregationist laws, here represented by a law enacted in Atlanta, Georgia, to prevent blacks from laughing in the street. When Greer finds out that the city's black citizens are only permitted to laugh "in a telefoam booth," he is so amused that he puts himself in the booth and cannot stop laughing. In order to return the situation to normal, the authorities are forced to send for an ambulance and pack him out of town.

Women poets of the Harlem Renaissance

The Harlem Renaissance was also an important moment for women poets, many of whom published in magazines like *Crisis* and *Opportunity* and in anthologies like Cullen's *Caroling Dusk* (1927) and James Weldon Johnson's *Book of American Negro Poetry* (1931). Though relatively few of these women published their own volumes of poetry (Georgia Douglas Johnson being the major exception), the work of such poets as Alice Dunbar-Nelson, Anne Spencer, Angelina Weld Grimké, Helene Johnson, Gwendolyn Bennett, and Mae Cowdery serves as a significant and often overlooked contribution to the African American literature of the period. The poetry of these women exhibits many of the same qualities as the work of their male counterparts: a strong racial identification, an anger at manifestations of racism and racial violence, a determination to fight social oppression, a rejection of white culture, and an attempt to reconstruct a sense of black heritage. At the same time, women poets addressed themes such as love and nature far more frequently than the male poets of the Harlem Renaissance, and their poems often reflected their awareness of gender oppression and well as racial oppression.

While the work of male poets such as Hughes, Toomer, McKay, and Cullen has remained within the canon of twentieth-century American poetry – at least as measured by its inclusion in standard anthologies – poetry by black women of the period has been largely overlooked. Most of the attention that has been paid to African American women writers of the 1920s and 1930s has focused on the prose fiction of Jessie Fauset, Nella Larsen, and Zora Neale Hurston. In fact, as Maureen Honey observes, many critical works do not mention the women poets at all, and others treat them as conventional, sentimental, and "out of step with the militant, rebellious race conciousness of the period."[5] The most celebrated woman poet of the Harlem Renaissance was certainly Georgia Douglas Johnson, who published three volumes of verse between 1918 and 1928, in addition to stories and plays. Johnson's poems, while carefully crafted, are conventional in form and now seem rather dated in their language and conception. Two less published but more strikingly original poets of the period were Anne Spencer and Angelina Weld Grimké.

Spencer published fewer than thirty poems between 1920 and 1931, and she never published a book of poetry. Having lived through conditions of extreme poverty as the child of former slaves, she was strongly committed to social justice; several of her poems deal with explicitly political and racial themes. Spencer's most powerful poem is "White Things," which was published in *The Crisis* in 1923. The poem was inspired by a story she had read about a pregnant black woman who was seized by a lynch mob and cut through the abdomen, killing both her and her unborn child. The poem moves from a quiet, positive tone to one of defiance and determination, climaxing in a powerful statement of its theme. In the first stanza, Spencer uses the traditional connotations of white and black (good versus evil, positive versus negative) only to reverse them through her imagery and language.

> Most things are colorful things – the sky, earth, and sea.
>   Black men are most men; but the white are free!
> White things are rare things; so rare, so rare
> They stole from out a silvered world – somewhere.
> Finding earth-plains fair plains, save greenly grassed,
> They strewed white feathers of cowardice, as they passed;
>   The golden stars with lances fine,
>   The hills all red and darkened pine,
> They blanched with their wand of power;
> And turned the blood in a ruby rose
> To a poor white poppy-flower.

Spencer, herself of partly Native American ancestry, comments on the colonization of the New World by Europeans who "stole from out a silvered world – somewhere" and "blanched" the colorful landscape of North America with "their wand of power." The whites act in stealth and cowardice, covering the green grass with "white feathers" and destroying the "red and darkened pine" of America's wilderness. As the color imagery suggests, the "red," "golden," and "darkened" races are included among the "colorful things" destroyed or whitened (perhaps through forced racial mixing) by the colonizers.

In the second stanza, Spencer shifts from an allegory of colonization to a denunciation of the terrorism perpetrated by whites against blacks:

> They pyred a race of black, black men,
> And burned them to ashes white; then
> Laughing, a young one claimed a skull,
> For the skull of a black is white, not dull,
>   But a glistening awful thing
>   Made, it seems, for this ghoul to swing
> In the face of God with all his might,
> And swear by the hell that sired him:
>   "Man-maker, make white!"

If we compare this poem with McKay's more famous "If We Must Die," we find in Spencer's poem a more inventive use of language and imagery. While still in the category of the "protest poem," Spencer's lyric is less strident in tone. Spencer skillfully interweaves images of nature with a powerful statement of historical protest. She states the main thesis of the poem in the second line: "Black men are most men; but the white are free." White men may be "free" – of slavery and other forms of social subjugation – but they are out of touch with nature, having erected an artificial hierarchy based on skin color. The poem reveals the desire on the part of white settlers to subjugate both the natural world and human nature to their desires, and to deprive other men of their right to freedom. The poem progressively narrows its scope from the general ("black men" referring to all the darker skinned races of the world) to the specific (the history of post-slavery racism in the United States).

The first stanza does not prepare us for the horrors of the second, in which we witness first-hand the effects of the white race's hostility toward the black race. After the lynching and burning of the "black, black men," a young white man picks up a skull from the ashes. The man – who is later described as a "ghoul," lending another negative connotation of the color white – represents not only the white man's desire to annihilate the black race, but also the perverse pleasure he takes in destroying blackness itself. As J. Lee Greene suggests, the man's actions recall the practice of whites collecting souvenirs from their victims at the lynching scene.[6] The poem ends with the man holding the skull (now ironically transformed into one of the title's "white things") and demanding that God create only white in the world: "Man-maker, make white!" Of course, the white man's hubris is a form of blasphemy, for in his desire to rid the world of "colorful things" and supplant them with "white things" he has spoken against the divine plan of God's creation. "White Things" provides a frightening vision of American racial history. As Greene argues, the poem shows how "God's cosmic force has been so undermined and perverted by humans that it is subject to the dictates of whiteness."[7]

As might be expected, color imagery pervades much of the poetry by African American women of the period: whiteness is often treated as a malevolent force associated with invisibility, suffocation, and death, while blackness is celebrated as a source of beauty or an assertion of the self against white control. In Angelina Weld Grimké's poem "Tenebris," for example, she compares a tree growing outside a white man's house to a hand "huge and black" that "plucks and plucks / At the bricks" of the house. The poem's use of color imagery is heightened by the description of the bricks as "the color of blood," suggesting the plantation house of the Southern states built and maintained with the blood of slave labor. The poem's title comes from the Latin word for darkness, subtly associating the black poet, and not the white householder, with the classical culture on which white society is supposedly built.

In another poem, "The Black Finger," Grimké sees a black cypress tree as "A black finger / Pointing upwards." The final two questions which end the poem suggest both the oppressed position of African Americans and the hope for their continued aspiration to something better:

> Why, beautiful still finger, are you black?
> And why are you pointing upwards?

In addition to the poem of racial protest, the genre at which the women poets of the Harlem Renaissance excelled was the love poem. Many of these poems were addressed to other women, as in the case of Grimké's haunting "A Mona Lisa." Grimké, a lesbian, could offer only a more muted version of her sexual feelings in her published poetry, although she made her attraction to other women more overt in her unpublished verse. In "A Mona Lisa," published in *Caroling Dusk*, she seeks a romantic union with another woman ("I should like to creep / Through the long brown grasses / That are your lashes"), but her unrequited love leads her to a vision of her own death. The metaphor of her lover's eyes as a pool of water becomes literalized in the second stanza: after she finds herself sinking to the bottom to "deeply drown," she wonders in a series of questions if she will be remembered as anything more than a "bubble breaking" or a wave "ceasing at the marge." Once again we find color imagery associating whiteness with death, as the speaker's "white bones" in the final image are contrasted with the highly erotic images of "long brown grasses" and "leaf-brown pools" used in describing her lover.

The middle generation: Tolson, Hayden, and Brooks

The Harlem Renaissance only lasted about a decade. In the early 1930s, the Great Depression closed down most avenues of economic and cultural opportunity for black writers, who depended heavily on the support of both white and black patrons. Though Hughes continued to write poetry until the 1960s, the production of poetry by African Americans began to fall off in the early 1930s and by 1935 the Renaissance was over.

In the mid-1940s, a new generation of African American poets began to emerge. If the work of poets such as Melvin Tolson, Robert Hayden, and Gwendolyn Brooks did not constitute either a "renaissance" or a "movement," it was at least an important revival of poetry by black Americans. Unlike the poets of the Harlem Renaissance, these poets did not seek to form a group or to promote African American cultural institutions in a more general sense. Both Tolson and Hayden were strongly influenced by the modernist writing of Eliot, Crane, and Pound. In a 1949 speech, Tolson explicitly distanced his writing from that of the Harlem Renaissance. Declaring that the time had come for "a New Negro Poetry for the New Negro," he proposed that African American poets present a "rich heritage of folk lore and history" while using the techniques developed by Eliot, Pound, Williams, and other white poets; conspicuously absent from his list were the names of any black writers. Four years later, Allen Tate praised Tolson's work as the first instance of a black poet having "assimilated completely the full poetic language of his time . . . the language of the Anglo-American poetic tradition."

Tolson was actually four years older than Langston Hughes, but because of his later development as a poet he is considered to be part of the post-Renaissance generation. Born in 1898 in Missouri, the son of a minister, he grew up is a succession of Missouri and Iowa towns. His family life was highly conducive to the study of literature and the arts: Tolson read voraciously, painted, and played in his family's musical gatherings. After attending Fisk University and Lincoln University (both all-black institutions), he taught at a black college in Texas and undertook a master's program at Columbia University, where he nearly completed a thesis on the writers of the Harlem Renaissance. In 1932, Tolson completed a book of poems, *A Gallery of Harlem Portraits*, that was never published during his lifetime. Tolson first achieved literary success when his poem "Dark Symphony" won a national contest sponsored by the American Negro Exposition of 1939. His first published volume, *Rendezvous with America*, followed in 1944. "Dark Symphony," with its formal structure based on a musical composition with six movements, set the tone for Tolson's formally rigorous and highly allusive later poems.

Tolson's most ambitious works were *Libretto for the Republic of Liberia* (1953) and *Harlem Gallery*, a projected long poem of which he only completed one out of five books by the time of his death in 1966. Both works have garnered high praise from critics but have found relatively few readers. *Libretto*, as David Perkins suggests, is made up of "metaphors, phrases in foreign languages, erudite puns, poeticisms, high rhetoric, motifs from black spirituals and blues, slang, and literary and historical allusions."[8] Its style, heavily influenced by experimental modernism, combines syncopated rhythms with highly intellectual discussions. Tolson had in fact been named poet laureate of Liberia, a West African nation founded with the idea of establishing an African homeland for former slaves. *Harlem Gallery*, Tolson's epic, is at least equally complex. The poet Karl Shapiro, who wrote a foreword for the poem, described it as "a narrative work so fantastically stylized that the mind balks at comparisons." The published volume, *Harlem Gallery, Book I: The Curator*, is divided into twenty-four sections corresponding to the letters of the Greek alphabet. The book examines the role of the black artist in America through the eyes of its narrator, a Harlem art curator of "afroirishjewish" origins. As Rita Dove suggests in her introduction to *Harlem Gallery and Other Poems*, the curator's gallery allows him the opportunity "to observe the shenanigans of the black bourgeoisie" and to examine "the position of blacks – and most specifically the black artist – in a white-dominated society."[9]

Like Tolson, Robert Hayden began his career deeply under the influence of modernism, and especially of Eliot. Hayden grew up in the "Paradise Valley" ghetto of Detroit, Michigan. After attending Detroit City College, he researched black history and folklore for the Federal Writers' Project during the Depression, and studied with W. H. Auden at the University of Michigan in the early 1940s. Hayden's most important poem is "Middle Passage," a kind of epic in miniature. The poem tells the story of Cinquez, the captive African prince who inspired and helped carry out the mutiny aboard the slave ship *Amistad*. Chronologically, the action of the poem begins with the exodus of African peoples from their villages and takes them across the Atlantic Ocean on slave ships. The first part of the poem is a description of the inhumane treatment of Africans aboard various slave ships. The second part is the reminiscences of a retired slave-trader. And the climactic third part is a poetic recreation of the *Amistad* mutiny. The poem was much reworked over time, and was published in four different versions between 1941 and 1966. Stylistically, the poem owes a debt to

Eliot's techniques of fragmentation, allusion, and the use of different voices in *The Waste Land*.

Like Tolson and Hayden, Gwendolyn Brooks was a product of the American midwest. Born in Kansas, she moved to Chicago soon after her birth and attended Wilson Junior College, meeting both James Weldon Johnson and Langston Hughes and writing a poetry column for the *Chicago Defender*. Less interested than either of Tolson or Hayden in imitating modernist models, Brooks published a first book of poems – *A Street in Bronzeville* (1945) – that provided a realistic portrayal of life in the black neighborhoods of Chicago. Using the long poem format as well as the shorter lyric, Brooks was consistent in presenting race as a public issue. *Annie Allen* (1949), a mock-epic in forty-three rhyming stanzas, was the first book of poems by an African American to win the Pulitzer Prize. Another long poem, "In the Mecca" (1968), depicts life in a Chicago slum building that was once an elegant apartment complex. In a short lyric like "We Real Cool" (1959), Brooks displays her gift for a formal compression that contributes to an ironic commentary on African American life.

The Black Arts movement

The Black Arts movement – also known as the Black Aesthetic, the New Black Consciousness, and the New Black Renaissance – began in the mid-1960s and lasted, in its most intense phase, until the mid-1970s. The poetry, prose fiction, drama, and criticism written by African Americans during this period expressed a more militant attitude toward white American culture and its racist practices and ideologies. Slogans such as "Black Power," "Black Pride" and "Black is Beautiful" represented a sense of political, social, and cultural freedom for African Americans, who had gained not only a heightened sense of their own oppression but a greater feeling of solidarity with other parts of the black world such as Africa and the Caribbean.

The new spirit of militance and cultural separatism that characterized the racial politics of the late 1960s had profound effects on the way African American poetry was written. The pressure on African American poets was greater than it had ever been to produce work that was explicitly political in nature and that addressed issues of race and racial oppression. The Black Arts movement was strongly associated with the Black Power movement and its brand of radical or revolutionary politics. As the critic Stephen Henderson suggested in the introduction to his 1972 anthology *Understanding the New Black Poetry*, the artists and writers of the Black Arts movement had "moved beyond the Harlem Renaissance" in their capacity to view their community "in the larger political and spiritual context of Blackness."[10] In the poems and critical statements of Amiri Baraka, Larry Neal, and others, Henderson claimed, "one can see the process of self-definition made clearer and sharper as the self-reliance and racial consciousness of an earlier period are revived and raised to the level of revolutionary thought." The writing of the Black Arts movement would not be "protest" art so much as "an art of liberating vision."

As a result of this change in emphasis, the younger black poets turned away from the modernist or formal styles of Tolson and Hayden and embraced a more militant poetic, one based on the language of the street. Among the most notable of these younger poets were Baraka, Audre Lorde, Nikki Giovanni, Don L. Lee (Haki Madhubuti), Etheridge Knight, David Henderson, June Jordan, Ishmael Reed, Michael S. Harper, Clarence Major, Sonia Sanchez, Jayne Cortez, and Lucille Clifton.

Henderson's appraisal of the new black poetry of the 1960s was a significant step in the legitimation of the Black Arts movement. Henderson identified three basic categories according to which African American poetry could be analyzed. The first of these was the poem's theme or specific subject matter; the second was its structure, including such elements as diction, rhythm, and figurative language; and the third was what he called the poem's "saturation," the extent to which it communicated its "blackness" and the accuracy of its presentation of black life in the United States.

The dominant theme in African American poetry, Henderson suggests, has always been that of "liberation," whether from slavery, from segregation, or from the false wish for integration into the mainstream of white middle-class society. A secondary theme in African American poetry has been the concern with a spiritual or mystical dimension (whether in religion, African mythology, or musical forms like hymns, blues, and jazz) which can provide a meaningful alternative to "the temporal, the societal, and the political."[11] In terms of structure, Henderson identifies a range of stylistic elements in contemporary black poetry involving references to both colloquial black speech and music, especially jazz and blues. Finally, the "saturation" of an African American poem involves the depth and the quality of its evocation of black experience. In order to illustrate this more elusive category, Henderson gives the example of the difference between a white Tin Pan Alley "blues" and a blues performance by the black musician Lightnin' Hopkins, in other words between a white imitation or appropriation of a form of black expression and an authentically black manifestation of it. While examples of such saturation are difficult to analyze in precise critical terms, they are an important part of the experience of reading this poetry. The younger black poets of the 1960s focused much more heavily than their predecessors on the contemporary idiom of urban blacks, on references to specifically black culture and cultural practices, and on a realistic depiction of life in the inner cities. These poems portrayed a level of life experience and used a form of language that was unfamiliar to most white readers; often, it seems, the intent of the poem was at least in part to shock such readers.

The most influential of the new black poets was Amiri Baraka. Born Leroi Jones in Newark, New Jersey, in 1934, Baraka published under that name until 1968. After graduating from Howard University, Baraka served in the Air Force until the age of twenty-four, when he moved to Greenwich Village in New York City and became part of the avant-garde literary scene, befriending poets like Allen Ginsberg, Charles Olson, and Frank O'Hara. During this period, Baraka was more drawn to the poetry and ideas of the Beats and other white avant-garde movements than to the politics of black separatism: he married a white woman; he wrote poems, essays, plays, and a novel within the context of the Beat counterculture; and he edited two magazines, *Yugen* and *Floating Bear*. Baraka's interest in racial issues was clear even in the early 1960s, as evidenced in his historical study *Blues People: Negro Music in White America* (1963) and in plays such as *Dutchman* and *The Slave* (both 1964).

In the mid-1960s, deeply affected by the death of Malcolm X, Baraka made a number of important changes in his life and focus. He divorced and moved to Harlem, he converted to the Muslim faith and took a new name, he founded the Black Arts Repertory Theatre/School in New York City and Spirit House in Newark, and he became a leading spokesman for the Black Arts movement. He was also nearly beaten to death in the Newark race riots of 1967. In 1968, Baraka co-edited *Black Fire: An Anthology of Afro-American Writing*, which included social essays, drama, and fiction as well as poetry, and in 1969 he published his poetry collection *Black Magic Poetry: 1961–1967*. As Jerry Gafio Watts suggests, *Black Magic Poetry* can be read "as a record of his progression from an entrapment in whiteness to an identification with blackness," from his "outsider status in [white] bohemia" to his "arrival at a black nationalist sensibility."[12]

Baraka's poetry changed radically during the 1960s, as he turned from a more general sense of social alienation to a vision that was politically revolutionary and that expressed a profound solidarity with black culture. In his 1964 volume *The Dead Lecturer*, Baraka begins to describe more explicitly his sense of political and social alienation as a black man whose former status as a bohemian poet has been "undone by my station . . . and the bad words of Newark" ("Political Poem"). But Baraka's real poetic revolution comes with the poem "Black Art" (1966). "Black Art" is Baraka's most famous poem and has been called the signature poem of the Black Arts movement, but it is one about which critics and readers are strongly divided. As Werner Sollors suggests, the poem is "striking for its venomous language and for its rhetorical violence."[13] The poem is a virtual barrage of language directed against white society in general, and more specific attacks are launched against Jews, white liberals, and bourgeois blacks:

> We want live
> words of the hip world live flesh &
> coursing blood. Hearts Brains
> Souls splintering fire. We want poems
> like fists beating niggers out of Jocks
> or dagger poems in the slimy bellies
> of the owner-jews. Black poems to
> smear on girldemamma mulatto bitches
> whose brains are red jelly stuck
> between 'lizabeth taylor's toes. Stinking
> Whores! We want "poems that kill."
> Assassin poems, Poems that shoot
> guns. Poems that wrestle cops into alleys
> and take their weapons leaving them dead
> with tongues pulled out and sent to Ireland. Knockoff
> poems for dope selling wops or slick halfwhite
> politicians Airplane poems, rrrrrrrrrrrrrr
> rrrrrrrrrrrrr . . . tuhtuhtuhtuhtuhtuhtuhtuh

Baraka finds that the normal boundaries of poetic language no longer contain the words he needs in order to express his rage. The use of obscenities and of raw sounds – "rrrr . . . tuhtuhtuh" – turns language into the verbal guns of "poems that kill." Jerry Watts, who is particularly critical of the poem, calls it "an insurrectionary statement of hilarious and demented imagery," and he dismisses it as "nothing more than mere thuggery superimposed on hurt black feelings, impotence, and defeat."[14] At the same time, however, there are reasons for the poem's success within the Black Arts movement. While the poem is certainly disturbing, especially in its anti-semitic references, it is rhetorically powerful in its suggestion that poetry can reverse many of the injustices perpetrated on African Americans. Lines like "Poems that wrestle cops into alleys / and take their weapons leaving them dead / with tongues pulled out" express the desire for social and political revenge by reversing the power relationships usually operating in American society. The poem's ending is more affirmative, calling for the "black poem" that can lead to a "Black World":

> Let the world be a Black Poem
> And Let All Black People Speak This Poem
> Silently
> or LOUD

Along with Baraka, perhaps the most significant poet to emerge from the Black Arts movement was Audre Lorde. In addition to several volumes of poetry, beginning with *The First Cities* (1968), Lorde wrote essays (collected in her book *Sister Outsider*), an autobiographical account of her battle with cancer (*The Cancer Journals*), and a fictionalized "biomythography" (*Zami: A New Spelling of My Name*). The daughter of West Indian immigrants, Lorde studied at both Hunter College and Columbia University. She worked as a librarian and taught at various colleges in New York City, including Hunter College, where she was a professor of English until her death in 1992.

Lorde's poems deal with her personal experience as an African American woman (or, as she called herself, "a black feminist lesbian mother poet"), as well as with the contemporary experience of blacks both in the United States and throughout the world. In her work, she makes frequent reference to historical events and figures, often juxtaposing events and images for ironic effect. In "The Day They Eulogized Mahalia," for example, she juxtaposes the public celebration of the black singer Mahalia Jackson with the death on the same day of six black children in an underfunded day-care center. In "Sisters in Arms" (1986) she comments on the situation of blacks in South Africa through a series of interlocking narratives: the violent death of a friend's fifteen-year-old daughter, the massacre and imprisonment of black children in a South African province, and the uprising by the warrior queen Mmanthatisi. Lorde is known for her evocative and very powerful use of imagery. In "Sisters in Arms," for example, she writes of the silence which "explodes like a pregnant belly / into my face / a vomit of nerves." Lorde's use of images is particularly effective in "Coal" (1968):

> In the total black, being spoken
> From the earth's inside.
> There are many kinds of open.
> How a diamond comes into a knot of flame
> How a sound comes into a word, colored
> By who pays what for speaking.

The image of the diamond is especially resonant here, as it evokes the history of racial oppression under which South African blacks have worked in the diamond mines. Yet at the same time the transformation of coal into diamonds represents the possibility of a revelatory opening of language. The significance of the image is made explicit in the final two lines:

> I am Black because I came from the earth's inside
> now take my word for jewel in the open light.

As a black woman poet, Lorde has had to "pay" for the privilege of speaking; but her poems remain as the permanent crystallization of her experience, the "jewels" that allow her to reflect her words outward into the world.

Another strong voice in African American poetry since the Black Arts Movement has been Michael S. Harper. Harper's "Dear John, Dear Coltrane," the title poem of his 1970 collection, represents an important subgenre within the poetry of the Black Arts movement: the poem dedicated to or deriving from the work of black musicians. As Günter Lenz puts it, black poetry of the 1960s and 1970s offered "the most promising medium to . . . transform the energy of the forms of black music into the structure and performance of literature."[15] For many black poets of the period, including Harper, the influence of music was just as crucial as that of poetry; while the poetry of Langston Hughes and others was an important model, so was the music of Charlie Parker, Miles Davis, Billie Holiday, Thelonius Monk, and John Coltrane. Of all the jazz musicians of the period, it was Coltrane who served as the most important model for black poets, the "shaping spirit," as Baraka put it, of the New Black Music. Poems interpreting and celebrating Coltrane's music were written by many African American poets.

In Harper's poem, he addresses both the man and his music. The poem begins and ends with the refrain "a love supreme," a phrase which Coltrane chanted on his record (and which Harper chants in his live performances of the poem). In between the appearances of the refrain, the poem moves through a series of focuses, from the personal and biographical to the cultural and historical. Images of Coltrane's suffering and aging body are juxtaposed with invocations of his music and affirmations of the black community. The opening lines of the poem end with first repetition of the refrain and the question, "What does it all mean?" The answer seems to come from Coltrane's music itself, which responds to the loss of Coltrane's physical manhood ("Loss, so great each black / woman expects your failure / in mute change, the seed gone") with a song "now crystal and / the blues."

In the concluding section, a call–and–response format invokes the process by which the black community as a whole has responded to a history of suffering:

> *Why you so black?*
> *cause I am*
> *why you so funky?*
> *cause I am*
> *why you so black?*
> *cause I am*
> *why you so sweet?*
> *cause I am*
> *why you so black?*
> *cause I am*
> *a love supreme, a love supreme*

So sick
you couldn't play *Naima*
so flat we ached
for song you'd concealed
with your own blood,
your diseased liver gave
out its purity,
the inflated heart
pumps out, the tenor kiss,
tenor love:
a love supreme, a love supreme –
a love supreme, a love supreme –

"Dear John, Dear Coltrane" uses many of the techniques Henderson identifies with the use of black music as a poetic reference: the allusion to song titles (Coltrane's classic composition "Naima"), the use of language from the jazz life ("funky"), quotations from a song ("a love supreme"), the generalized reference to a musical form ("the blues"), the musician as subject (Coltrane), and the incorporation of an emotional response to the music ("so flat we ached / for song you'd concealed"). Finally, the poem incorporates the tonal memory of jazz as a basis of poetic structure. This effect is most clear in a passage like "fuel / the tenor sax cannibal / heart, genitals and sweat," where a memory of the complex rhythms of Coltrane's music helps the reader to experience the highly syncopated rhythm of the lines.

If Coltrane's music enabled Harper to articulate his vision of history, it also helped him to formulate his own poetic style and voice. The alternation of vernacular speech patterns ("Why you so black? . . . Why you so funky?") with more traditionally lyric language reenacts the harmonic and melodic counterpoint of Coltrane's music. At the same time, the use of the call-and-response format echoes the repetition of Coltrane's own refrain; in thematic terms, the call-and-response tradition is linked with the tradition of black music, and, by extension, of African American poetry.

Chapter 7

The New Criticism and poetic formalism

In the early 1920s, a group of brilliant young poets initiated what would be-come one of the most important movements in twentieth-century American literature: the New Criticism. The oldest of these poets, John Crowe Ransom, had been teaching at Vanderbilt University in Nashville, Tennessee, since 1914. Along with another Vanderbilt instructor, Donald Davidson, as well as undergraduate students Allen Tate and Robert Penn Warren, Ramsom founded a literary magazine, *The Fugitive*. The members of Ransom's circle – who contributed both poetry and critical essays to the magazine – called themselves "Fugitives."

The Fugitives began as a group concerned with producing and publish-ing good poetry, and their magazine – which ran from 1922 to 1925 – was an important literary publication that included in its pages poems by many of the leading writers of the day. In the course of the decade, how-ever, the focus of the group shifted from the study of poetry to an explo-ration of the intellectual and artistic problems of Southern writing, and to a still broader examination of the economic and social issues facing the rural South. By 1930 the Fugitives were calling themselves "Southern Agrarians," and were making the argument that the South's distinctiveness lay in a predominantly agricultural society which stood as a bulwark against the industrial materialism and consumerism of the Northern states. *I'll Take My Stand: the South and the Agrarian Tradition* (1930) was a collection of essays by twelve Southerners, including Ransom, Davidson, Tate, and Warren.

At the same time that they were turning their attention to regional issues, Ransom and the other Fugitives were also leading a movement to legitimize a different kind of criticism from that currently practiced in most English departments in the United States. Influenced by the critical essays of T. S. Eliot and by the books of English critics I. A. Richards and William Empson, Ransom and the other Fugitives increasingly turned their attention to the actual texts of poems instead of the biographical information surrounding their composition. This "close reading" of poetry – often performed by critics who were poets in their own right – was a departure from the kind of historical and philological study that had dominated the field. In 1937

Ransom published an essay entitled "Criticism, Inc," which argued that literary criticism "must become more scientific . . . precise and systematic." The following year, two of Ransom's former students – Robert Penn Warren and Cleanth Brooks – published what would be the single most influential book of the New Critical movement: *Understanding Poetry*. That book, and its companion volumes *Understanding Fiction* and *Understanding Drama*, codified many of the New Critical ideas into a coherent approach to literary study and revolutionized the teaching of literature. Ransom himself published two highly influential volumes of essays – *The World's Body* (1938) and *The New Criticism* (1941) – the latter of which would give the movement its name.

In the 1930s, most of the New Critics left Vanderbilt and spread their ideas to universities across the country: Ransom went to Kenyon College in Ohio and founded *The Kenyon Review*; Warren and Brooks both went to Louisiana State University, where they founded *The Southern Review*; and Tate went on to teach at Princeton, New York University, and the University of Minnesota. The New Critical mode, propelled by influential books of criticism like Brooks' *The Well-Wrought Urn* (1947) and W. K. Winsatt's *The Verbal Icon* (1954), would dominate the academic study of poetry until the end of the 1960s. The success of the New Criticism during these years is not difficult to explain: as Terry Eagleton suggests, the New Criticism evolved at a time when American literature programs were struggling to become professionalized, and when the study of English Literature was attempting to compete with both the sciences and the social sciences as an academic discipline. The New Critical methodology, with its emphasis on the close reading of short poems, provided a "convenient pedagogical method of coping with a growing student population," particularly in the period following World War II.[1]

Though each of the New Critics pursued a somewhat different set of ideas about poetry, the fundamental nature of their inquiry followed similar lines. In general, the argument of the New Criticism was that the most successful works of literature displayed an "organic unity" which could best be discovered through an understanding of their words, images, figures of speech, and symbols. The New Critics insisted on treating the poem as a self-sufficient verbal object (the "well-wrought urn" or "verbal icon"), and in recognizing, in the words of Ransom, "the autonomy of the work itself as existing for its own sake." They warned against critical practices that distracted the reader from the poem itself, such as the "intentional fallacy" (the idea that a work should be judged according to the intentions of its author) and the "affective fallacy" (the idea that a work should be judged according to its emotional effects on the reader). Finally, they avoided readings that relied on biography, psychology, or historical and social context.

According to the New Critics, the primary focus of the reader should be on a poem's verbal construction, and especially on its use of such elements as "tension," "irony," and "paradox" in achieving an equilibrium of opposed forces. Ransom's more particular version of this argument was that a poem consists of two basic elements – structure (its argument or logical discourse) and texture (its imagery, rhythm, sound, and diction). In order for a poem to be successful, these two elements should exist in a sort of dramatic tension. The primary methodology of the New Criticism was the close reading or "explication" of the poem, which would reveal the complex interrelations of meanings and ambiguities within the text.

The New Criticism was highly successful in training a generation of readers in the methods of close literary analysis. But in creating a new critical orthodoxy it also limited the range of possible responses to poetry, and as a result engendered an academic poetry establishment that was conservative in its literary tastes. The spirit of experimentation that had characterized the modernist era was replaced by an often rigid and unimaginative brand of literary formalism, and during the Cold War the New Criticism provided a convenient means of avoiding an engagement with current social and political issues. Many poets of the 1950s and 1960s conceived of their work as a rebellion against what they saw as the highly conventional poetic practices of the New Critics and their followers.

The formalist mode of poetic writing can be divided into three generational moments. The first of these moments was that associated with the New Criticism of the 1920s and 1930s; the second included the formalists of the generation who emerged in the 1940s and 1950s under the influence of the New Critics as well as Eliot and W. H. Auden. A third wave of formalist poetry, identified as the "New Formalism," began in the 1980s and lasted until the end of the century. This chapter will be concerned primarily with the first of these generations, and to a somewhat lesser extent with the second and third.

John Crowe Ransom

Ransom was born in 1888 in rural Tennessee, the son of a Methodist minister. A precocious student, he entered Vanderbilt at the age of fifteen and graduated in 1909. Ransom studied classics at Oxford from 1910 to 1913, before returning to Vanderbilt as an instructor in the English department. He began writing poetry in about 1916, and in 1919 he published his first volume, *Poems about God*. In the early 1920s, Ransom discovered his mature poetic voice, publishing his two most important books of poetry: *Chills and Fever* (1924) and *Two Gentlemen in Bonds* (1927). From that point on, he wrote relatively few poems, preferring to focus on his teaching and on the critical essays for which he is most famous.

Ransom should rightly be seen as a minor poet of the 1920s rather than a major poet of the modernist era, but he nonetheless wrote a handful of poems in which he achieves a true mastery of poetic form and expression. His poetry is traditional in both form and subject matter, yet it displays a sensibility more typical of modernism in its biting irony and its refusal of nineteenth-century modes of sentimentality. Stylistically, Ransom's best work is characterized by its skillful prosody, its metaphysical wit, and its satirical constrast of formal literary language with the colloquial idiom. In his most famous poem, "Bells for John Whiteside's Daughter" (1924), Ransom presents a seemingly sentimental situation – the death of a young girl – only to undermine that sentimentality in the poem itself:

> There was such speed in her little body,
> And such lightness in her footfall,
> It is no wonder her brown study
> Astonishes us all.
>
> Her wars were bruited in our high window,
> We looked among orchard trees and beyond
> Where she took arms against her shadow,
> Or harried unto the pond.
>
> The lazy geese, like a snow cloud
> Dripping their snow on the green grass,
> Tricking and stopping, sleepy and proud,
> Who cried in goose, Alas,
>
> For the tireless heart within the little
> Lady with rod that made them rise
> From their noon apple-dreams and scuttle
> Goose-fashion under the skies!
>
> But now go the bells, and we are ready,
> In one house we are sternly stopped
> To say we are vexed at her brown study.
> Lying so primly propped.

As in many of Ransom's poems, we find the theme of mortality, but his treatment of the theme is very unusual. The poem is certainly not a typical elegy, in which the primary purpose is to express grief at the death of a loved one; further, the poem's resolution provides no sense of consolation or compensation for the loss of the young girl. Both the somewhat prose-like rhythms and the oddly stiff diction of the poem create a distance from the events described. In Ransom's own terminology, the *structure* of the poem is that of a traditional elegy, but the *texture* remains in an uneasy tension with the elegiac form. Even the poem's title distances us from its subject: the girl, whose first name is never given, is referred to only as "John Whiteside's daughter." In the poem itself, the words "astonishes" and "vexed" suggest that rather than an outpouring of grief at the death of the little girl, the narrator experiences surprise and vexation at an event which "has upset our human calculation." Throughout the poem, Ransom plays with the discrepancy between the very simple theme and the unusual diction and phrasing. Ransom adopts a mock heroic language in evoking "wars . . . bruited in our high window" and "arms" taken against shadows. This language, evoking an epic battle rather than a girl's play, is contrasted with the humorous scene of the geese who are herded by the girl and made to "scuttle / Goose-fashion under the skies." The word "bruited," perhaps the most unusual usage in the poem, suggests that the girl's battles with the geese are rumored far and wide, but it also has the less pleasant connotation of a noise or roar which may have disturbed the speaker in his "high window."

The first stanza begins with an evocative portrait of the girl, informing us of her youth, vivacity, and grace (the syntactic parallelism of the "speed in her little body" and the "lightness in her footfall" providing a perfectly balanced portrait). But in the final two lines of the stanza, this imagery is strongly contrasted with the image of the girl's body laid out in her coffin (her "brown study"), a sight which "astonishes us all." The contrast between the almost violently active little girl, who "harried" the geese with her "rod," and the still body now in the coffin, is very effective. This effect is accentuated by the final line of the poem, which presents her as "lying so primly propped." Here there is an unnaturalness or formality about her appearance: her primness in death contrasts with her boldness and recklessness in life; her "propped" posture in the coffin contrasts with her former activity; and the "brown study" of her death contrasts with the natural world of orchard, pond, and geese with which she was associated in life.

The poem avoids falling into pathos in several ways: by its contrasts of tone and language, by its use of epithets that create ironic distance ("the little / Lady with rod"), and by never departing from the perspective of an uninvolved adult neighbor who appreciates the girl's innocence and energy but appears not even to know her name. We can easily see why Randall Jarrell called the poem "perfectly realized . . . and almost perfect." The poem subtly blends humor with pathos, connecting both through a simple yet elegant imagery. The simile of the geese dropping their white feathers "like a snow cloud / Dripping their snow on the green grass" suggests the possibility of natural process into an aesthetic appreciation, but the death of the girl affords no such luxury, only the vexation of being "sternly stopped" by her "brown study." The absurdity of the conceit of the geese themselves mourning the girl's death ("Alas" they cry in goose language), adds to the general starkness of the poem's tragi-comic vision. The bells of the poem are church bells, but they are also the bells of mortality that toll, as John Donne put it, for us all.

Allen Tate

The second poet to emerge from the New Critical nexus was Allen Tate. Tate's brilliant intellect and precocious poetic talent were a match for Ransom, and as an undergraduate he dazzled his classmates and teachers (including Ransom) with his knowledge of the French symbolists. On the recommendation of Hart Crane – with whom Tate began corresponding in the early 1920s – he also began reading the modernists. Tate and Ransom did not agree about *The Waste Land* (Tate admired the poem while Ransom attacked it) and their attitudes toward poetic modernism in general would remain markedly different throughout their careers.

Tate left Vanderbilt in 1924 and moved to New York City, where he lived until 1928. While in New York, Tate published his first collection of poems (*Mr. Pope and Other Poems*), as well as a biography of the Confederate general Stonewall Jackson. Tate's most famous poem, "Ode to the Confederate Dead," was composed in 1926 and revised in 1930. The irregular form of the "Ode" is not typical of Tate's poetry of the 1920s, which more often conformed to the formal style associated with the New Criticism. Nevertheless, the "Ode" remains Tate's most important composition.

Tate's poem represented his own "quest of the past," as he put it in a 1928 letter. It was a quest to recover not only the cultural past of the South, but also the history of his family, which had been "scattered to the four winds" after the Civil War. The poem is formally complex: though lacking a regular verse form, it contains a varied rhyme scheme and makes use of frequent repetition and internal rhyme. The action of the poem takes place at the gate of a Confederate graveyard on a late autumn afternoon. A lone man views the falling leaves, which remind him of the "seasonal eternity of death" as they pile up on the gravestones. In the second stanza, the man pauses for what Tate calls "a baroque meditation on the ravages of time":

> Autumn is desolation in the plot
> Of a thousand acres where these memories grow
> From the inexhaustible bodies that are not
> Dead, but feed the grass row after rich row.
> Think of the autumns that have come and gone!
> Ambitious November with the humors of the year,

With a particular zeal for every slab,
Staining the uncomfortable angels that rot
On the slabs, a wing chipped here, an arm there:
The brute curiosity of an angel's stare
Turns you, like them, to stone,
Transforms the heaving air
Till plunged to a heavier world below
You shift your sea-space blindly
Heaving, turning like the blind crab.

The man experiences autumn's changes as a "desolation"; he is deeply troubled by the "brute curiosity" of the angel's stare, perhaps because he can no longer participate in the "active faith" enjoyed by his ancestors. He goes through a series of metamorphoses that reflect the torpor of his psyche: he is turned into stone, descends into "sea-space," and is finally transformed into a "blind crab."

While Tate's theme of death and the inexorable passage of time is universal, the narrative situation is specific to the South. The protagonist, a Southern intellectual who is clearly a version of Tate himself, is reminded by the Confederate military cemetery of how profoundly the South has changed. As Louis Rubin suggests, the "New South of cities and factories" has begun to replace the South beloved of the Fugitives and later the Agrarians. "Surveying the heroic past and the empty present," Rubin notes, "the young Southerner could only feel himself in isolation from what were now his region's ways."[2] Later in the poem, the speaker finds that he is unable to address even the bones of the Confederate dead: "What shall we say to the bones, unclean, / Whose verdurous anonymity will grow? . . . We shall say only the leaves whispering / In the improbable mist of nightfall." The heroic world of Confederate soldiers is lost to the modern Southerner, who cannot experience nature in anything other than predatory or alienated terms: the grass nurtured by the soldiers' bodies has turned an "insane green"; the graveyard is a place where "gray lean spiders come, they come and go"; and the willow trees growing above the graves form a "tangle" that blocks out all light. In this haunted place, only the "singular screech-owl's tight / Invisible lyric" can be heard.

Tate plays effectively with sound throughout the poem, especially in his use of end rhymes. In the stanza quoted above, the first four lines have a traditional rhyme scheme (abab), but in the rest of the stanza the rhymes are looser in organization. After rhyming "year" with "there," Tate disrupts the rhyme scheme by adding the unexpected rhymes of "stare" and "air." In other cases, rhyming words are so far removed from each other that we almost forget they are rhymes at all: "below" comes eight lines after "row," and "crab" follows a similar distance after "slab." The effect of these delayed and irregularly repeated rhymes is to create a feeling of anxiety, mirroring the attitude of the narrator as he contemplates the eerie graveyard.

The rhythms are similarly irregular, ranging from three to six beats per line and working strongly against the fluidity of regular iambic meter. As Tate himself suggested in his essay on the poem, the rhythm of the poem was intended to match its theme. Just as the dramatic tension of the poem resides in the contrast between two ideas – the "heroic theme" of "active faith" represented by the Confederate dead, and the "fragmentary cosmos" which results from the solipsism of the modern world – the poem's rhythm was meant to be a modulation between a formal regularity and a "broken rhythm" which would capture the failure of heroic emotion. Thus we find the alternation between lines of heroic pentameter ("Autumn is desolation in the plot," "Think of the autumns that have come and gone!") – which evoke a romanticized sense of the past – and the shorter lines toward the end of the stanza that comment on the modern speaker's situation. After the image of the broken statue, "a wing chipped here, an arm there," the lines become shorter and less elegiac, suggesting the fragmentary and impotent nature of the viewer's experience. The double caesura of "Turns you, like them, to stone" creates a heavy, stonelike feeling, while the opening trochees of the final line, "Heaving, turning like the blind crab," accentuate the image of the awkwardly moving crab itself.

This second stanza alone gives an indication of the complexity of Tate's poem. Yet at the same time it also displays the limitations of Tate's style. Tate's "Ode" does not rise to the level of dense formal achievement found in Crane's best work or in Eliot's *Four Quartets*, nor does it achieve the ironic compression of Ransom's strongest poems. And while the poem contains moments of lyric brilliance and effective imagery, it lacks the formal and thematic possibilities represented by modernist poems such as Pound's *Cantos*, Eliot's *Waste Land*, and Williams' *Paterson*.

The New Criticism and postwar poetry

Although the New Criticism was an American phenomenon, it was part of a more general trend toward poetic formalism on both sides of the Atlantic. During the mid-1930s, volumes by William Empson, C. Day Lewis, Louis MacNeice, and W. H. Auden helped establish a period style in the work of younger English poets. The most influential of these poets was Auden, whose work was formal, casually ironic, and technically accomplished. Auden's poetry exerted an influence on an emerging generation of American poets, including John Berryman, Randall Jarrell, Delmore Schwartz, Karl Shapiro, Richard Wilbur, Richard Howard, and James Merrill. In 1939,

Auden emigrated to the United States; he became a United States citizen in 1946. Auden's presence in American literary life – as a teacher and lecturer in various colleges and universities, as an actively publishing poet, and as the editor of the prestigious Yale Series of Younger Poets – made the 1940s and early 1950s the "Age of Auden." John Ashbery, who wrote his senior thesis on Auden in 1949, claimed that when he began reading modern poetry, Auden was "*the* modern poet," just as Eliot had been the quintessential modern poet for the previous generation. Auden never became fully Americanized, however, and despite the importance of his influence on a generation of poets, anthologists and literary historians have generally not included him among the ranks of American poets.

In the years following World War II, many younger poets adopted the formal style popularized by Auden and the New Critics. Much of the poetry written during the late 1940s and 1950s – a period identified as the "Age of Conformity" (Irving Howe) and the "tranquillized Fifties" (Robert Lowell) – paid more attention to matters of technique and formal method than to novelty of idea or conception. Many poets preferred to remain within the relative safety of fixed forms like the sonnet or rhymed quatrain; the social and political conservatism of the period was reflected in the poems themselves, which often avoided taking stylistic, thematic, or formal risks. The typical poetry of the period can be found in a number of anthologies that served to solidify the shared vision of an academic or mainstream style. Such collections as John Ciardi's *Mid-Century American Poets* (1950), Rolfe Humphries's *New Poems by American Poets* (1953), W. H. Auden's *Criterion Book of Modern American Verse* (1956), and Donald Hall, Robert Pack, and Louis Simpson's *New Poets of England and America* (1957) introduced a new generation of formal poets, including Wilbur, Merrill, Howard Nemerov, Anthony Hecht, John Hollander, Donald Justice, and William Meredith.

This generation of postwar formalists were all born between 1920 and 1930, and they were well educated, well traveled, and cosmopolitan. Merrill, for example, was the son of a prominent financier, the principal founder of one of America's largest brokerage houses. As a group, these poets represent the core of the academic poetry establishment over the last several decades of the twentieth century, and they have been highly feted by that establishment. Merrill received the National Book Award, the Bollingen Prize, and the Pulitzer Prize. Justice and Nemerov both won the Pulitzer, and both Nemerov and Meredith served as Poetry Consultant to the Library of Congress. Wilbur was appointed the nation's Poet Laureate, succeeding Robert Penn Warren.

The typical poems produced by academic poets of the 1950s and 1960s reflect strongly the influence of the New Critics and of the more formal poets of the modernist generation, such as Frost, Yeats, and Stevens. They are formal, witty, and impersonal, seeking an elegance of phrasing and often a relaxed or insouciant tone. A good example of such polished writing is Richard Wilbur's poem "A Simile for Her Smile":

> Your smiling, or the hope, the thought of it,
> Makes in my mind such pause and abrupt ease
> As when the highway bridgegates fall,
> Balking the hasty traffic, which must sit
> On each side massed and staring, while
> Deliberately the drawbridge starts to rise:
>
> Then horns are hushed, the oilsmoke rarefies,
> Above the idling motors one can tell
> The packet's smooth approach, the slip,
> Slip of the silken river past the sides,
> The ringing of clear bells, the dip
> And slow cascading of the paddle wheel.

Wilbur displays a good deal of technique here, but he does so in a seemingly effortless manner. There is none of the tension between form and theme we find in Ransom's poetry, and the poem is easily appreciated both for its charming use of the extended simile and for its manipulation of form and sound. The end rhymes bring a sense of unity to the stanzas, which achieve an ideal balance between strict iambic pentameter and frequent but never jarring variation from it. Wilbur makes effective use of alliteration, especially in the second stanza, and he makes us feel the motion of the water in the "slip, / Slip of the silken river past the sides." The simile itself is inventive yet does not strain the powers of the imagination: the smile of the young woman to whom the poem is addressed is compared (somewhat unexpectedly) to the rising of a drawbridge which slowly allows the passage of a paddle-wheel boat. Finally, Wilbur indulges in both wordplay (in the title's play of similarity between "simile" and "smile"), and paradox ("abrupt ease").

Despite all the ways in which the poem is successful, however, we cannot consider it an *important* poem. It manages a nice conceit, but it also avoids any engagement with larger ideas or issues. No specificity is given about the relationship between the speaker and the woman he hopes will smile at him; no real emotion is expressed or portrayed, despite the attempt to capture the sense of a potentially emotional moment; and no larger social or philosophical statement is made. The use of the urban imagery of cars, highways, bridges, and oilsmoke is made to serve no purpose other than as an analogy for a moment of personal happiness; as a result, such imagery comes to seem almost gratuitous.

In the 1960s, poets such as James Merrill began adopting formalist, post-New Critical techniques in more obviously autobiographical poems. Merrill's "The Broken Home" (1967), an autobiographical account of his parents and their divorce, is written in the form of seven consecutive sonnets. While "The Broken Home" relates details about Merrill's life, it is not a "confessional" poem in the way that we will see in the work of Robert Lowell or Sylvia Plath. Instead, it remains distanced from the rawness of personal experience both by its formal structure and by its somewhat detached, ironic tone. Merrill's "wit" can be compared to Ransom's: like Ransom, Merrill uses packed phrasing to evoke a complexity of feeling and awareness, and he makes frequent use of puns and wordplay, especially in his manipulation of familiar clichés. We see Merrill's technique at work in the second sonnet:

> My father, who had flown in World War I,
> Might have continued to invest his life
> In cloud banks well above Wall Street and wife,
> But the race was run below, and the point was to win.
>
> Too late now, I make out in his blue gaze
> (Through the smoked glass of being thirty-six)
> The soul eclipsed by twin black pupils, sex
> And business; time was money in those days.
>
> Each thirteenth year he married. When he died
> There were already several chilled wives
> In sable orbit – rings, cars, permanent waves,
> We'd felt him warming up for the green bride.
>
> He could afford it. He was "in his prime"
> At three score ten. But money was not time.

If, as Don Adams suggests, the speaker's central quest is "to rediscover who his parents really were and are," this sonnet begins that task by examining the life of his father.[3] The sonnet turns on the cliché "time is money," an expression associated both with the father and with the era in which he made his fortune. By the final couplet, the cliché is turned around as the father's death ironically suggests that "money was not time": despite all the money he has made and the fact that he still claims to be "in his prime" at the age of seventy, he cannot buy back the years he wasted in the pursuit of money and a succession of ever younger wives. The other crucial phrase in the sonnet is "too late now," suggesting that the son has failed until now to recognize his father's failures. In these lines, however, he makes up for lost time by offering a crushing denunciation of his father's life and values.

The form of the poem contributes to Merrill's theme of an emotional and spiritual emptiness in his father's life: each quatrain contains one full rhyme and one rhyme in which the vowel has been changed (one/win, sex/six, wives/waves). The use of these slant rhymes suggests that the apparent solidity of the father's life fails to disguise a hollowness or lack of integrity at its center.

The most obvious stylistic tendency of the poem is Merrill's use of puns. The pun on "cloud banks" turns the father's apparently solid profession of brokering and investment banking into an insubstantial and transitory object. Merrill also puns on "sable" (denoting both the dark color of the outer space where the satellite wives orbit and the fur coats he has given them) and "rings" (the orbits of the wives around the father as well as their wedding bands). The "chilled wives" evoke "chilled" cocktails, suggesting the father's superficial and decadent life.

Merrill's language is packed not only with such wordplay, but also with metaphors, clusters of imagery, and mythic structures. The father, for example, is introduced as having "flown in World War I," and the discourse of flight and air is continued in "cloud banks," "eclipsed," and "orbit." Through the sequencing of these metaphors, the apparently heroic fact of the father's having been a pilot in the war is ironized: now he is no longer the war hero, but a stationary figure around whom the various ex-wives orbit.

Like Ransom, Merrill creates further ironies by playing with the tension between a highly compressed poetic idiom ("The soul eclipsed by twin black pupils") and a more relaxed, colloquial diction and phrasing ("the point was to win," "he could afford it"). Like Ransom, too, Merrill places heavy demands on the reader's intelligence and sensitivity to language. Such poetry appeals to the pleasures of the intellect; at times, however, its ironic cleverness can come to seem strained and almost arch. Merrill's preoccupation with style at times prevents the poem from making a direct emotional connection with the reader.

The poems that made the greatest impact on the development of American poetry during the 1950s and 1960s were not those written in the formal style of Merrill and Wilbur. By the late 1950s, American poetry was already undergoing what James Breslin has referred to as a "radical transformation of poetic theory and practice."[4] The poetry of New Critical formalism, a style that had "rigified into orthodoxy" and begun to feel "limited, excluding [and] impoverished," was rejected by many poets who participated in a sweeping "antiformalist revolt."[5] The dramatic change in postwar American poetry was the result of a feeling of deep dissatisfaction with inherited models of language and form. Robert Lowell, for example, remarked that while poets had become extremely proficient at writing in set forms, such writing no longer seemed relevant to the conditions of contemporary life:

> [T]he writing seems divorced from culture somehow. It's become too
> much something specialized that can't handle much experience. It's
> become a craft, purely a craft, and there must be some breakthrough back
> into life.[6]

Robert Creeley put this same critique of formalist poetry in even stronger
terms:

> Poems were equivalent to cars insofar as many could occur of a similar
> pattern – although each was, of course, "singular." But it was this
> assumption of a mold, of a means that could be gained beyond the literal
> fact of the writing *here and now*, that had authority. It is the more ironic to
> think of it, remembering the incredible pressure of *feeling* in those years,
> of all that did want "to be said," of so much confusion and pain wanting
> statement in its own terms.[7]

What Lowell and Creeley both experienced was the sense of a cultural
crisis, a moment when poetry needed once again to become "disruptive –
critical of its culture, of its immediate past, of itself."[8] The desire to enact
some "breakthrough back into life," as Lowell put it, to critique its own
conventions as well as aspects of American culture and society as a whole,
was the central motivating force of American poetry in the decades after
World War II.

   In terms of its impact on American poetry as a whole, Lowell's 1959 volume *Life Studies* represented such a breakthrough. Not only did *Life Studies*
contain a number of striking and memorable poems – including "Skunk
Hour," "Waking in the Blue," "Memories of West Street and Lepke," "Man
and Wife," "During Fever," and "My Last Afternoon with Uncle Devereux
Winslow" – but it marked a dramatic departure from a style of poetry that
had already earned Lowell significant literary success. Lowell's 1946 volume
Lord Weary's Castle had won him the Pulitzer Prize, a Guggenheim fellowship, an award from the American Academy of Arts and Letters, and the
prestigious post of Consultant in Poetry at the Library of Congress. The
most powerful poems in *Lord Weary's Castle*, such as "The Quaker Graveyard in Nantucket," are written in a densely rhetorical and almost Miltonic
style. In this wartime elegy for his cousin Warren Winslow, who died at sea
when his navy ship sank, Lowell writes in what can be described as a high
literary mode:

> Whenever winds are moving and their breath
> Heaves at the roped-in bulwarks of this pier,
> The terns and sea-gulls tremble at your death
> In these home waters. Sailor, can you hear
> The Pequod's sea wings, beating landward, fall
> Headlong and break on our Atlantic wall

> Off 'Sconset, where the yawing S-boats splash
> The bellbuoy, with ballooning spinnakers,
> As the entangled, screeching mainsheet clears
> the blocks: off Madaket, where lubbers lash
> The heavy surf and throw their long lead squids
> For blue-fish?

The rhyming pentameter lines – broken by frequent enjambment and caesura – and the highly pressurized energy of the language create an undeniable effect. That effect might be described as dizzying: we need to read the poem several times before we can get past the sounds of the language (propelled by alliteration and the onomatopoetic descriptions of splashing boats and screeching sails) and the syntactic complexity. The poem's literary modes are traditional: personification (the winds's breath), metaphor (the ship's sails as wings), and the pathetic fallacy (the gulls and terns mourn the sailor's death). We might contrast this passage with lines from *Life Studies* such as those at the beginning of "Memories of West Street and Lepke":

> Only teaching on Tuesdays, book-worming
> in pajamas fresh from the washer each morning,
> I hog a whole house on Boston's
> "hardly passionate Marlborough Street"

Here, the line-lengths are uneven and there is no longer a discernable impulse toward iambic pentameter. The language is more casual and even colloquial: the speaker is not reading but "book-worming," and he "hogs" a whole house. The initial gesture of the poem is a deflationary one: beginning with the word "only," Lowell then tantalizes the reader with the alliteration of "teaching on Tuesdays" and the somewhat intriguing image of "book-worming" before offering the thoroughly flat second line (its verbal flatness emphasized by the addition of an extra foot). Even the visual appearance of the poem is more relaxed and prose-like: for example, Lowell no longer capitalizes the words on the left-hand margin.

The energy Lowell creates in "The Quaker Graveyard" comes largely from his use of active verbs: "heaves," "tremble," "hear," "fall," "break," "splash," "clears," "lash," and "throw." The opening stanza of "Memories of West Street and Lepke," in contrast, has only two active verbs in eleven lines, and both of these actions can be read ironically: the poet "hogs" a whole house on Marlborough Street, and his daughter "rises" ("like the sun") in her "flame-flamingo infants' wear." The two most energetic verbs in the stanza – "book-worming" and "scavenging" – are presented in a more passive tense (the present progressive), a tendency that continues throughout the rest of the poem: "telling off the state and president," "waiting sentence," "strolling," "wearing chocolate double-breasted suits," "piling towels on a rack," "dawdling off," "hanging like an oasis." In a poem that is at least in part about Lowell's "lost connections" with his past, the mood of dissipation created by the passive verb tenses conveys his own sense of uselessness and ineffectuality. The poetry of "A Quaker Graveyard" may be more inspired, more obviously "poetic," but it is the poetry of "Memories of West Street and Lepke" that comes closer to capturing the feeling of "real life" in the postwar era as Lowell and others perceived it.

The New Formalism

The revival of metered and rhymed poetry in the 1980s among a group of younger poets constituted the third generational wave of formal verse in the twentieth century. Adopting the somewhat pretentious title the "New Formalism," poets disaffected by the unstructured free verse of the "workshop" lyric (the dominant style in university creative-writing programs during the 1970s and 1980s) sought to reinvigorate the practice of American poetry in traditional forms and meters. Depending on where one stood within the verse culture of the period, these New Formalists (or neo-formalists) were either reactionaries attempting to turn back the clock to the days of the New Critics, poetic revolutionaries seeking to counter the tide of vapid free verse, or a small and ultimately negligible thorn in the side of mainstream poetry.

The New Formalists, though relatively few in number compared with practitioners of free verse, were a vocal and articulate minority. Members of a generation born in the 1940s and 1950s, many of them were professors, critics, translators, and editors as well as poets, and they were connected with periodicals such as *The Hudson Review*, *The New Criterion*, and *The New England Review*. In 1985, Philip Dacey and David Jauss edited *Strong Measures: Contemporary American Poetry in Traditional Forms*, the first significant anthology of formal poetry to be published in the United States since the early 1960s. This was followed by a book of essays on the New Formalism, *Expansive Poetry*, edited by Frederick Feirstein in 1989. Finally, in 1996, the publication of *Rebel Angels: 25 Poets of the New Formalism*, solidified the "canon" of New Formalist poets. *Rebel Angels* brought together the best-known New Formalists – Dana Gioia, Brad Leithauser, Molly Peacock, Mary Jo Salter, and Timothy Steele – along with formalists like Marilyn Hacker and Rafael Campo who had not previously been included under the banner of the New Formalism.

The work of the New Formalists ranges from the fairly traditional use of fixed forms to a more innovative use of formal techniques and structures. An example of the latter would be Brad Leithauser's sonnet "Post-Coitum Tristesse," written entirely in monosyllable lines. Another strategy is to create tension between traditional forms and more challenging content. Molly Peacock's sixteen line "exploded" sonnet "Those Paperweights with Snow Inside" plays a narrative of domestic violence against the apparent solidity of the sonnet form. Hacker's "Cancer Winter" describes in a series of Italian sonnets the poet's battle with breast cancer. R. S. Gwynn's three-sonnet sequence "Body Bags" tells tragic stories in miniature. The sestet of the second poem is particularly brutal in its use of rhyming iambic meter:

> I saw him one last time. He'd added weight
> Around the neck, used words like "grunt" and "slope,"
> And said he'd swap his Harley and his dope
> And both balls for a 4-F knee like mine.
> This happened in the spring of '68.
> He hanged himself in 1969.

Here the form is used with ironic intent. When read aloud, the final line comes out in perfect iambic pentameter; yet the shortness of the line makes it appear to be visually cut off, just as the young man's life was prematurely ended by his suicide.

Unfortunately, not all the poems by the New Formalists are this successful or innovative in their use of form. In fact, many of the poems in *Rebel Angels* seem to substitute the requirement of formal consistency for any originality of poetic voice or vision. As a fairly typical example, I quote two stanzas from Elizabeth Alexander's "Who I Think You Are":

> Baba's home is different from my daddy's:
> the sofa arms are draped with quiet lace,
> Does he fix fish with cardamon and mace?
> Coupons in a cookie tin. Meat patties,
>
> Steaming Cream of Wheat and ripe banana,
> juice cups with the little paper hats
> the guava jelly jars on plastic mats.
> We are your children and receive your manna.

Technically, these lines are competent: they rhyme in a neat *abba* pattern, they sustain a regular though not overly insistent iambic pentameter, and they use caesura to vary the rhythmic effect within the stanzas. But one might well ask what the New Critics would have made of such poetry. There is little of the complexity – on the level of diction, imagery, figurative language, wordplay, argument, or voice – that formal verse at its best makes possible. Even in terms of what Ransom would call the poem's "texture," there is nothing striking in terms of the manipulation of form. The closest the stanzas come to any kind of ironic tension is in the witty rhyme of "banana" with "manna," but even here it is not clear whether any irony is intended.

The New Formalism can be usefully contrasted with the other most visible poetic movement of the 1980s: the Language Poetry. Both the New Formalists and the Language Poets rejected mainstream free-verse lyric as it was practiced in writing workshops across the country. But while the Language Poets were participants in a poetic avant garde that sought to revitalize the linguistic and formal procedures of American poetry (see chapter 10), the New Formalists seemed curiously retrogressive in their attempt to resurrect the practices of a half century or more ago. The argument of the New Formalists for a greater attention to poetic form, and more specifically to traditional metrical forms, no longer seems as convincing as did the argument made by the New Critics of the 1930s and 1940s for a more rigorous attention to form. The critical methods developed by the New Critics were an important advance on the dominant critical practice of the time, and their poetry can be seen primarily as a logical extension of their critical practice rather than vice versa. In the case of the New Formalism, on the other hand – which seems to have evolved as an aesthetically conservative reflex against what was perceived as the "laxity" of the 1960s and 1970s – the poetry has developed no new critical or theoretical apparatus to support it. The claims by the movement's advocates that it represents a "revolution" in the practice of American poetry seem at best hyperbolic and at worst demagogic. First of all, there is nothing revolutionary about writing in sonnets and quatrains. And secondly, there has been no "fundamental change" in the writing of American poetry, since the vast majority of published poetry continues to be in free verse.

All this is not to question whether traditional forms have a place in American poetry (clearly they do), but rather to ask whether consecrating a "movement" to the writing of formal verse – far from being an act of revolutionary potential – is merely to perpetuate the notion that "real" poetry must include such elements as rhyme, regular meter, and stanzaic form. Over the course of the century, the strongest American poets have shown that poetic language emerges out of the poet's confrontation with the texture and meanings of individual words rather than as a result of the insertion of these words into prefabricated forms. If, as Robert Creeley put it, "form is never more than an extension of content," then the decisions poets make about what forms to write in are ultimately of less importance than the things they have to say.

Chapter 8

The confessional moment

Among those poets who were inclined to challenge certain aspects of the New Criticism, Robert Lowell, Anne Sexton, and John Berryman introduced [a poetry] which some maligned as "confessionalism" but others hailed as a liberation from the tyranny of poetic decorum.

Joseph Conte[1]

Throughout the 1960s, 1970s, and well into the 1980s the confessional model remained influential with academic critics and literary historians across a wide spectrum, perhaps because it offered a humanly compelling and rather clear-cut way of evaluating poetry. Poems involving daring self-revelation could be assumed to be bold and sincere.

Thomas Travisano[2]

The antics and agonies of the celebrated confessional generation might be seen, in part, as a desperate flailing of mortals deceived by their predecessors into the divinity of the poetic calling.

Jed Rasula[3]

I place these varied statements about confessional poetry at the beginning of the chapter in order to illustrate the extent to which the definition of "confessionalism" has itself been the subject of contention. Was confessionalism an important movement in American poetry, a significant break from New Critical and modernist models? Or was it simply a convenient, and ultimately reductive, critical label used to explain certain developments in postwar poetry? Does the term describe a generation of poets who sought desperately to fulfill their lofty poetic ambitions by means of a self-indulgent display of raw emotion? Or does it celebrate a liberating and daring move away from a pervasive "tyranny of poetic decorum"?

Robert Lowell's shift during the decade of the 1950s from a poetic modeled on New Critical formalism to a more relaxed, colloquial, and self-revelatory free verse was certainly a dramatic change, but it was hardly unique among poets of the period. Similar trajectories can be traced in the careers of John Berryman, Randall Jarrell, Adrienne Rich, and James Wright, among others. There is no doubt that the so-called "confessional" movement represented an important change in the way the American poetic mainstream approached the writing of poetry. The poems were presented in the first-person voice with little apparent distance between the speaker and the poet; they were highly emotional in tone, autobiographical in content, and narrative in structure. The personal reflections of poets were no longer couched in the distanced idiom characteristic of both modernism and New Criticism. The mode of confessionalism – whether one approved of the term or not – served as a model for poets who chose to reject modernist difficulty and New Critical complexity in favor of a more relaxed or personal voice. It also allowed poets to articulate feelings, thoughts, and emotions that challenged the decorum of an era marked by its containment of psychic needs and desires. Responding to the "tranquillized Fifties," as Lowell called them, these poets resisted midcentury cultural norms that demanded "the repression of grief [and] the plowing under of traumatic experience."[4]

As Diane Middlebrook suggests, one of the chief characteristics of confessional poetry was its investigation of "the pressures on the family as an institution regulating middle-class life"; more specifically, confessional poems focused on such issues as "divorce, sexual infidelity, childhood neglect, and the mental disorders that follow from deep emotional wounds received in early life."[5] The appeal of confessional poetry was heightened by its seemingly direct portrayal of poets' tempestuous lives. In fact, it was often the biographies of the confessional generation as much as their poetry that attracted the attention of scholars, critics, and readers. Plath, Berryman, Anne Sexton, and Delmore Schwartz were all suicides, and Jarrell attempted suicide. Other confessionals experienced problems with alcoholism (Lowell, Bishop, and Berryman), emotional breakdowns and depressions (Lowell, Berryman, Bishop, Plath, and Sexton), and divorces (Lowell, Berryman, Jarrell, and W. D. Snodgrass).

Historically, most critics trace the beginnings of confessional poetry to the poems Lowell began writing in the late 1950s. The most extreme phase of the confessional mode lasted until the mid-1960s, and included Lowell's *Life Studies*, W. D. Snodgrass's *Heart's Needle*, Sylvia Plath's *Ariel*, Anne Sexton's *To Bedlam and Part Way Back* and *All My Pretty Ones*, and John Berryman's *77 Dream Songs*. Other poets of the period, such as Elizabeth Bishop, Delmore Schwartz, Randall Jarrell, and Theodore Roethke, have also been grouped with the confessionals. The confessional mode continued to exert an important influence on the poetry of the 1970s and 1980s. In fact, the "postconfessional" lyric was to become the dominant stylistic mode of American poetry in the late twentieth century. Poems dealing with relationships, sex, marriage, and domestic life became so common in the wake of the confessionals that they were no longer seen as daringly provocative; instead, such poems were written in creative-writing workshops across the country and soon came to constitute the new mainstream of American poetry. Poets such as Louise Gluck and Sharon Olds, both from the generation after the confessionals, have focused much of their work on family relation-ships and on such subjects as divorce, adolescent anorexia, and childhood abuse. Olds' volume *The Father*, one of the most successful adaptations of the confessional mode, is a sequence of poems devoted to her conflicted feelings about the death of her father.

Robert Lowell

Lowell's "Skunk Hour" is often cited as the quintessential poem of the confessional movement, though its landmark status is due less to its content – which now strikes us as rather tame compared to some of the later products of the confessionals – and more to its historical place as the first poem to be written in the new style. In fact, "Skunk Hour," which appears as the last poem in *Life Studies*, was the first poem in the volume to be finished and the work that Lowell considered "the anchor poem of the sequence." He began the poem in August 1957 while he was visiting the coastal town of Castine, Maine. As Lowell tells it, he had been struck with the sense of "having nothing to write, of having, at least, no language." With the writing of "Skunk Hour," he was able to abandon his previous formal style and, inspired by his friend Elizabeth Bishop's poem "The Armadillo," write a poem in "short line stanzas with drifting description." Though different from Lowell's previous style, the poem is in fact highly crafted. It is composed in eight six-line stanzas with a variable meter and rhyme scheme; the first four stanzas address the decay of the town, and the second four deal with his personal ordeal, the "dark night of the soul" from which he is saved by the appearance of a family of skunks.

The style of the first half of the poem is gently mocking of the town and its inhabitants. There is the eccentric heiress who prefers "Queen Victoria's century" to the present; now, "in her dotage," she tries to resist the modern world by buying "all / the eyesores facing her shore," but then "lets them fall." Below her on the social scale is the "summer millionaire" who repre-sents the superficiality and lack of taste among the town's newer inhabitants; he "seemed to leap from an L. L. Bean catalogue," but even he has now left the town and sold his "nine-knot yawl" to lobstermen. Finally, the town's "fairy decorator" has painted everything in his antique shop orange, perhaps attempting to promote his now useless objects (a cobbler's bench and awl) to tourists. Lowell's portrait of the town presents everything as somehow out of key; or, as he more emphatically puts it, "the season's ill." The town, which seems devoid of productive labor or ideas and in the process of social and physical decay, serves as an analogue for the state into which Lowell fears his own poetry has fallen.

In the second half of the poem, the tone dramatically shifts as the "illness" of the "season" turns into Lowell's own "ill-spirit" and his disturbing sense that "my mind's not right":

> One dark night,
> my Tudor Ford climbed the hill's skull;
> I watched for love-cars. Lights turned down,
> they lay together, hull to hull,
> where the graveyard shelves on the town.
> My mind's not right.
>
> A car radio bleats,
> "Love, O careless Love . . ." I hear
> my ill-spirit sob in each blood cell,
> as if my hand were at its throat . . .
> I myself am hell;
> nobody's here –

The poem's most striking lines are those in which he implicitly compares the landscape of "love-cars" lying "hull to hull" with his own mental state. He is isolated in his "Tudor Ford" (its name – a pun on "two door" – created by the era's tastemakers to enhance its appeal), and can only experience the encounters of lovers within their parked cars as perverted and morbid. The hill is transformed into a "skull" – intensifying the earlier imagery of the town's illness and the "red fox stain" covering "Blue Hill" – and the line of parked cars is placed right next to the town's cemetery. Lowell packs the stanza with a densely figurative language: there is a metonymic substitution in which the cars stand for the lovers within, followed by an implied metaphor comparing the cars to boats. The nautical metaphor of cars' bumpers as ships' hulls is perhaps suggested by the proximity of the sea and the imagery of boats and fishing nets in the early section of the poem, but it lends an almost surreal feeling to the stanza, which is in turn intensified by the haunting image of the graveyard which "shelves on the town." Lowell is presumably using the word "shelves" in the sense of sloping or inclining, but the word remains ambiguous in its connotation. Do the shelves here suggest the interlocking fates of the living and the dead, or do they suggest a "shelving," or putting aside, of a town that has become useless?

At the poem's climactic moment, Lowell contrasts a popular song playing on the car radio with a quote from Milton's *Paradise Lost*: "I myself am Hell." The song's lyrics in fact contain another buried reference to death – "Now you see what careless love will do . . . Make you kill yourself and your sweetheart too" – and Milton's Satan is the agent behind the destruction of the earthly paradise created around the love of Adam and Eve. But what brings Lowell back from the brink of suicidal despair is a group of skunks searching "in the moonlight for a bite to eat." The sudden appearance of the skunks – who seem to wander into the poem out of nowhere – once again shifts the tone from agonized to humorous:

> They march on their soles up Main Street:
> white stripes, moonstruck eyes' red fire
> under the chalk-dry and spar spire
> of the Trinitarian Church.
>
> I stand on top
> of our back steps and breathe the rich air –
> a mother skunk with her column of kittens swills the garbage pail.
> She jabs her wedge-head in a cup
> of sour cream, drops her ostrich tail,
> and will not scare.

Here, as James Breslin suggests, Lowell makes his first movement toward an "authentic connection with otherness."[6] The skunks present such a comical sight, marching unabashedly up Main Street and sticking their heads in cups of sour cream, that Lowell cannot maintain the high seriousness of his nocturnal vision. The pun on "soles" ("souls") suggests that these physical creatures are unconcerned with human forms of religious and moral doubt: they simply go about their business, in contrast with both the "chalk-dry and spar" morality of the Trinitarian Church and the social and political realities represented by "Main Street." Charles Altieri sums up the symbolic significance of the skunks:

> By returning to the prereflective natural order . . . Lowell makes the skunk
> embody the determination and self-concern of all living beings and
> beyond that, as mother, a willingness to face danger in order to accept the
> responsibility of her role . . . Now one sees both a parody of the Eucharist
> and, on another level, a genuine moment of communion, for, as the skunk
> swills from the garbage pail, Lowell finds precisely the image of
> endurance and survival he had sought in vain in the rest of the
> volume . . . As the skunk makes her way beneath the "chalk-dry church
> spire" reminding the reader of the dead vertical world, she embodies
> whatever possibilities Lowell can find for restoring a context of value
> within secular and biological necessity.[7]

The skunk's appearance is at best a partial restitution of meaningful value in the life of the poem's speaker. Having rejected the options of both civic responsibility (Main Street) and organized religion (the Trinitarian Church), the speaker finds value only in an animal associated with garbage and noxious odors. As Altieri suggests, the figure of the skunk resists our attempt to see it as some form of redemption: the identification of man and skunk is "too foreign to one's sensibilities for there to be completely affirmative resolutions." Lowell's use of this highly untraditional metaphor for the poet's survival suggests his new understanding of the "confessional" poet. In a strategy that will be adopted by other confessional poets as well, the association of the speaker or protagonist with an image of debasement maps the poet's damaged psyche onto the outside world.

Sylvia Plath

We see this strategy even more clearly in the work of Plath, who was in fact a student of Lowell's at Boston University. In the intensely self-dramatizing poems she wrote shortly before her own suicide in February 1963, Plath adopted highly strained metaphors to describe her psychic state. "Lady Lazarus," written in the fall of 1962, begins with a comparison between the poem's speaker and the Jews tortured and killed in World War II:

> A sort of walking miracle, my skin
> Bright as a Nazi lampshade,
> My right foot
>
> A paperweight,
> My face a featureless, fine
> Jew linen.

Plath pushes beyond poetic convention in her choice of metaphors, assaulting the reader's sensibilities with the lurid violence of her images. As Jon Rosenblatt notes, Plath's comparison of the sufferings of her speaker to "the sadistic medical experiments on the Jews by Nazi doctors and the Nazis' use of their victims' bodies in the production of lampshades and other objects" is intended not to make realistic historical comparisons but to "draw the reader into the center of a personality and its characteristic mental processes."[8] Though some readers have objected to what they see as Plath's misappropriation of the holocaust for use in a poem about individual suffering, Rosenblatt argues that imagining her own psychic drama against the backdrop of Nazism is justified as a means of universalizing the personal conflict. Nevertheless, the question of Plath's direct appropriation of traumatic historical imagery remains a troubling one in poems such as "Lady Lazarus" and "Daddy," and it raises fundamental questions about the use of historically specific imagery or personae in the service of personal or "confessional" poems. Does the fact that Plath herself was not Jewish, for example, have any bearing on the legitimacy of her use of the holocaust as a defining metaphor for her own struggles?

Another fundamental difference between "Lady Lazarus" and a poem like Lowell's "Skunk Hour" is that Plath subordinates the poem's "confessional" aspect (its status as personal or biographical revelation) to its dramatic structure. Whereas Lowell's speaker was clearly a version of Lowell himself, Plath's speaker is a composite based on her own life experience as well as other, fictional personae. Though the poem deals in a general sense with Plath's own suicide attempts and their aftermath, the personal details are left vague, and the poem's speaker focuses more on the creation of her mythic persona. The cultural complexity of this created persona is suggested by the title's conflation of the biblical Lazarus (who rises from the dead in an ironized version of the failed suicide) and the "Lady" (with echoes of Lady Godiva, the Madonna, and various other figures from literature and fable) who becomes legendary in her suffering and ability to withstand various forms of torture. If the title is not immediately seen as comic, the grotesque comedy of the poem soon becomes apparent both in its form and in its presentation of the persona. Lady Lazarus compares herself to a carnival freak, whom the "peanut-crunching crowd / Shoves in to see." She feels herself to be on display, both as a suicide and as a woman: later in the poem, she describes the viewing of her scarred and emaciated body as "the big strip tease" and as a theatrical "comeback in broad day."

At this point, Plath uses the form of the poem – and in particular the repetition of rhyming words – for a darkly comic effect:

> There is a charge
> For the eyeing of my scars, there is a charge
> For the hearing of my heart –
> It really goes.
>
> And there is a charge, a very large charge
> For a word or a touch
> Or a bit of blood
>
> Or a piece of my hair or my clothes.

Plath's use of the three-line stanza – as in other late poems like "Ariel" and "Fever 103" – carries echoes of the terza rima form of Italian tradition; but Plath's use of the stanza provides only a general structure for her experimentation with a variable rhyme scheme and metrical pattern. Most of the rhymes in the poem are off-rhymes (put/brute; goes/clothes; stir/there), and the pure rhymes often work through repetition of the same word or through combinations of internal and end rhymes that create a kind of syncopated feeling ("I turn and burn, / Do not think I underestimate your great concern"). In the above passage, the word "charge" is repeated four times within five lines, the last time accentuated by the internal rhyme with "large." This kind of insistent rhyme highlights the pun implicit in the word "charge": it is both an electrical charge (consistent with the imagery of lamps, burning, and the body as machine) and the monetary charge for those who want to see Lady Lazarus. The lines mock the reader, who, like the "peanut-crunching crowd" which pays to see Lady Lazarus, is implicated in the voyeuristic act of watching Plath's "act" of self-revelation, a kind of biographical "strip tease." The reader is drawn into the poem by this conceit, invited to watch, listen, and even touch the woman, who is herself reduced to a set of mechanized body parts: her heart, for example, is like a wind-up toy that "really goes." The sound of the words here – especially the repetition of the harsh "ar" sound in "charge," "scars," "heart," and "large" – adds to the brutally ironic tone of the passage. This disturbing effect is intensified by the relatively short lines and the use of meters more typical of light verse (for example, the rocking anapests of "For a piece of my hair or my clothes").

Throughout the poem, Plath not only portrays her own torment, but parodies her attempts at suicide. This self-parody, however, is mixed with a sense of pride at her ability to manipulate both herself and her readers. Plath's persona of performer in the poem – whether it takes the form of stripper, sideshow freak, or vaudeville comedian – allows her to declare herself a success. The implicit comparison between Plath as poet and as suicide is clear in the following lines:

> Dying
> Is an art, like everything else.
> I do it exceptionally well,
>
> I do it so it feels like hell.
> I do it so it feels real.
> I guess you could say I've a call.

Plath's virtuosity as poet – which she displays in her manipulation of voice, image, form, and rhythm throughout the poem – is mapped onto her skill at "dying," which she perversely claims to do "exceptionally well." By writing poems about her own suicide attempts, Plath is also selling herself as poet to the reader.

> Ash, ash –
> You poke and stir.
> Flesh, bone, there is nothing there –
>
> A cake of soap,
> A wedding ring,
> A gold filling.
>
> Herr God, Herr Lucifer
> Beware,
> Beware.
>
> Out of the ash
> I rise with my red hair
> And I eat men like air.

The poem ends with another image of resurrection: that of the phoenix myth. The female speaker returns as a fiery spirit whose physical body has been burned away, and who can now enact vengeance on the various male figures who have tortured, oppressed, and humiliated her throughout the poem: doctors, Nazis, and even God himself. Plath's final image can be read in a more directly biographical way – in the context of her anger toward her now estranged husband Ted Hughes – but it also a more general statement of liberation from the male-dominated society in which she lived.

Anne Sexton

Sexton's "The Truth the Dead Know," from *All My Pretty Ones* (1962), can be considered "confessional" in the sense that the poem's speaker can be clearly identified with the poet herself; yet at the same time, the poem is a meditative lyric which raises fundamental questions about the nature of death. The primary philosophical tension of the poem opposes the societal construction of death as an occasion for social and religious ritual and the poetic construction of death as an occasion for creative and personal exploration. The poem begins at the funeral of Sexton's father – who had died only three months after the death of her mother – and it takes the form of a bitter elegy for both her parents:

> Gone, I say and walk from church,
> refusing the stiff procession to the grave,
> letting the dead ride alone in the hearse.
> It is June. I am tired of being brave.
>
> We drive to the Cape. I cultivate
> myself where the sun gutters from the sky,
> where the sea swings in like an iron gate
> and we touch. In another country people die.
>
> My darling, the wind falls in like stones
> from the whitehearted water and when we touch
> we enter touch entirely. No one's alone.
> Men kill for this, or for as much.
>
> And what of the dead? They lie without shoes
> in their stone boats. They are more like stone
> than the sea would be if it stopped. They refuse
> to be blessed, throat, eye and knucklebone.

The highly symmetrical form of the poem – four quatrains with interlocking (abab) rhymes – suggests a sense of confinement or enforced order from which the speaker is trying to escape. Yet the speaker's utterance of the single word "gone" represents her inability to make any public comment about her parents' death. The word cuts in two ways: the parents are "gone" to the grave, but she too is already "gone," mentally and spiritually absent from the scene, as she walks out of the church. Instead of joining in the funeral procession and thus participating in the expected rituals of mourning, Sexton refuses "the stiff procession to the grave" and instead drives to Cape Cod. This escape into a new landscape – one which suggests the desire to be surrounded by sea and sky rather than by artifacts of the human world – allows her to regain at least a partial sense of being alive.

The dominant gesture of the poem is one of refusal: the speaker refuses to ride in the funeral procession; the parents "refuse / to be blessed" in their dying; and the poem itself refuses to allow the familiar poetic tropes of nature as consolation or of the elegy as redemption. Nature is presented in terms that suggest indifference or even menace: in a series of striking images, the sun "gutters from the sky," the sea "swings in like an iron gate," and the wind "falls in like stones." Even in her attempt to escape human society for the natural world, the speaker can only find metaphors taken from the human realm. Gutters and gates both represent liminal zones, boundaries between one space and another: between the speaker and her dead parents, or in psychological terms between the speaker and her ability to experience the cathartic emotions of grief and mourning. At the same time, the stones seem to be hurled at the speaker and her lover by an angry, "whitehearted" sea, as if punishing her for her refusal to behave in a more respectful way. These images reinforce the speaker's sense of isolation: if people die "in another country," then we can never know "the truth the dead know." Yet if the characteristic posture of the speaker in Sexton's poetry is that of the lone or isolated female, "The Truth the Dead Know" offers at least the possibility of interpersonal contact. The two middle stanzas show the speaker with her lover, and their touch reassures her that "no one's alone." The progression of pronouns in the poem – from "I" in the first stanza to "we" in the second and third to "they" in the fourth – suggests the psychological journey of grief from a focus on the bereaved self to an engagement with the dead.

The final stanza is perhaps the most deeply engaging. Sexton returns to the question posed by the title, which seems to have been forgotten in the trip to the Cape: "And what of the dead?" The question is of course a rhetorical one, since it is formulated in such vague terms as to offer no possibility of a response. Sexton herself responds by suggesting an analogy in the form of a metaphor that is almost riddle-like in its formulation: "They lie without shoes / in their stone boats." The "stone boats" – echoing the stones of stanza III but also suggesting a coffin or grave that transports the body to the land of the dead – are described further as "more like stone / than the sea would be if it stopped." These lines – though at first paradoxical – work according to a definite poetic logic. The absence of motion suggested by the sea stopping is perceived as even more still than an object that never moved, such as a stone. The poem ends with the curious reduction of the dead to "throat, eye, and knucklebone": rather than souls waiting to be blessed, the dead are represented by seemingly random parts of the physical body. But while the strange choice of body-parts might seem to emphasize the arbitrariness of death, we can read Sexton's choices symbolically as well. The throat and the eye represent speech and vision, respectively, and thus suggest primary modes of interaction between human beings. The "knucklebone" can be read in different ways. On one level, it is that recalcitrant part that cannot be elevated to any transcendent level of meaning; on another level, it can be associated with violence or abuse. The rhyme of "knucklebone" with "stone" emphasizes the finality of death, one that allows no access to an abstracted "truth" which the dead might be privileged to know.

John Berryman

Like Robert Lowell and other poets of what has been called the "middle generation" of American poetry, Berryman began writing under the influence of the New Criticism and only gradually came to formulate his own highly individual style. Though older than Lowell by three years, Berryman had to wait longer for his most important poetic breakthrough, which would come in the mid-1960s with the first of what would be a total of 385 poems entitled *The Dream Songs*. Berryman was both an exceptionally talented and an extremely ambitious poet, whose work is so idiosyncratic that it has not yet been fully understood by critics and readers. His most important poem before *The Dream Songs* – *Homage to Mistress Bradstreet* (1953) – was a long interior monologue in the voice of the first American poet, Anne Bradstreet. In its imaginative creation of a poetic persona and in its exploration of extreme psychological and spiritual states it can be seen as a descendant of Yeats and Eliot, the two twentieth-century poets who had the most profound influence on his work. In *The Dream Songs*, Berryman turned to Whitman's "Song of Myself" for inspiration. Though the Dream Songs are formally and stylistically very different from Whitman's work, they resemble Whitman's poem in that they strive for the same combination of the personal and the epic. Like "Song of Myself," whose hero is the poet himself, *The Dream Songs* feature a central protagonist who is given the name of Henry but who is modeled quite closely on Berryman's own life, thoughts, and emotions.

Much of the critical discussion of *The Dream Songs* has involved an attempt to determine the degree to which Henry is in fact a thinly disguised

version of Berryman himself. Berryman tried to discourage such biographical readings of the poems, stating that Henry was "an imaginary character
(not the poet, not me) . . . a white American in early middle age sometimes in blackface, who has suffered an irreversible loss." In one interview,
Berryman quipped: "Henry is accused of being me and I am accused of
being Henry and I deny it and nobody believes me." Such disavowals are
difficult to accept at face value, however, given the overwhelming evidence
that Henry and Berryman are, for the most part, one and the same.

The Dream Songs were published in two collections – 77 *Dream Songs*
(1964) and *His Toy, His Dream, His Rest* (1968) – and Berryman continued
to use the character of Henry in his poems until his suicide in 1972. The form
of the poems is distinctive: three stanzas of six lines, sporadically rhymed and
with varied line lengths. Within this form, Berryman uses syntax and diction
in highly idiosyncratic, jarring, and often very powerful ways: his goal, he
claimed, was to "make the reader's nerves jump." Clearly the poems are not
meant to be sung, but their designation as "songs" is only partly ironic: it
alludes to the title of Whitman's poem and to the whole tradition of English
lyric verse, on which the poems trope in various ways. At times, Berryman
plays the idea of lyric as song against other generic conventions such as epic,
fairy-tale, minstrelsy, or prose fiction. For example, in "Dream Song" 1,
he mixes a flatly conversational prose ("I see his point – a trying to put
things over") with effusive lyric ("Once in a sycamore I was glad / all at
the top, and I sang") and with lines echoing the Old English alliterative
meter ("Hard on the land wears the strong sea / and empty grows every
bed"). Berryman (who was also an accomplished Shakespeare scholar) had an
unusually nuanced command of language and a deep knowledge of English
and American literary tradition. Rather than showing off his erudition in his
poems, however, he used it to accomplish brilliant manipulations of voice
and style. Lowell described the poem's style as "a conglomeration of high
style, Berrymanisms, Negro and beat slang, and baby talk." The tone of the
poems is often comic, but it is a comedy tinged with a great deal of sadness
and an overwhelming sense of loss and frustration.

These emotions are clearly an expression – if not exactly a "confession" –
of Berryman's own emotional makeup. Berryman began writing what would
become *The Dream Songs* after undertaking written analyses of his dreams.
Henry is plagued by thoughts of death (Berryman's own father committed
suicide when he was a boy), depression, disappointment, despair, sexual
hunger, failed marriages, boredom, guilt, and alcohol. Many of the poems
are elegies to dead poets, including Frost, Williams, Theodore Roethke,
Delmore Schwartz, and Randall Jarrell. Some of the songs have titles –
for example, no. 76 is called "Henry's Confession" and nos. 78 to 91 are
jokingly labelled "Op. Posth." – but most carry only a number, as in a

typical sonnet sequence. While the poems are better read in order, several of them are strong enough to stand on their own as individual lyrics. In addition to the first poem, the most successful include no. 4 ("Filling her compact & delicious body"), no. 5 ("Henry sats in de bar & was odd"), no. 14 ("Life, friends, is boring"), no. 16 ("All the world like a woolen lover"), no. 29 ("There sat down, once, a thing on Henry's heart"), no. 40 ("I'm scared a lonely. Never see my son"), no. 45 ("He stared at ruin. Ruin stared right back"), no. 76 ("Nothin very bad happen to me lately"), no. 382 ("At Henry's bier let some thing fall out well"), and no. 384 ("The marker slants, flowerless, day's almost done").

Berryman's poetic skill can clearly be seen in a poem like "Dream Song" 14:

> Life, friends, is boring. We must not say so.
> After all, the sky flashes, the great sea yearns,
> we ourselves flash and yearn,
> and moreover my mother told me as a boy
> (repeatingly) "Ever to confess you're bored
> means you have no
>
> Inner Resources." I conclude now that I have no
> inner resources, because I am heavy bored.
> Peoples bore me,
> literature bores me, especially great literature,
> Henry bores me, with his plights & gripes
> as bad as achilles,
>
> who loves people and valiant art, which bores me.
> And the tranquil hills, & gin, look like a drag
> and somehow a dog
> has taken itself & its tail considerably away
> into mountain or sea or sky, leaving
> behind: me, wag.

Berryman considered organizing *The Dream Songs* as a kind of mock epic, in which Henry would be a hero fighting "late in a long war" against all those who sought to destroy him. In this poem, the only connection to such heroism is the mention of the Greek hero Achilles. The speaker is bored of everything, including literature, society, and himself. Berryman overturns the cultural pretensions of the middle-class society represented by his mother: we must never admit to boredom, because to do so is to admit the weakness of having no "Inner Resources." He satirizes such attitudes by deflating Western culture (Achilles himself is reduced to lower case and his heroic wrath to a series of "plights and gripes") and by parodying the gestures of Romantic poetry ("the sky flashes, the great sea yearns"). Each assertion is undercut by its ironic repetition. The idea that the sea "yearns" (an assertion of nature's preternatural power) is turned on its head by the nonsensical suggestion that "we ourselves flash and yearn"; the idea of "inner resources" as an adequate response to the alienation or dissatisfaction felt by Berryman is undercut both by the repetition of the term and by the slyly parenthetical reminder of his mother's lack of originality ("repeatingly").

After reading the final stanza, with its reference to the tranquilizing effects of "gin," one is tempted to reread the poem as an interior monologue spoken while under the influence of alcohol. This would help explain the rapid changes in tone, from self-important proclamation ("Life, friends, is boring") to guilty retraction ("We must not say so"), as well as the loose syntax (three lines begin with "and") and the detached, almost trance-like quality of the final stanza. The ambiguous syntax of the final line makes possible the pun on the word "wag": the dog has left Henry behind with a wag of his tail, but Berryman/Henry also identifies himself as a "wag," a mischievous person, joker, or truant. This secondary meaning – more common in the English of Shakespeare's day – has a thematic resonance: just as Henry hides from the world behind a haze of gin, Berryman plays truant from the poem's reader by denying any sense of closure or transcendent meaning. The motion of the wagging tail visually represents the back and forth or sideways movement of the poem, which never goes anywhere but only returns (repeatingly) to its beginnings; the "sea or sky" of the penultimate line is an ironic allusion to the sky's dramatic flashings and sea's passionate yearnings of the first stanza. The wagging dog and the "tranquil hills" of the final stanza are images that suggest little consolation. Unlike Lowell's skunks, which in their specificity could be made to stand for a kind of heroism in the face of human mediocrity and despair, the dog is presented with no identifying features: even its gender is neutral as it takes "itself & its tail considerably away."

Elizabeth Bishop

Bishop's poetry resists easy classification, and despite her friendship with Lowell and her generational affinities with the confessionals, her work displays a greater degree of reticence and restraint than that of poets like Lowell, Berryman, Plath, and Sexton. I have decided to conclude this chapter with a discussion of Bishop not because I think her poetry falls neatly or easily into the confessional mode, but because her work – by its very resistance to the more intimate styles of her contemporaries – tests the limits of the confessional paradigm as a strategy for reading poetry that is personal or autobiographical in nature. According to at least one of the definitions of the confessional poem – "a type of narrative and lyric verse . . . which deals with the facts and intimate mental and physical experience of the poet's own life"[9] – several of Bishop's poems would qualify.

Bishop's life history would seem to have made her an ideal candidate for the confessional mode. Her father died eight months after she was born and her mother – deeply disoriented by her father's death – spent the next five years in and out of mental asylums. She was declared permanently insane in 1916, and Bishop would never see her again. After spending a year with her maternal grandparents in Nova Scotia, Bishop was brought back to Massachusetts to live with other relatives. Problems with her health as a child prevented her from attending school regularly, and as a result she felt more comfortable with books than with most other people. Her life was spent in various parts of the world, much of the time living as a guest in other people's homes. As a woman poet who was a lesbian, who was never part of any literary "movement," and virtually all of whose poetic contemporaries were men, she felt marginalized within both literary culture and American culture at large. Many of Bishop's poems deal either directly or more covertly with themes of isolation, alienation, or loss. This is particularly true of the poems written after 1967, when her longtime lover and companion Lota de Macedo Soares (with whom she had lived in Brazil since the early 1950s) committed suicide.

But while Bishop wrote a number of poems in the first-person voice – some of them personal or autobiographical narratives based on her childhood and later life – her style and overall approach to this material remains more distanced than that of the confessionals. Bishop's poetic clearly differed from that of poets like Plath and Sexton, who felt that the more deeply they mined their own psychic histories in their poems, the more powerful the resulting poetry would be. And though she continued to admire the work of her close friend Robert Lowell, Bishop expressed reservations even about *his* capacity to reveal so much about himself and his private life in his poetry. Bishop explicitly rejected the confessional mode in both essays and letters to other poets. She considered the poetry of Sexton and W. D. Snodgrass to be "egocentric – simply that," and she considered the general tendency in poetry of the 1960s to substitute anguished self-revelation for more subtle self-presentation to be a peculiarly "American sickness." The "sickness" or "morbidity" exhibited by confessional poets made Bishop feel that such poets – rather than boasting about their private catastrophes – should "keep some of these things to themselves."

Even the poems in which Bishop allows moments of personal revelation can hardly be called "confessional." The poems in her final volume, *Geography* III (1979), illustrate the difficulty of reading her work under the aegis of confessionalism. "In the Waiting Room" is a narrative poem in which a seven-year-old girl (generally accepted as being some version Bishop herself) is waiting in a dentist's office and reading a magazine

(*National Geographic*) while her aunt is being treated by the dentist. The pictures in the magazine – of African women's breasts – horrify the girl; at the moment in the poem when she believes she hears her aunt's cry of pain from inside the dentist's room, the girl realizes that it is her own voice she is hearing:

> Suddenly, from inside,
> came an *oh!* of pain
> – Aunt Consuelo's voice –
> not very loud or long,
> I wasn't at all surprised;
> even then I knew she was
> a foolish, timid woman.
> I might have been embarrassed,
> but wasn't. What took me
> completely by surprise
> was that it was *me*:
> my voice, in my mouth.
> Without thinking at all
> I was my foolish aunt,
> I – we – we falling, falling,
> our eyes glued to the cover
> of the *National Geographic*,
> February, 1918.

At this apparently climactic moment, the poem takes a turn that is in some ways the opposite of the typical "confessional" movement toward self-revelation. Rather than enacting a more direct contact with the reader by offering an intensified vision of the self (for example, if the poem had more explicitly focused on the young Bishop's discovery of sexuality or gender identity), Bishop confuses the very definition of self by refusing to offer up any single version of the personal and poetic self for analysis. Not only is the aunt's cry of pain conflated with that of the girl (identified later in the poem as "Elizabeth"), but both of them are implicated in the larger social and historical reality represented by the *National Geographic* of February 1918. As Elizabeth Dodd has noted, the focus of the poem is not only on the personal awareness suggested by Elizabeth's cry of painful self-recognition, but also on the larger awareness of humanity in general: "the young Elizabeth is not really discovering her sexuality so much as her own participation in the human race."[10] The poem ends, in fact, with a deliberate turn away from the personal and toward the larger historical context:

> The War was on. Outside,
> in Worcester, Massachusetts,
> were night and slush and cold,
> and it was still the fifth
> of February, 1918.

By specifying the exact date, place, and historical context, Bishop works against the tendency of the confessional lyric to focus on the personal to the exclusion of outside forces or events. Bishop is more self-analytical than self-dramatizing. Her characteristic poetic gesture is not that which typifies the work of Lowell, Plath, or Sexton, who tend to use images and metaphors as tropes for a personal self which is mythologized in a dramatic narrative of discovery or revelation. Instead, we find a distancing or self-reading suggested by the strategic shift from first person to second person:

> I said to myself: three days
> and you'll be seven years old.
> I was saying it to stop
> the sensation of falling off
> the round, turning world
> into cold, blue-black space.
> But I felt: you are an *I*,
> you are an *Elizabeth*,
> you are one of *them*.

Here, as C. K. Doreski notes, Bishop conflates the adult poet with the "cautiously authorial" child in the poem.[11] The girl is already self-conscious in a way that is painstakingly analytical and reflective rather than dramatic (a tendency that we also see in the curiously reticent and undramatic protagonist of a poem such as "Crusoe in England"). In order to prevent the sensation of "falling off / the . . . world" – a trope that may indicate a fear of losing control over her life or of falling into a fixed social identity like that of her "foolish" Aunt Consuelo – the young Elizabeth turns to a detail that is at once prosaic and secure: she will soon be seven years old. This knowledge is not threatening in the way the *National Geographic* pictures are, but it places her in a social realm: we are defined by our age as well as by factors such as our race, class, and gender.

The doubling of pronouns at the end of the passage creates a kind of vertigo of self-consciousness: "But I felt: you are an *I*." The movement from "I" to "you" doubles back on itself, as the narrating self ("I") changes to an observed self ("you") and then to a socially constructed self which is both an "I" and an "Elizabeth." This "Elizabeth," now named and thus inserted into a social role, is somewhat ominously identified as one of "them." The identification with "them" – not only her aunt but all the people in the waiting room, with their "shadowy grey knees, / trousers and skirts and boots" – is perplexing to the young Elizabeth, who until now has only been herself, not part of a social group to which she is required to belong. "Why should I be my aunt, / or me, or anyone?" she asks. "What similarities . . . held us all together / or made us all just one?" Where another poet might have used such speculations as an occasion for tortured self-doubt or anger towards the pressures of conformity, Bishop reaches a place of characteristic reticence and control: "How − I didn't know any / word for it − how 'unlikely.'" The quotation of the word "unlikely" suggests that it may be a word she has heard adults like her aunt using. Ironically, she has had to adopt the language of "them" in order to describe her feelings about the change in herself. The placing of the word in quotes suggests that such moments as that experienced by her younger self in the waiting room do not have any special status as sources of insight or epiphany.

In the poems of *Geography III*, Bishop adopts three different strategies for examining the self: the use of a fictional persona (as in "Crusoe in England"), the presentation of some version of the poet's younger self ("In the Waiting Room," "The Moose"), and, most directly, the presentation of her current, adult self. "One Art" is the most successful example of the final category. In this poem, Bishop thematizes both her profound sense of loss and her refusal to engage in certain forms of emotional self-revelation. As the form of the poem suggests (it is written in the traditional and highly regulated form of a villanelle) this discussion of the "art of losing" will take place within a controlled poetic environment; there will be none of the aesthetic or emotional "messiness" that can be associated with the free-verse confessional lyrics of her contemporaries.

The poem was, in fact, not only extremely worked over (there are seventeen extant drafts of the poem) but also purposefully restrained in its emotional expression. Changes in the title itself from earlier to later drafts indicate the gradual turn away from raw "confession" to more artistically controlled oration, which Brett Millier compares to "a speech in a brave voice that cracks [only] once."[12] The first title was "How to Lose Things," followed in later drafts by "The Art of Losing Things" and finally the non-committal "One Art." Similarly, changes in the body of the poem indicate a shift toward greater emotional subtlety. As Millier puts it in her excellent study of the poem's successive drafts, "each version of the poem distanced the pain a little more, depersonalized it, moved it away from the tawdry self-pity and confession that Bishop disliked in many of her contemporaries." Even in its final version − which seems highly controlled compared with earlier drafts − Bishop felt somewhat uncomfortable with the degree of its self-revelation: "I'm afraid it's a sort of tear-jerker," she wrote in a letter to one of her friends.

The poem's early stanzas adopt an ironic tone, suggesting that "the art of losing isn't hard to master" and that we should "lose something every day" in order to learn how to accept the inevitability of loss. As the poem progresses, however, the losses become deeper and more serious:

I lost my mother's watch. And look! my last, or
next-to-last, of three loved houses went.
The art of losing isn't hard to master.

I lost two cities, lovely ones. And, vaster,
some realms I owned, two rivers, a continent.
I miss then, but it wasn't a disaster.

– Even losing you (the joking voice, a gesture
I love) I shan't have lied. It's evident
the art of losing's not too hard to master
though it may look like (*Write* it!) like disaster.

From the loss of valued objects such as her mother's watch she moves to ever larger losses: houses, cities, rivers, and finally continents. The three houses were her house in Key West, Florida, and two houses in Brazil; the continent is South America, which she felt she had lost with the death of Lota. As Millier suggests, the emotionality and confessionality of the poem are deflected by the emphasis on objects and places rather than on people and relationships.

The most forceful expression of loss is reserved for the final stanza, which underwent more revision than any other part of the poem. The "you" addressed here is a younger woman with whom Bishop had been involved at the time the poem was written, and whose desire to end the relationship was the final, intolerable loss that occasioned the writing of the poem. The earlier drafts referred to the "exceptionally beautiful" blue eyes of her lover, who is later dematerialized as "a joking voice, a gesture / I love."

But perhaps the most important evolution takes place in the final line. In an earlier draft, Bishop had expressed a sense of desperation, suggesting that we can master losing "anything at all anything but one's love. (Say it: disaster)." The interposed parenthetical phrase – "(Say it: disaster)" – later becomes the more writerly and less obviously confessional "(Write it!) this disaster" and later still "(*Write* it!) like disaster." By the final draft, Bishop cannot even admit, without equivocation, that such a loss does in fact constitute a disaster: it may only "look like" disaster.

Depending on how we read the poem, this change may seem like the heroic reserve of a woman who – like her predecessor Marianne Moore – refuses to make her poetic art a place for expressing her personal grief. Or it may look like the gesture of a poet who so deeply repressed her own feelings that she can only express herself in the most restrained and equivocal manner. In either case, Bishop's poem remains a monument to the process of poetic composition in the late twentieth century.

Chapter 9

Lyric as meditation

One of the striking features of American lyric poetry during the last half of the twentieth century is the predominance of lyrics written in what can be called the "meditative" mode. I am using the term "meditative" in its most general sense, to indicate a state of prolonged or concentrated contemplation in which the poet engages with ideas, objects in the natural world, the self, or some combination of these. The meditative mode of lyric is certainly not a new one: meditative poetry has a long history that includes the visionary strain of the Romantics as well as Emersonian and Whitmanic transcendentalism, Yeatsian mysticism, Stevensian philosophical meditation, and the Surrealism of European and South American poets such as Georg Trakl, Federico García Lorca, César Vallejo, and Pablo Neruda.

The turn toward meditative modes of poetry in the 1950s and 1960s is attributable to several factors: the increasing visibility of paradigms of the subconscious or unconscious adopted from Freudian and Jungian psychology; the growing acceptance of Surrealism in art and literature; and the experimentation with ideas taken from occult and mystical traditions. Finally, there was a broadly based shift from a Depression-era poetry more concerned with immediate social conditions to a postwar poetry more concerned with an exploration of the (lyric) self and its place in the world. This exploration, which took a variety of different forms, explains the increasingly symbolic, introspective, and metaphysical character of much postwar writing.

Eliot's *Four Quartets*

The *Four Quartets* – published during the late 1930s and early 1940s – remains the most impressive achievement in the twentieth-century meditative lyric. Eliot wrote the *Four Quartets* in England, where he had been living and working since the 1910s. The poem has been claimed by both American and British readers as a part of their respective national literatures. By the time he wrote the *Four Quartets*, Eliot appeared to identify more strongly with the traditions of his adopted country than those of his native land: three of the poem's four sections are set in England, and the elegiac style is a definitive return to English poetic tradition. Since the publication of *The Waste Land*, his social and religious beliefs had changed dramatically: he had converted to Christianity and become a member of the Anglican Church. Not surprisingly, the poem is saturated with both the language and the history of England. Nevertheless, the influence of *The Four Quartets* on the development of American poetry cannot be doubted: in the work of Theodore Roethke, for example, we see clear echoes of the poem. Though Roethke claimed to reject "the meditative T. S. Eliot kind of thing,"[1] he turned in his later works such as "North American Sequence" to an intensely meditative style reminiscent of the *Four Quartets*.

The *Four Quartets* is a metaphysical exploration of both the poet's personal history and the more public history of the two countries in which he lived. The importance of landscape and geographical place is suggested by the titles of the poem's four sections, each of which is a place name. The first section, "Burnt Norton," focuses on the rose garden of an English country house; the second quartet, "East Coker," is set in the village in Somerset from which Eliot's ancestor Andrew Eliot traveled to the New World in the seventeenth century in search of religious freedom; the third section, "The Dry Salvages," focuses on both the Mississippi River of Eliot's Missouri childhood and the rocky coastline of New England; and the last quartet, "Little Gidding," takes place in an English village founded as a seventeenth-century Anglican religious community.

The poem is a meditation on time as well as place. Eliot explores temporality and the way in which human beings experience time: as historical progression, as temporal moment, or as a part of eternity. The poem begins with the famous proposition,

> Time present and time past
> Are both perhaps present in time future,
> And time future contained in time past . . .

All moments in time, Eliot goes on to say, are "eternally present": thus there is no need to divide our experience into that of the historical past, the lived present, and the expected future. The temporal meditation of the poem is also reflected in its musical structure. Each section of the poem is itself a "quartet" (analogous to the string quartet as classical musical form) consisting of five "movements." These movements are used to explore and develop the language, ideas, and symbols introduced in the poem.

The primary tension in the poem lies between the temporal and phenomenal mode in which we generally experience reality and the search for a pattern, form, or design that could help us to experience the spiritual or eternal ("the still point of the turning world"). Eliot proposes certain images that allow us to attain this "stillness" – a Chinese jar, for example – but he finds that language itself is incapable of conveying such a pattern:

> Words strain,
> Crack and sometimes break, under the burden,
> Under the tension, slip, slide, perish
> Decay with imprecision, will not stay in place,
> Will not stay still.

Other symbolic structures in the poem are the four elements (air, earth, water, and fire), and the four seasons. The final quartet, "Little Gidding," begins with a fusion or confusion of the seasons which symbolizes the intersection of earthly time with the timeless realm of the eternal:

> Midwinter spring is its own season
> Sempiternal though sodden towards sundown,
> Suspended in time, between pole and tropic.

Each quartet is also dominated by a particular element: the primary element of "Little Gidding," for example, is fire, as we see in Eliot's brilliant use of fire imagery in the opening section:

> When the short day is brightest, with frost and fire,
> The brief sun flames the ice, on pond and ditches,
> In windless cold that is the heart's heat,
> Reflecting in a watery mirror
> A glare that is blindness in the early afternoon.
> And glow more intense than blaze of branch, or brazier,
> Stirs the dumb spirit: no wind, but pentecostal fire
> In the dark time of the year.

Awed by the unusual combination of "frost and fire" which creates a blinding glare in the midst of winter's darkness, Eliot is moved to an evocation of the "pentecostal fire" by which the Holy Ghost came to Christ and his disciples. The references to fire in the poem also suggest the air raids conducted by the Germans on London during the war. The German dive-bomber is figured as a "dark dove with . . . flickering tongue," an image that is more fully developed in the fourth movement:

> The dove descending breaks the air
> With flame of incandescent terror
> Of which the tongues declare
> The one discharge from sin and error.
> The only hope, or else despair
>   Lies in the choice of pyre or pyre –
>   To be redeemed from fire by fire.

Here we find Eliot's writing at its most compressed and most visionary. Adopting the formal structure of rhymed tetrameter, Eliot plays on both a formal and a metaphoric level with resemblance and difference. The stanza's three rhyme sounds are nearly identical; at the same time, the two kinds of "tongues" represented here (that of the firing dive-bomber and that of the Holy Ghost) display a structural identity but an opposite effect on the world. We can only be redeemed from one kind of fire (that of war and human destructiveness) by the other (the refining fire of religious belief). At the end of the poem, Eliot unites this fire image with that with which he began: the rose. As he enters the garden once again (simultaneously the rose garden and the Garden of Eden from which the human race was banished), he hears the voices of children and the song of the thrush first introduced in "Burnt Norton." The poem has come full circle, as has the speaker, who now realizes that "the end of all our exploring / Will be to arrive where we started / And to know the place for the first time." The collapse of the distinction between temporality and eternity ("Quick now, here, now, always") brings about a sense that "all shall be well and / All manner of thing shall be well." The poem's final image, that of "the crowned knot of fire," contains within it three ideas: the spiritual intensity of fire, the beauty and ideal pattern of the rose, and the solid knot tying them together.

Theodore Roethke's "North American Sequence"

In "North American Sequence," the opening section of Roethke's posthumous collection *The Far Field* (1964), the poet appears at times to draw almost too heavily on the *Four Quartets*. Nevertheless, "North American Sequence" is one of the most important meditative poems of the century. Roethke is a difficult poet to categorize: he was not a confessional, although there are clearly confessional aspects to his work, nor was he a New Critical formalist, although many of his poems adopt formal structures. Among the poets of his generation (the generation of poets who began publishing mature work in the 1940s and early 1950s), Roethke was arguably the most important heir to the American tradition of meditative poetry.

"North American Sequence" is a series of visionary landscape poems written in the final years of his life. As James Dougherty suggests, the sequence resembles the *Four Quartets* in several respects: it "reflects upon specific landscapes with a mind trammeled in memories but in quest of the eternal";[2] it adopts a sequential and quasi-musical structure; and it even ends with the symbol of the rose. Yet at the same time, Roethke's poem can equally well be linked with other predecessor poems, such as Whitman's "Song of Myself" and his two seaside meditations "As I Ebb'd with the Ocean of Life" and "Out of the Cradle Endlessly Rocking," and Wordsworth's Romantic landscape meditation "Tintern Abbey." One important difference between Roethke's sequence and Eliot's is that, as Dougherty observes, Roethke's "spiritual insight and deliverance from the egoistic self . . . come not from ascetic detachment but from the plenitude of his experience of nature." For example, Roethke rewrites Eliot's imagery in substituting a wild rose blowing in the sea wind for Eliot's domesticated rose garden.

"North American Sequence" is divided into six poems, each of which charts a portion of a physical and spiritual journey taken by the speaker. David Perkins characterizes the journey enacted by the poems as one "out of frozen self-disgust, darkness, fragmentation, and isolation into vital wholeness and union with Being."[3] The sequence is a powerful synthesis of landscape poetry and mystical or symbolic poetry; it can also be read as a continuation or rewriting of Whitman's quest in "Song of Myself" and other poems to discover the self through contact with the physical world. At every step along the speaker's journey, the state of the poet's consciousness is correlated with the landscape that surrounds him, as the poem alternates between highly emotional moments of self-exploration and precise descriptions of nature. The personal sections of the poem become increasingly ecstatic and mystical as Roethke moves more deeply into the organic world he contemplates within himself; yet this movement toward an ecstatic reunion with the self is constantly prevented or nullified by nature's presentation of its "dying face."

I will focus here on the fifth poem in the sequence, "The Far Field," a poem which presents Roethke's meditative poetic at its most powerful. The poem is itself divided into four sections, the first of which presents a quasi-surreal dream vision:

> I dream of journeys repeatedly:
> Of flying like a bat deep into a narrowing tunnel,
> Of driving alone, without luggage, out a long peninsula,
> The road lined with snow-laden second growth,
> A fine dry snow ticking the windshield,
> Alternate snow and sleet, no on-coming traffic,
> And no lights behind, in the blurred side-mirror,
> The road changing from glazed tarface to a rubble of stone,
> Ending at last in a hopeless sand-rut,
> Where the car stalls,
> Churning in a snowdrift
> Until the headlights darken.

The central motif of the journey is established here through the evocation of a dream which also sets the meditative tone of the poem as a whole. The image of the bat entering its tunnel suggests the return to an imagination based in the subconscious, and the imagistic narrative of the stalled car is the first of a series of images suggesting frustration or paralysis.

In the next section, Roethke moves into a series of childhood memories which are evoked by images of nature that suggest death, decay, and hidden danger. In a corner of the field that has been "missed by the mower" and that now serves as a "flower-dump" and a repository for "tin cans, rusted pipes, broken machinery," the speaker (now a child) finds "the shrunken face of a dead rat, eaten by rain and ground-beetles" as well as young rabbits "caught in the mower," and "the tom-cat, caught near the pheasant-run, / Its entrails strewn over the half-grown flowers, / Blasted to death by the night watchman." The discovery of these dead bodies provided a knowledge of "the eternal," allowing him to understand the cycle of life and death:

> I suffered for birds, for young rabbits, caught in the mower,
> My grief was not excessive.
> For to come upon warblers in early May
> Was to forget time and death:
> How they filled the oriole's elm, a twittering restless cloud, all one
>   morning,
> And I watched and watched till my eyes blurred from the bird shapes –

As a result of his direct contact with nature, the child learns "not to fear infinity, / The far field, the windy cliffs of forever . . . The wheel turning away from itself, / The sprawl of the wave, / The on-coming water." Roethke's evocative series of images combines both mystical and natural elements in a synthesis that takes us beyond customary understandings of life and death. He experiences "a weightless change, a moving forward / As of water quickening before a narrowing channel / When banks converge, and the wide river whitens." The young poet has taught himself how to remain calm in the face of natural process. He can now experience his life as "a still, but not a deep center, / A point outside the glittering current," and he moves into a kind of meditative state: "My mind moves in more than one place, / In a country half-land, half-water."

Roethke's search for a "still, but not deep center" is certainly reminiscent of Eliot's quest for a "still point of the turning world"; however, the conclusion of the poem takes Roethke's speaker in a very different direction from that taken by Eliot's more philosophically introspective narrator. As Roethke travels deeper into his reunion with nature, he finds his "lost self" changing into "a sea-shape turning around." Faced with "his own immensity," he experiences "all the waves, all their loose wandering fire." The waves of the ocean are at the same time the waves of his own physical being, bringing to him "the murmur of the absolute." He discovers the eternal not in the neat patterns of gardens or in the historical experience of religious tradition, but in the plenitude and endless variety of nature:

> The mountain with its singular bright shade
> Like the blue shine on freshly frozen snow,
> The after-light upon ice-burdened pines;
> Odor of basswood on a mountain-slope,
> A scent beloved of bees;
> Silence of water above a sunken tree:
> The pure serene of memory in one man –
> A ripple widening from a single stone
> Winding around the waters of the world.

Roethke's use of sound, and especially the alliteration of several different consonants, brings a sonic richness to the passage that matches its rich presentation of aural, visual, and olfactory imagery. The synthesis of sound, image, and idea brings us to the deepest point in Roethke's meditative process, where the speaker is finally reconciled with his natural surroundings as well as his own physical and psychic nature.

Deep Image: Robert Bly and James Wright

In the 1960s and 1970s, the most prominent expression of the meditative impulse was the "Deep Image" movement. The poetry of Deep Image sought to use the visual image as a means of accessing deeper levels of feeling or consciousness, often in the form of sudden epiphanies or revelations of insight. In the words of Robert Bly, the Deep Image poem could be distinguished from the Imagism of the 1910s and 1920s by its use of the image to enact "psychic leaps" between the conscious and the unconscious. According to Bly's theory, the poet should not only attempt to capture images apprehended by the conscious mind, but should "ask the unconscious . . . to enter the poem and contribute a few images that we may not fully understand."

While the Deep Image poets shared certain elements with poetic Surrealism – including the desire to use the image to access deep or unexplored levels of consciousness – they did not go as far as the Surrealists in their attempt to overturn social and artistic convention or to challenge the rationality of poetic language and syntax. While we may find dreamlike or nightmarish scenes in the work of Deep Image poets, we do not find the type of free association or the kind of bizarre and shocking images found in Surrealist writing. Among the poets who have been associated with the Deep Image aesthetic, we can divide the field into those whose work comes closer to a

Surrealist mode (W. S. Merwin, Mark Strand, James Tate, Charles Simic) and those whose work borrows surreal elements while remaining closer to a realist or descriptivist aesthetic (Bly, James Wright, Galway Kinnell, Gary Snyder, William Stafford). For the purposes of this chapter, I will focus on the poets of the latter group, since their work is more easily understood within the meditative tradition as it has been defined by American poets like Whitman, Stevens, Eliot, and Theodore Roethke.

The poems in Robert Bly's volume *Silence in the Snowy Fields* (1962) felt radically new to readers of the early 1960s, since they appeared to reject both the religious symbolism of Eliot and the overt Romanticism of Roethke. Bly's most famous poem, "Driving Toward Lac Qui Parle River," contains a notable lack of obvious narrative or psychic drama. The poem is written in an understated language and style, and its intense subjectivity is achieved within the context of a commonplace setting and event:

> I am driving; it is dusk; Minnesota.
> The stubble field catches the last growth of sun.
> The soybeans are breathing on all sides.
> Old men are sitting before their houses on carseats
> In the small towns. I am happy,
> The moon rising above the turkey sheds.
>
> The small world of the car
> Plunges through the deep fields of the night,
> On the road from Willmar to Milan.
> This solitude covered with iron
> Moves through the fields of night
> Penetrated by the noise of crickets.

Here we find a relatively commonplace scene – a Minnesota bean-field at dusk – witnessed by the speaker driving in his car. The first two stanzas evoke a private, pensive, and calmly joyful mood. The mood is expressed largely through the poem's imagery. Although the description of the landscape plays a key role in the poem, the images which comprise this description do not aim at accuracy in objective detail. Instead, images such as "The soybeans are breathing . . ." and "the small world of the car . . ." reveal the speaker's emotional state, as the speaker's mood permeates the description of surrounding landscape. Even those images which are comparatively traditional seem highly selective, such as the reference to old men sitting on car seats and the moon above turkey sheds. We might say that subjectivity is welcomed into the poem; in one instance, the subjective element enlarges to such a degree that description lapses into declaration: "I am happy." The images become progressively more laden with emotional weight through the first two stanzas, from the stark recounting of fact in the opening line ("I am driving; it is dusk") to the extended image of the moving car presented in the final three lines of the second stanza.

It is in the third stanza that we shift from the use of more conventional images to the poem's "deep image," an almost magical description of the river with its small bridge and the people talking in the boat, just out of hearing:

> Nearly to Milan, suddenly a small bridge,
> And water kneeling in the moonlight.
> In small towns the houses are built right on the ground;
> The lamplight falls on all fours in the grass.
> When I reach the river, the full moon covers it;
> A few people are talking low in a boat.

The clue that we are now turning to the speaker's mystical vision comes with the word "suddenly." From here on, considerable effort is made to remove the division between objectivity and subjectivity. The speaker's solitude allows him to descend into a state of mind in which ordinary things suddenly become defamiliarized and are perceived in a new and unusual fashion. As in many Bly poems, things are seen as gravitating toward the earth, as if in a rejection of any gesture of transcendence. The houses are "built on the ground"; the moonlight is shining down upon the water; the people in the boat are below the road; and even their talking seems drawn down away from the speaker. The speaker's mystical vision comes to be expressed as physical proximity to the earth, a state in which aesthetic vision is possible. Many of the images intermingle elements of both speaker and world to express a deep union between the two. Even the name of the Lac Qui Parle ("lake which speaks") River – an actual river in western Minnesota – has an important symbolic significance. The river is felt to be speaking or communing with the poet/narrator, communicating an intuitive sense of nature's purpose.

Bly also heightens his poetic rhetoric through the use of figures of speech which contribute to the meditative feeling. In two striking metaphors, water "kneel[s] in the moonlight" and lamplight "falls on all fours in the grass." The meditative quality of the poem is enhanced by its syntax as well. The flatness of syntax and language throughout the poem draws our attention more strongly to the images and metaphors, and the spareness of the syntactic connections brings a sense of simplicity and rightness to the poem.

This deliberate use of syntax for poetic effect can be seen in the first three lines of the third stanza, which begin with the elliptical structure of "Nearly to Milan, suddenly a small bridge." We feel along with the speaker the suddenness of this unexpected sight, which when combined with the personification of the river in the next line offers a strong visual impression.

In contrast, the repeated monosyllables and somewhat elongated syntactic movement of the third line (the longest of the stanza) provide a larger view of the landscape. The almost childlike observation of the houses being built "right on the ground" (as opposed to the more elevated houses in cities) involves another shift in the reader's consciousness. In the context of the poem as a whole, this image can perhaps qualify as a "deep image," one which resonates with the poem's other images of depth and downward movement.

The mood of the speaker also evolves in the course of the poem. The first stanza establishes a contented mood as the speaker is seen driving in his car: this mood is reflected in the pastoral imagery and the explicit declaration of happiness in the penultimate line. In the second stanza, however, the mood becomes more ominous, as the speaker focuses on darkness and isolation. It is no longer "dusk" but "night." Correspondingly, the diction is more fraught with tension: the word "plunges" suggests a possibly violent act, and "penetrates" can suggest negative connotations. There is also an absence of visual images in the stanza, and the only aural image is the faint sound of the crickets outside the car.

In the third stanza, the mood shifts once again, but this time there is no explicit statement of the speaker's emotion as in the first stanza. The deeper and more meditative emotion here is established by the suggestion of nearness and contact with things in the world. The stanza begins with the word "nearly," which gives both a sense of expectation and a feeling of proximity to something of importance. The poet has almost reached his goal (the town of Milan), and at the same time he is nearing a more essential aim. The sound of "nearly" is repeated in "kneeling" in the second line, a word suggesting prayer. The full moon "covers" the river, an image which can be either maternal (a mother covering her child with a blanket) or sexual. These images of protectiveness, acquiescence, and contact inform the final line, in which the poet hears the voices of people talking in a boat. Through the use of this understated image, Bly seems to be suggesting a kind of community or communion. Yet the poet remains somewhat apart from that human communication; he hears only the sound of the talking, not the actual words. The ambivalence in the poet's final vision differs markedly from the sense of an achieved revelation at the end of both Eliot's and Roethke's poems.

James Wright is the other poet most closely associated with the poetry of Deep Image. Wright's poetic training – first as an undergraduate student of John Crowe Ransom, and then as a graduate student under Theodore Roethke at the University of Washington – prepared him for a career as a formalist in the New Critical mode. In his first two volumes – *The Green Wall* (1957) and *St. Judas* (1959) – he wrote in a style derived from Robinson, Frost, and Roethke. *The Branch Will Not Break* (1963) was a breakthrough volume for Wright. Inspired by his friendship and collaboration with Bly (they translated such poets as Neruda, Vallejo, and Trakl together), he abandoned traditional forms and began to express his feelings more directly, at once relaxing and modernizing the language in which he wrote. Wright felt that his work in a traditional style had reached a "dead end," and that while he had written poetry that was "very strict and careful in its form," he had left out "so much of life." He had been "trapped," he claimed in a letter to Roethke, "by the very thing – the traditional technique – which I labored so hard to attain." The idea of the limitations imposed by poetic form was hardly a new one – Pound had come to much the same realization a half century earlier – but each generation of poets must go through the same process of discovery. In the early 1960s, Wright succeeded in breaking through the "ten-mile-thick granite wall of formal and facile 'technique' " that was imprisoning him.

In a poem like "Lying in a Hammock at William Duffy's Farm in Pine Island, Minnesota," Wright's style went beyond even Bly's in its apparent simplicity.

> Over my head, I see the bronze butterfly,
> Asleep on the black trunk,
> Blowing like a leaf in green shadow.
> Down the ravine behind the empty house,
> The cowbells follow one another
> Into the distances of the afternoon.
> To my right,
> In a field of sunlight between two pines,
> The droppings of last year's horses
> Blaze up into golden stones.
> I lean back, as the evening darkens and comes on.
> A chicken hawk floats over, looking for home.
> I have wasted my life.

The poem's narrative situation is extremely straightforward. The speaker lies in a hammock on a late afternoon, observing and listening to the world around him. As he becomes increasingly absorbed by the act of observing his surroundings, he makes the sudden realization that he has, as he bluntly puts it, "wasted his life." Clearly, the interpretation of the poem hinges on our understanding of this final line and its implications, though our appreciation of the poem need not end there. Wright himself commented on the line in the following way:

> I think that final line – "I have wasted my life" – is a religious statement, that is to say, here I am and I'm not straining myself and yet I'm happy at this moment, and perhaps I've been wastefully unhappy in the past . . . and in my blindness, I haven't allowed myself to pay attention to what was around me.

Wright's identification of the line as a religious statement points not to any particular set of religious or spiritual beliefs, but to a universal human capacity for the kind of sudden insight or epiphany described. In Bly's early review of the poem, he pointed to a psychological reading as well: the speaker's realization that he had "found nothing in his life to be sure of, that he had arrived nowhere," was achieved by a process of self-analysis that required "slipping past the defenses of the ego." What makes this poem particularly appealing as an expression of self-discovery is the combination of universality and specificity. The central idea may be general, but the images that lead up to it are detailed and specific. Even the title, with its specification of the fact that the speaker was lying in a hammock on the farm of a person named William Duffy (and not just in any hammock on any farm) and that that farm was located in Pine Island, Minnesota, provides a necessary counterbalance to the very general statement of the last line. The idea of the poem is not simply that we should spend more time lying in hammocks, but that the particularity of our experience is crucial to our ability to break through to a new awareness.

Let us look at the specific images Wright uses to structure the poem. There are four main images presented, each divided syntactically and spatially from the others. The first is the butterfly he sees sleeping on the tree above him; the second is the sound of the cowbells in the ravine behind the house; the third is the droppings of last year's horses, seen to his right; and the fourth is the chicken hawk floating over him and "looking for home." Each image is heightened by the use of figurative language: the butterfly is compared to "a leaf in green shadow"; the cowbells act as metonymies for the cows themselves which "follow one another" down the ravine; the horse droppings blaze metaphorically into "golden stones"; and the chicken hawk is personified as "looking for home." Though narratively the poem falls into four sections of roughly equal length, there is an important change in the syntax at the end, where each sentence is given its own line. Thus the final three events of the poem – the arrival of evening, the passage of the hawk, and the speaker's realization of having wasted his life – receive additional emphasis.

The range of symbolic meanings that have been assigned to Wright's images indicate the extent to which – as we have already seen in the work of Bly – the "deep" image can take on a symbolic function. The chicken hawk, for example, like the famous hawk at the end of Whitman's "Song of Myself" who "swoops by and accuses" the poet, is clearly linked with the speaker himself. The hawk "floats," suggesting an affinity with the speaker's motion in the hammock, but he is also "looking for home," just as the speaker appears to be lost in his search for a meaningful existence. Significantly, the house mentioned in the poem is "empty": the world of human society can provide no answers for the poet/speaker. We also find a symbolism in the linked pattern of the images themselves. The butterfly is "bronze," its metallic appearance analogous to the metallic clinking of the cowbells and to the "golden stones" into which the horse droppings are transformed. This metallic imagery suggests permanence and value, but Wright does not seek to transform the natural world into emblems of artistic creation as Yeats does in his Byzantium poems. Both the butterfly and the horse droppings remain essentially part of nature: the butterfly is in "green shadow," suggesting the potential for generation, and the droppings indicate a process of decay that is itself productive of new life.

The final line clearly comes as a surprise, both in the suddenness of its utterance (there has been nothing in the poem so far to prepare us for this kind of self-revelation) and in its verbal abruptness. Wright does not say, for example, "I now realize that I have wasted my life," or "the beauty and tranquillity of nature remind me that my life until now has been wasted"; instead, he puts his most important statement in succinct terms that make no pretense of being "poetic." We are woken from the spell cast by the poem, and perhaps awoken to another level of consciousness about our own existence.

Gary Snyder and Galway Kinnell

I conclude with a somewhat briefer discussion of two other meditative poems from the late 1950s and early 1960s: Gary Snyder's "Mid-August at Sourdough Mountain Lookout" and Galway Kinnell's "Flower Herding on Mount Monadnock." Kinnell's poem, published in 1964, can be seen as a midway point between the Deep Image poems of Bly and Wright and the more overtly surrealist mode of a poet like W. S. Merwin; Snyder's poem, from his 1959 volume *Riprap*, moves toward a kind of linguistic clarity and simplicity that can be associated with the practice of Zen Buddhism.

Snyder's "Mid-August at Sourdough Mountain Lookout" presents its first-person speaker in understated terms and emphasizes the simplicity of his needs:

> Down valley a smoke haze
> Three days heat, after five days rain
> Pitch glows on the fir-cones
> Across rocks and meadows
> Swarms of new flies.
>
> I cannot remember things I once read
> A few friends, but they are in cities.
> Drinking cold snow-water from a tin cup
> Looking down for miles
> Through high still air.

Snyder's speaker is not overawed by his natural surroundings; instead, he seems completely at peace with them. His actions are simple: drinking water, gazing down from the mountain. In this way, his method resembles that of Zen Buddhist meditation, in which insights can occur in the course of the most mundane activities. His language avoids the kind of abstractions that characterize Kinnell's style, remaining close to the physical details of his surroundings. (Snyder was in fact working as a forester in the Pacific Northwest at the time the poem was written.) In the first stanza, he describes with precise detail the pitch on the fir-cones, the humidity coming up from the valley, and the swarms of flies in the August heat, not embellishing the images through the use of figurative language.

In this sense, Snyder's technique is a radical departure from the tradition of Eliot, Roethke, and the Deep Image poets: Snyder's aim is not to make metaphors or symbols out of the images he presents, but simply to capture the particularity of a feeling or sensation. This idea is stated more explicitly in the second stanza, where Snyder contrasts the intensity of physical sensation (drinking "cold snow-water from a tin cup" and looking down "through high still air") with the seeming transcience of human and intellectual contact (friends far away in cities and forgotten books). Like Bly in his car and Wright in his hammock, Snyder is presented in a state of isolation; but Snyder is far more explicit in his polarization of the human, civilized world with the world of nature.

Snyder's poem gains much of its effect through its verbal compression and ellipsis of unnecessary words. The speaker conveys everything he needs to say about his physical situation and state of mind in ten relatively short lines. In the first two lines, for example, the compression of language is almost Poundian. "Down valley a smoke haze" presents a clear visual image, leaving out the connective words of a more typical sentence such as "Down in the valley I see a smoke haze." Similarly, in the second line, Snyder leaves out the verb, giving us only the bare statement of two types of weather (heat and rain), divided formally by a mid-line caesura. Rhythm and sound are also used effectively in the poem. Snyder's free-verse lines are irregular in length – ranging from four to ten beats – but each of the two stanzas ends with a line of four monosyllables, giving added emphasis to the images he presents. The sounds of the poem are densely packed and resonant: the use of sybillants, along with the repetition of long vowels in the first stanza (haze – days – days – rain, down – glows – smoke – cones) create a richness of sound that reflects the richness of the poet's sensory experience.

In "Flower Herding on Mount Manadnock," Kinnell narrates a physical and psychic journey up the side of a mountain. The mountain itself is located in southern New Hampshire, but Kinnell's mountain is as much a symbolic as a geographical place. The poem begins before dawn, as the speaker awakens and chastises himself for the nightmare he has experienced: "Damned nightmarer!" As in the poems of Bly and Wright, the time of day is important. Bly's poem takes place at night, and Wright's at the moment when afternoon turns to evening. "Flower Herding" is a morning poem, suggesting the hopefulness of the speaker after his nightmare-filled sleep.

The structure of the poem – with its ten short free-verse sections – suggests the passage of time as the hiker ascends the mountain. One moment appears to follow the next without interpretive or narrative connection, the flow of the speaker's experiences and associations taking us from one image or thought to the next. When time does appear, it is expressed through the rhythms of nature rather than through human measurement: for example, in the first two stanzas, the nighttime song of the whippoorwill is replaced by the morning song of the "peabody bird." The poem's narrative is told by the passage of discreet moments, as experience leads to memory and back again. The sweat in the speaker's nostrils as he climbs triggers a memory of the sea, which in turn causes a confusion of sea and land, past and present:

> One summer off Cap Ferrat we watched a black seagull
> Straining for the dawn, we stood in the surf,
>
> Grasshoppers splash up where I step,
> The mountain laurel crashes at my thighs.

In section 5, time enters the poem in a different way, as the poet imagines the birds' songs as elegies. From this point on, the tone of the poem becomes more serious, as images of loss, decay, and mortality predominate. In section 6, the poet rests at a pool of water and thinks he sees bacteria beneath his reflection. In a haunting image, the poet sees a vision of physical decay and dissolution behind his self-reflection: "My face sees me, / The water stirs, the face, / Looking preoccupied, / Gets knocked from its bones."

The speaker perceives the mountain now, not as a place of stillness and permanence ("dimensions of depth"), but as a place of emptiness and disintegration. The vines encircle him so that he must "turn" and "crane" in order to make out the "shimmering nothingness" of the sky. The trees take on an almost surreal appearance as "Green, scaly moosewoods . . . tenants of the shaken paradise." The utter stillness of nature is replaced by the wind blowing, and the water from last night's rain comes "splattering" down to the ground.

In the final two sections, the poet struggles between the need for transcendence and the realization of mortality. The flight of birds is offset by the "hug of the earth," which "wraps / with moss their graves." The ending of the poem is particularly striking in its use of the natural world as a reflection of the speaker's own troubled psyche:

In the forest I discover a flower.

The invisible life of the thing
Goes up in flames that are invisible
Like cellophane burning in the sunlight.

It burns up. Its drift is to be nothing.

In its covertness it has a way
Of uttering itself in place of itself,
Its blossoms claim to float in the Empyrean,

A wrathful presence on the blur of the ground.

The appeal to heaven breaks off.
The petals begin to fall, in self-forgiveness.
It is a flower. On this mountainside it is dying.

The speaker finds the flower to be representative of the dual forces he finds in nature. Its blossoms "claim to float in the Empyrean," but in fact the flower is subject to the same process of physical decay and death as the speaker. As in the poems of Roethke, Bly, Wright, and Snyder, a concreteness in the description of the physical world leads to an apprehension of deeper levels of experience. Here again we find a moment of epiphany, but it is of a more philosophical and less direct kind. The speaker realizes that life and death are inseparable, defined by each other. As Kinnell wrote in his 1971 essay "The Poetics of the Physical World," the knowledge of mortality can enhance our experience of life: there is "a kind of glory in our lives which derives precisely from our inability to enter . . . paradise or to experience eternity." The desire of the poet to see the flower as an object of perfection, as some kind of "appeal to heaven," is shattered by the realization that the only thing we can hope for is "self-forgiveness."

Chapter 10

The New American Poetry and the postmodern avant-garde

American poetry in the late 1950s and early 1960s was divided between two distinct poetic communities and two very different conceptions of what poetry should be. On the one hand, American poetry was still dominated by the mainstream lyric as represented by the work of poets like James Merrill, Robert Lowell, Theodore Roethke, and other members of the established literary culture. On the other hand, there was a growing body of work by poets who defined themselves as a new poetic counterculture. Where the poetic mainstream still regarded Eliot and Auden as their primary poetic models, the new avant-garde modeled itself on an experimental tradition of poets whose work could hardly be read by the methods of the New Critics: Pound, Williams, Gertrude Stein, and Louis Zukofsky. By the end of the 1950s, this postwar avant-garde was just beginning to be recognized by readers and publishers.

The decisive literary event of 1960 was the publication of an anthology entitled *The New American Poetry*. Published by Grove Press and edited by Donald Allen, the anthology would for the first time bring together many of the innovative young writers who were to constitute the next significant generation of avant-garde poetry. *The New American Poetry* was the most important anthology of American poetry to be published in the second half of the twentieth century. The poets included varied considerably in their backgrounds, styles, and attitudes, but they were alike in their experimental focus and in their rejection of the kind of academic verse represented by the New Criticism. Allen's collection was highly unusual among mid-century anthologies: the poets whom he identified as "our avant-garde, the true continuers of the modern movement in American poetry" were not only young (few of them were over forty and several were still in their twenties) but also relatively unpublished by the standards of the day. Allen was extremely prescient about the importance these poets would have over the next three to four decades. A number of them – including Allen Ginsberg, Charles Olson, Gary Snyder, John Ashbery, Frank O'Hara, Robert Duncan, Jack Spicer, Robert Creeley, Denise Levertov, and Leroi Jones (Amiri Baraka) – were to play a central role in the development of late-twentieth-century poetry.

The Beat Generation

The most prominent of the groups presented in Allen's anthology was certainly the Beats, who had attracted attention through their poetry readings – in particular the Six Gallery reading in San Francisco. Though the San Francisco Bay area had been a site of important avant-garde activity since the mid-1940s, it was the Six Gallery reading that brought together East Coast writers of the Beat Generation (Allen Ginsberg and Gregory Corso) with West Coast poets such as Michael McClure, Gary Snyder, Philip Whalen, and Philip Lamantia. The reading accomplished two important things. First, as Paul Hoover has argued, it "galvanized media interest in a variety of alternative poetries"[1] which could now challenge the dominant New Critical mode. And second, it introduced the concept of poetry as public performance at a time when poetry was seen primarily as a form of written literature meant to be experienced in private study or contemplation.

To understand the symbolic importance of the "Six Poets at the Six Gallery" reading, we need to realize how radically different it was from the kind of formal, academic readings that were then (and remain today) the norm on college and university campuses. The gallery itself – a converted auto-repair shop which had been set up as a kind of informal theater – was hardly a traditional venue for poetry readings. While Ginsberg read "Howl," performing it more like an orgiastic chant than a traditional poem, Kerouac cheered him on by yelling "Go!" at the end of each line. The poem began with powerful lines that would have grabbed the attention of the audience: "I saw the best minds of my generation destroyed by madness, starving hysterical naked, / dragging themselves through the negro streets at dawn looking for an angry fix." Ginsberg's use of long Whitmanic lines, his stark presentation of contemporary urban life, and his unique synthesis of surrealist imagery, visionary proclamation, and political invective made the poem unlike anything that had been heard before. The "generation" that Ginsberg's poem represented felt alienated from much of American life, and it was "Howl" more than any other poem of the era which captured that spirit of alienation.

The poetry of the Beats took a number of forms, reflecting a range of influences from the poetry of Whitman, Blake, Pound, and Williams to Surrealism and Buddhist philosophy. The Beats also embraced the musical forms of jazz and blues, which helped them develop experimental techniques involving spontaneity and unpredictability. Like the confessionals, the Beats were responding to the alienating social and ideological structure of America during the Cold War, but their response was framed in very different terms: where the psychic violence of confessional poems was directed inward and largely contained by the use of traditional forms and language, the poetry of the Beats was more outwardly defiant and countercultural, the "howl" of a generation of cultural outlaws. The mainstream literary establishment – which celebrated the work of the confessionals as a socially acceptable expression of personal and social *angst* – found it more difficult to accept the work of the Beats, which made no concession to traditional codes of language or social behavior.

In May 1957, a few months after the publication of *Howl*, the book's publisher Lawrence Ferlinghetti was charged with publishing and selling an obscene book. The obscenity trial that ensued brought national attention to Ginsberg, to Ferlinghetti's City Lights Bookstore, and to the Beat movement as a whole: by the end of the trial, more than ten thousand copies were in print, making the book a bestseller by the standards of American poetry.

In the trial, Ferlinghetti defended Ginsberg's poetry against the charge of obscenity, claiming that it not the poet but American society which was obscene. In October, Judge Clayton Horn ruled that the book was not obscene because, although it included "coarse and vulgar language" and presented "unorthodox and controversial ideas," it was not without "redeeming social importance." Clearly, lines like "who let themselves be fucked in the ass by saintly motorcyclists, and screamed with joy" would have been offensive to many readers, as would references to distributing "Supercommunist pamphlets in Union Square," "whoring through Colorado in myriad stolen night-cars," or taking a variety of illegal drugs including peyote, marijuana, and heroin.

But what is most striking about "Howl" is less the targeted offensiveness of its material than the originality of its language. As Fred Moramarco and William Sullivan suggest, the poem represents "the first important poetic use of the American hip vernacular," while at the same time intensifying its vision through the use of startling combinations of words: "angelheaded hipsters," "hotrod-Golgotha jail-solitude watch," "hydrogen jukebox," "bop kaballa."[2] Ginsberg achieved brilliant effects of sound within phrases such as "shuddering mouth-wracked and battered bleak of brain all drained of brilliance in the drear light of Zoo"; or he created chains of images as in "Peyote solidities of halls, backyard green tree cemetery dawns . . . storefront boroughs of tea-head joyride neon blinking traffic light." Finally, he organized the poem through the use of anaphora, creating the feeling of a Whitmanic chant. The first section is built around a series of actions by him and the members of his generation; the second is constructed around the actions of "Moloch," the Canaanite fire god who symbolizes a merciless postwar society to which the nation's youth is being sacrificed; and the third section deals with Carl Solomon, the young poet to whom the poem is dedicated and whose madness and incarceration in a series of mental hospitals ("I'm with you in Rockland") is the result of that society.

Neither Ginsberg nor any of the other Beats were able to replicate the extraordinary success of "Howl." Though Ginsberg was to write a number of memorable poems – including "America," "A Supermarket in California," "Kaddish," and "Wichita Vortex Sutra" – none of them matched the power and originality of "Howl," and the continuing notoriety he achieved in the ensuing decades was more the result of his social and political activities than of the new poems he was writing. When he died in 1997, Ginsberg was the most famous poet in America and the most easily recognizable poet in the world; as a serious poet who nonetheless achieved and maintained a public status, he was a unique figure among American poets of his time.

Robert Duncan and the San Francisco Renaissance

A far less public figure than Ginsberg, but one who had an equally important impact on the development of the New American Poetry, was Robert Duncan. Duncan, who was born in 1919 and attended the University of California, Berkeley, in the late 1930s, was one of the founding members of the "San Francisco Renaissance" in poetry. While the San Francisco poets were by no means a homogeneous group, their shared concerns with the creation of an alternative artistic and literary community and their commitment to a more egalitarian social order resulted in a strong group identity. The poets of the renaissance tended to see the poet's role as that of articulating a social and political vision as well as a purely literary sensibility: Kenneth Rexroth, for example, was a longtime agitator for leftist and anarchist causes and Duncan himself wrote many poems of an explicitly political nature. The group was further solidified by an active literary culture in the San Francisco area, including readings at coffeehouses, courses, and seminars at the newly founded Poetry Center at San Francisco State College, and the existence of little magazines such as *Circle*, *City Lights*, *Ark*, and *Golden Goose* and presses like City Lights Books.

During the late 1940s and early 1950s, Duncan met the poets who would become his closest literary allies: Charles Olson, Robert Creeley, and Denise Levertov. It was in the 1960s that he published the three volumes that contain much of his strongest work: *The Opening of the Field*, *Roots and Branches*, and *Bending the Bow*. These volumes introduce, among other poems, the two open-ended poetic sequences that he worked on throughout his later career: "The Structure of Rime" and "Passages." In addition to "Often I Am Permitted to Return to a Meadow," some of Duncan's most important poems are "My Mother Would Be a Falconress," "Poem Beginning with a Line by Pindar," "The Fire: Passages 13," "Torso: Passages 18," and "Up Rising: Passages 25." Duncan was unique among American poets in being equally comfortable with traditional stanzaic forms and free-verse or open forms. In Duncan's radically eclectic style, each poem was allowed to achieve its own specific form; according to an aesthetic system he referred to as "grand collage," the poem would collect and arrange various ideas, symbols, myths, and images in a new and complex constellation. In this sense, his poetics are clearly influenced by the model of Pound's *Cantos* and by Pound's "ideogrammatic method." But Duncan, who described himself as a literary "magpie," derived his idiosyncratic poetics from a wide range of sources, including the experimental modernism of Stein and H. D. and the mythical and prophetic lineage of Pindar, Dante, Shelley, Whitman, Blake, and Rimbaud. As Michael Davidson observes, "many of Duncan's finest poems are readings of other texts, his own poem serving as meditation and transformation."[3] Perhaps the most complex example of this "intertextual" writing is "Poem Beginning with a Line by Pindar," in which he finds aspects of the story of Eros (Cupid) and Psyche in Pindar's first Pythian Ode, Apuleius's *The Golden Ass*, a Goya painting, a Whitman poem, Pound's *Pisan Cantos*, and his own dreams.

Duncan addressed a number of the public issues of his day. In "The Multiversity," he defends the free speech movement at the University of California and attacks the administration for its use of authoritarian violence: "the club, the gun, the strong arm / gang law of the state." In "Up Rising" and several other of the "Passages" poems he protests against America's involvement in the Vietnam War. Here he excoriates Lyndon Johnson as a president whose "name stinks with burning meat and heapt honors." Finally, Duncan had the courage to address the issue of homosexuality at a time when openly declaring himself to be homosexual was a professional as well as a personal risk. After he published the essay "The Homosexual in Society" in 1944, John Crowe Ransom decided not to publish an already accepted poem in *The Kenyon Review*.

In "The Torso," Duncan addressed the question of homosexuality in poetic form:

> Most beautiful!   the red-flowering eucalyptus,
> > the madrone, the yew
> > Is he . . .
>
> So wouldst smile, and take me in thine arms
> The sight of London to my exiled eyes
> Is an Elysium to a new-come soul
>
> > If he be Truth
> > I would dwell in the illusion of him
>
> His hands unlocking from chambers of my male body
> > such an idea in man's image
> > rising tides that sweep me towards him
> > > . . . *homosexual*?

The trees of the opening images suggest the male torso of the poem's title, but the ellipses after "Is he" introduce the topic of male homosexuality on a more pragmatic level that seems to disrupt the lyric effusiveness of the first two lines. The question "Is he a homosexual?" – itself a social cliché – is interrupted by a passage from Marlowe's play *Edward II*, by the speaker's own romanticization of a relationship ("If he be Truth . . .") and by a description of a sexual embrace. These interruptions serve to elevate the importance of the question "Is he a homosexual" from the level of speculation or gossip to one of mystery or metaphysics. The object of the speaker's love is "a trembling hieroglyph" who later in the poem becomes materialized through the enumeration of various body parts. As Cary Nelson remarks, the italicized word "homosexual," followed by a question mark and placed on its own line, forces the reader to question the use of a single name for such a complex combination of emotions. What does it mean, Duncan asks, to be a homosexual in erotic, interpersonal, historical, sociopolitical, and aesthetic terms? As in so many of his poems, the literary, the personal, and the political are brought together in a weave that reveals new possibilities of meaning.

The Black Mountain poets

The third grouping of the New American Poets was the Black Mountain school, consisting of those poets identified with Black Mountain College and its charismatic teacher, rector, and poet-in-residence Charles Olson. The Black Mountain group consisted of poets who taught at the college (Olson and Creeley), poets who studied there in the early 1950s (Edward Dorn, Joel Oppenheimer, Jonathan Williams, and John Wieners), and poets such as Denise Levertov who were more loosely affiliated with the college or its literary magazines. Located in rural North Carolina, the college was conceived as a kind of utopian community where writers, painters, musicians, dancers, and other intellectuals could work in an open educational environment. The most important poetic influences on the work of the Black Mountain poets were Pound, Williams, and Olson, though the Objectivists were admitted as a secondary influence.

Olson's essay "Projective Verse" (1950) was the guiding text for the Black Mountain poets. Not since Pound's Imagist manifestoes of the 1910s had a declaration of poetic ideas made such an profound impact on contemporary writing. "Projective Verse" proposed a poetics based on a technique Olson called "composition by field." As opposed to "closed verse" (i.e. traditional poetic form), the "open-form" poem would be written in such as way as to maximize the energy and spontaneity of the poet's language. Olson's essay left the details of the process of "composition by field" rather vague, but he emphasized the importance of a more active attention to the properties of sound and rhythm in creating a verbal energy: a "kinetics" of poetic form. Olson defined the poem as a "high-energy construct" that enacts the process of its own creation. Perhaps the most famous statement to come from "Projective Verse" was one Olson had borrowed from his friend Creeley: "form is never more than an extension of content." The principal units of form for Olson were the line (which should serve to move the poem forward rather than to emphasize the polish of its construction) and the syllable (which should provide a rhythmical and sonic base for the poem). One of the more controversial aspects of Olson's essay was its emphasis on the physical presence of the breath as a basis for poetic composition: according to Olson, it was the breath which generated the "speech-force of language" and which determined the length and shape of the poetic line. Such ideas were influential on the free-verse poetics of the 1950s and 1960s: Ginsberg, for example, credited Olson's theories as a partial explanation for the style of "Howl."

The poet whose work and ideas were most clearly in dialogue with those of Olson was Robert Creeley. Olson and Creeley were in almost daily contact during the early 1950s, and their voluminous correspondence (published in ten volumes thus far) chronicles one of the most important literary friendships of the late twentieth century. Creeley's peripatetic lifestyle – he moved from New Hampshire to southern France and then to Mallorca before coming to teach at Black Mountain in 1954 – made letters a convenient form in which to express his developing sense of poetry and poetics.

Creeley published several books of poetry with small presses during the 1950s, but it was not until the publication of *For Love: Poems, 1950–1960* (1962) that he received widespread recognition. In Creeley's early work, his dual preoccupations were the attempt to understand and describe human relationships, and the analysis of language as a medium for communication and self-expression. Creeley's characteristic poems are short meditations on some aspect of life; they are remarkable for their psychological complexity and their highly compressed, even minimalist style. In Creeley's most famous poem, "I Know a Man" (1954), he displays a unique ability to make us feel the weight of every syllable:

>As I sd to my
>friend, because I am
>always talking, – John, I
>
>sd, which was not his
>name, the darkness sur-
>rounds us, what

can we do against
it, or else, shall we &
why not, buy a goddamn big car

drive, he sd, for
christ's sake, look
out where yr going.

The form of the poem owes something to the example of Williams, with its short free-verse lines and compact stanzas. But Creeley takes Williams' nontraditional use of form a step further: the highly syncopated rhythm of his lines is inspired less by Williams' lyrics than by the jazz improvisations of Charlie Parker and Miles Davis. The most striking aspect of the poem's rhythm, as Charles Hartman has observed, is an extreme form of enjambment in which Creeley seems constantly to be pushing the last word of the line into the next line: "to my / friend," "which was not his / name," "for christ's / sake." Creeley disrupts the normal flow of meaning by continually breaking words across line breaks, stanza breaks ("what // can we do," and even in the middle of a word ("the darkness sur-/rounds us"). This disruption also takes place on the level of punctuation (the frequent use of commas to create caesuras in the middle of the line), orthography (ampersands and abbreviations like "sd" and "yr"), and syntax ("shall we & / why not, buy a goddamn big car").

These formal devices are not simply intended to make the poem more difficult or experimental; they play an important role in defining the voice and mood of the poem's speaker. This speaker is not the articulate confessionalist of Lowell's "Skunk Hour," nor is he the self-dramatizing persona of Plath's "Lady Lazarus." Instead, this is a speaker who stumbles through his narrative – interrupting himself with self-analysis ("because / I am always talking") and clarifications ("which was not his / name") – until he is cut off by his friend's warning to watch where he is going. Further, his speech act takes place in a very untraditional setting for a lyric poem: he is talking while driving a car. Though the speaker appears to be having a conversation with his friend, the rhythm of the poem is not typically conversational: instead, as Lynn Keller observes, "The crowding of stresses and the unnatural pauses communicate both the speaker's anxious restraint and his need for release."[4]

If the climax of the poem clearly comes in stanza III – where we feel the tension between the speaker's fear of the darkness that surrounds us and the escapism latent in the desire to buy a big car – it is difficult to know how to interpret this moment and its interruption in the fourth stanza by the friend's warning to "look out where yr going." Charles Altieri reads line 9 as the speaker's desperate attempt to "cover the emptiness" through an appeal to a "purely verbal universe."[5] In this reading, looking out where we are going becomes a metaphor for a greater attention to life experience. Michael Davidson, on the other hand, emphasizes the poem's social context as an expression of the Beat counterculture: for the Beats and other New American Poets of the 1950s, "the world [was] perceived as alien and hostile, an undifferentiated 'darkness' created and maintained by forces beyond the individual's control."[6] The two alternatives to that darkness suggested by the poem are the endless talk of the hipster-poet (suggested by the dialogic form of the poem itself) and the need to "take the open road," in this case in a "big car." We might also read the fantasy of buying the "goddamn big car" as a reference to the materialistic consumerism of the 1950s, an era marked by the increasing size and social significance of the automobile. Creeley himself, who was plagued by money problems throughout the early 1950s, managed to buy a car in 1950, but it was a 1928 Hupmobile which he purchased for $15. In the poem, Creeley at once acknowledges his own material desires (for a better car, for an easier or more comfortable life) and satirizes the postwar spending binge that led Americans to define their lives and aspirations through the acquisition of material possessions.

The New York school

The last of the groups constituting the New American Poetry was the New York poets, who included Ashbery, O'Hara, Kenneth Koch, and James Schuyler. The New York poets were associated with the avant-garde art world of New York City, and especially with the Abstract Expressionists who had made Manhattan the center of the international art scene. The New York poets – some of whom worked in the art world as curators and reviewers – wrote in an abstract and witty style that combined literary and artistic influences to create a new postwar aesthetic. Unlike the academic poetry of the period, their work incorporated such elements as gossip heard at parties, the lives of Hollywood stars, and the ironic humor associated with homosexual "camp." Their experiments with language – influenced by the French Surrealist poets, the Abstract Expressionist painters, and the work of American avant-gardists such as William Carlos Williams and Gertrude Stein – were among the most radical of the postwar era, and led to the even more programmatic experiments carried out by the Language group.

The most charismatic and influential member of the New York school – up to the time of his accidental death in 1966 – was Frank O'Hara. After serving in the navy during World War II, O'Hara attended Harvard, where he met both Ashbery and Koch. The late 1940s was a golden age of poetry at Harvard (among the other poets studying there at the time were Robert Bly, Robert Creeley, Donald Hall, and Adrienne Rich) and its heightened intellectual climate encouraged young writers like O'Hara and Ashbery to scour both American and European poetic traditions for examples of innovative writing. After O'Hara moved to New York City in 1951, he took a job selling books and postcards at the Museum of Modern Art, where he eventually became a curator of exhibitions. O'Hara's involvement with the New York art world, and especially with the Abstract Expressionists, was crucial to his development as a poet: Abstract Expressionism provided O'Hara with the idea of art as process rather than as finished product: the poem was to be "the chronicle of the creative act that produces it." Like the paintings of Franz Kline and Jackson Pollock, O'Hara's poetry would be one of richly varied surfaces instead of symbolic depth. Rather than the layers of meaning provided by symbols or "deep images," O'Hara sought a language that resisted interpretive strategies based on reading "behind" the words. Unlike poets such as Lowell and Bishop, who labored over many drafts of a poem before considering it finished, O'Hara often composed his poems very fast, achieving a verbal and emotional energy through the speed of his composition.

In its emphasis on energy and spontaneity, O'Hara's poetics resembled that of the Black Mountain poets, though O'Hara found Olson too serious in his proselytizing for a new poetry; O'Hara would in fact parody "Projective Verse" in his own mock-manifesto "Personism." In the mid-1950s, O'Hara developed what was to be his distinctive style. Taking his cue from William Carlos Williams, O'Hara moved away from the surrealist-inspired language of earlier poems like "Second Avenue" (1953) and wrote poems that were more relaxed, colloquial, and evocative of everyday urban existence. O'Hara's poems of dailiness have been called "lunch poems" (referring to their descriptions of his actions and motions during the lunch hour) and "I do this I do that poems." In these poems, O'Hara goes beyond the example of Williams in recreating the routine of daily life. In "The Day Lady Died," for instance, he details his wanderings during a particular lunch hour:

> It is 12:20 in New York a Friday
> three days after Bastille day, yes
> it is 1959 and I go get a shoeshine

It is only after he has eaten lunch and run a series of mundane errands (buying a magazine, going to the bank, etc.) that O'Hara hears the shocking news of Billie Holiday's death. The contrast between the ordinariness of everyday experience and the powerful memories evoked by the singer's death generates the poem's unique poignancy.

O'Hara also wrote a number of poems about art and artists, and was involved in collaborative projects with painters like Larry Rivers and Joe

Brainerd. O'Hara's most famous poem on the artistic process is "Why I Am Not a Painter" (1957):

> I am not a painter, I am a poet.
> Why? I think I would rather be
> a painter, but I am not. Well,
>
> for instance, Mike Goldberg
> is starting a painting. I drop in.
> "Sit down and have a drink" he
> says. I drink; we drink. I look
> up. "You have SARDINES in it."
> "Yes, it needed something there."
> "Oh." I go and the days go by
> and I drop in again. The painting
> is going on, and I go, and the days
> go by. I drop in. The painting is
> finished. "Where's SARDINES?"
> All that's left is just
> letters, "It was too much," Mike says.

On one level, "Why I Am Not a Painter" is an extended verbal joke on the difference (or lack of difference) between poetry and painting. While the poem begins by suggesting that O'Hara would rather be a painter than a poet – not a surprising feeling at a time when the Abstract Expressionist painters had achieved an extraordinary measure of both critical and financial success – it fails either to justify this preference or to explain his decision not to be a painter. Instead, the poem takes a number of sudden and witty turns, its progress determined more by O'Hara's free association than by any narrative or poetic logic. Most of the poem concerns the activities of a painter (Mike Goldberg) and a poet (O'Hara himself), whose distinct artistic projects are ironically conflated. O'Hara uses no visual images in describing Goldberg's painting, telling us only that in its first version it contained the written word "SARDINES"; his own poem, on the other hand, has a title that makes it sound more like a still life painting ("Oranges"), and it is written in an indeterminate form: "a / whole page of words, not lines." Nevertheless, the opposition between painting as a primarily visual medium and poetry as a primary verbal form is made clear by the end the poem: the color orange which was the original inspiration for O'Hara's poem remains only as the title, and the word "SARDINES" which was originally written across Goldberg's painting is retained only in the form of random letters in its abstract composition.

On a more serious level, "Why I Am Not a Painter" is an *ars poetica* about the unpredictability of the creative act. The poem's rather offhanded style, casual narrative structure, and loose formal construction evoke the

sense of play and experimentation that O'Hara and his fellow artists and
poets saw as an antidote to the social rigidity of the Cold War era. O'Hara's
refusal to provide a direct answer to the question posed by the title stands
for a larger refusal to play by society's rules: the explanation of why he
is a poet rather than a painter cannot be reduced to the kind of simple
formula demanded by postwar America. As a homosexual and a participant in the bohemian art culture of the 1950s, O'Hara was well versed in
the strategies of evasiveness, and "Why I Am Not a Painter" is not only a
rejection of the kind of poetic high seriousness represented by Eliot, Lowell, and the New Critics but a camp response to the tradition of what he
derided as "the important utterance." The poem is divided into three asymmetrical stanzas: the first poses the central question, the second purports to
answer the question but digresses into an anecdote about going to see Goldberg's painting, and the third contains a description of O'Hara's own poetic
process:

> But me? One day I am thinking of
> a color: orange. I write a line
> about orange. Pretty soon it is a
> whole page of words, not lines.
> Then another page. There should be
> so much more, not of orange, of
> words, of how terrible orange is
> and life. Days go by. It is even in
> prose, I am a real poet. My poem
> is finished and I haven't mentioned
> orange yet. It's twelve poems, I call
> it ORANGES. And one day in a gallery
> I see Mike's painting, called SARDINES.

O'Hara proceeds through a series of statements – all uttered with deadpan
irony – about his work as a poet. The tone of the poem is never entirely
clear: like an Abstract Expressionist painting, it leaves much of the work
of interpretation to the reader. On the one hand, there is an obvious joke
in his proclamation that the poem "is even in / prose. I am a real poet."
(O'Hara may be thinking of Pound's declaration that poetry should be as
well written as prose, or celebrating the "prose poem" as the epitome of
avant-garde poetry). Yet at the same time, O'Hara hints at a deeper layer
of meaning in his statement that "There should be / so much more . . . of
how terrible orange is / and life." In his sudden juxtapositions of language,
O'Hara is constantly seeking to disrupt the reader's expectations. The line
break between "orange" and "life," for example, also emphasizes the lack
of logical connection between the two. What is the relationship between
a color (orange) and life? Is life terrible, and if so, is it terrible in the same

way that orange is? Or are these statements merely intended to mock the reader's desire to find a deep message in the poem?

Formally, O'Hara's use of a combination of caesuras and abrupt line breaks creates a feeling of spontaneity: "I go and the days go by / and I drop in again. The painting / is going on, and I go, and the days / go by." The chatty repetition of words and phrases – "I go," "the days go by," "I drop in" – is clearly intended to be humorous, but it has another effect as well. In his conflation of his own actions and the creation of the painting, O'Hara seeks to break down the separation between life and art. Life, like art, is inherently unpredictable; it can be dramatic (as in "The Day Lady Died") or it can rest on a more quotidian plane, merely "going on" until something of value (a poem or a painting, for example) emerges out of it.

Had John Ashbery died in 1966 as O'Hara did, he might be remembered only as a talented but relatively minor poet of the postwar generation. Since his poetic career spans over half a century, however, his achievement clearly outstrips his involvement with the New York school. Ashbery was a controversial figure in American poetry, and his poems served as a kind of litmus test for the reader of contemporary verse. Some readers found his writing overrated, self-indulgent, and wilfully difficult; others considered it to be among the strongest and most innovative poetry of the late twentieth century. Ashbery was one of the few poets of his generation to be accepted both by the experimental community and by the more mainstream poetry culture. Though he abandoned a self-consciously experimental style after the publication of *The Tennis Court Oath* in 1962, his work continued to be characterized by its difficulty and its disjunctiveness: the typical Ashbery poem juxtaposes radically different discourses, shifts rapidly between registers of tone and diction, resists conventional explanation and paraphrase, refuses to present a coherent speaker or a unified lyric self, and avoids traditional subject matter, preferring surreal or comic-book narratives. Like O'Hara, Ashbery was more interested in process than in finished product: he claimed that his poems were less about the outside world than about the act of the "poem creating itself." Since "things are in a continual state of motion," the poem should convey "the experience of experience."

In addition to his stylistic innovations (the influence of which can be seen in the Language Poets, among others), Ashbery is noted for his ability to capture the tenor of the postmodern "information age." His major themes include the nature of consciousness and temporality; the fundamental instability of the self; the impossibility of closure; and the falsity of fixed absolutes. "Syringa," from his 1977 collection *Houseboat Days*, is one of Ashbery's characteristic and deservedly famous poems; the opening section provides a good sense of Ashbery's style.

Orpheus liked the glad personal quality
Of the things beneath the sky. Of course, Eurydice was a part
Of this. Then one day, everything changed. He rends
Rocks into fissures with lament. Gullies, hummocks
Can't withstand it. The sky shudders from one horizon
To the other, almost ready to give up wholeness.
Then Apollo quietly told him: "Leave it all on earth.
Your lute, what point? Why pick at a dull pavan few care to
Follow, except a few birds of dusty feather,
Not vivid performances of the past." But why not?
All other things must change too.
The seasons are no longer what they once were,
But it is the nature of things to be seen only once,
As they happen along, bumping into other things, getting along
Somehow. That's where Orpheus made his mistake.
Of course Eurydice vanished into the shade;
She would have even if he hadn't turned around.
No use standing them like a gray stone toga as the whole wheel
Of recorded history flashes past, struck dumb, unable to utter an
    intelligent
Comment on the most thought-provoking element in its train.
Only love stays on the brain, and something these people,
These other ones, call life.

Ashbery revisits the famous myth of Orpheus, in which Orpheus (the son of Apollo) goes to the underworld to rescue his wife Eurydice and is later torn apart by a group of women (the Bacchantes) when he refuses their advances. Orpheus is best known as a supremely talented musician who could make animals, trees, and stones follow him and who even managed to charm Hades and Persephone into letting Eurydice go. In Ashbery's revision of the myth, the Bacchantes tear Orpheus apart not because they are angered by his fidelity to Eurydice but because they are maddened by the agonizing power of his art, "driven / Half out of their minds by his music, what it was doing to him."

The title of the poem is itself a pun: "syringa" is a flower, a member of the saxifrage family, but the word is also derived from "syrinx," the Greek word for the reed from which musical pipes were made. In another myth, a nymph named Syrinx is transformed into a reed so as to escape being raped by Pan; that reed is in turn made into a musical pipe by Pan. Here the story of Orpheus overlays that of Syrinx, which is alluded to only obliquely in the poem. Both the syringa and the syrinx are important elements in the poem's symbolic structure: Orpheus represents music (and by extension poetry) and his song is compared to the "sparkling yellow flowers / Growing around the brink of the quarry." Both flowers and music break rocks: the song with its beauty, the flowers with their roots (the word saxifrage means "rock-breaker"). But music is also associated with loss for both Orpheus and Ashbery, who laments that "it isn't enough / To just go on singing."

"Syringa" is a poem about the power of song, and it is also an *ars poetica*, a poem about the making of poetry. According to Ashbery, there are two modes of poetry. On the one hand, there is the high Orphic strain which is "emblematic," presenting a "tableau" or "stalled moment" of life. On the other hand, there is the music associated with Syrinx, "In whose tale are hidden syllables / Of what happened," and who asks for no lasting artistic glory, no "stellification." When Syrinx transforms herself into a reed, she loses her individual identity and becomes part of the "flowing, fleeting" process of life itself: "the tossing reeds of that slow, / Powerful stream, the trailing grasses / Playfully tugged at." Ashbery clearly sees his own poetry as falling into the latter mode, since "Stellification / Is for the few, and comes about much later."

While Ashbery's poem is in part a lament for Orpheus, it also makes fun of him, depicting him as an almost comic-book figure. The opening lines are written in an exaggeratedly simple style: "Of course, Eurydice was a part / Of this. Then one day, everything changed." For Ashbery, the mere fact that a story has become canonized as "myth" does not give it any special status. Unlike Pound, who sought in the myths of the past the "luminous details" that would express the essence of a particular culture, Ashbery treats the stories of the mythic past as he would any story of contemporary life. After all, the stories of most people and their lives – even those which are important in their day – disappear "into libraries, onto microfilm," where only a few "are still interested in them." The myths of the past are by nature no more interesting than modern life or the artifacts of popular culture which Ashbery explores in poems like "Daffy Duck in Hollywood" and "Farm Implements and Rutabagas in a Landscape." In the end, the poem enacts a deflation of the Orpheus myth: the story ends halfway through the poem and we are left with the anti-climax of the ending. Like O'Hara, Ashbery resists the temptation to move toward symbolic depth. His juxtapositions of classical myth with popular culture, and of intense lyricism with flatly prosaic style, suggest an ironic detachment from any gesture that could be seen as conferring an aura of "truth" or a claim of aesthetic transcendence.

Language Poetry and the postmodern avant-garde

While the idea of poetry as "language experiment" can be traced as far back as Whitman, the evolution of American poetry from Whitman to the modernists to the postmodern Language writers involves a gradually increasing attention to the potential of poetry as a medium for the exploration of

language itself. Like their predecessors in the New American Poetry movements of the 1950s and 1960s, the Language Poets of the 1980s and 1990s
were strongly committed to the idea of poetry as an agent of social and
political critique. But whereas the New American poets tended to express
their critique of contemporary society through direct statements of anger,
outrage, or disgust, the Language writers were more interested in using
poetry to examine the ways in which language operates within a range of
social, cultural, and literary discourses.

The difference between the New American Poets and the Language writers is in part generational. The Beats and other postwar poets reached their
poetic maturity at a time when the country was enjoying a period of economic expansion accompanied by a restriction of certain forms of social
expression: from within their bohemian communities in New York and San
Francisco, they used their poems to express a rebellion against the conformity, materialism, and social hypocrisy of the late 1940s and 1950s. The
poets of the Language group, on the other hand, came of age at a time
when the initial "boom" of postwar economic expansion had ended, and
when the impact of the media-driven commodity culture was so pervasive as to be universally recognized. Whereas the poets of the 1950s and
1960s were guided by what Paul Breslin has called the "psycho-political
muse" of poetry – spurred on by a communal goal of liberating the psyche
from "the false consciousness imposed by society" – the Language Poets
were responding to a very different set of concerns.[7] Their poetics were
based less on a conception of remaining "open to experience" and more
on a project of foregrounding the operations of language itself. Language,
they argued, is not merely a vehicle for explaining or translating experience
but a generative agent in the poem's composition. The poem is written
not as a means of expressing emotions or personal qualities of the author,
but as an expression of a complex grid of social and historical relations.
Where a poet like Allen Ginsberg had used his poems to comment on
the distorted values of the dominant American culture ("America") or to
chronicle the anti-establishment gestures of his generation ("Howl"), the
Language Poets tended to avoid direct pronouncements, preferring to critique society through reference to the underlying structures of language and
ideology.

There are two primary explanations for this shift. The first is that by the
1970s and 1980s American culture had become so saturated with language
in all its debased and mediatized forms (advertising, television talk-shows,
bestsellers, political "sound-bites") that it was no longer possible to conceive of poetry in terms of a "natural" language generated by the poet
himself or herself for a particular occasion. In other words, the Language

Poets suggested, there was no longer the possibility of achieving either the modernist ideal of the "direct treatment of the thing" or the postwar ideal of a poetry based on an expression of the "self" and on the actuality of human speech. In the group manifesto "Aesthetic Tendency," several of the Language writers used a post-Marxist analysis to attack the narrowness of mainstream poetic norms, and especially of the "expressivist" lyric which had become the dominant form of American poetry.

The second reason for the fundamental change in poetics had to do with the proliferation of literary theories challenging the notion of language as a transparent medium for the communication of thoughts, concepts, and images. The poststructuralist ideas of such theorists as Jacques Derrida suggest that language is fundamentally a system of differences in which words ("signs") do not capture or represent meanings but only refer to other signs in an infinite deferral of meaning. The seminal works of Derrida and other poststructuralists such as Roland Barthes and Michel Foucault appeared during the 1960s and early 1970s, at exactly the time when the Language movement was coalescing. The Language Poets, like the poststructuralists, rejected the ideal of linguistic transparency: the idea that language can reflect in some immediate and direct way the objects or experiences it attempts to describe.

Over the last two decades of the century, the Language Poets explored the intersection of language, history, and ideology in a number of different ways. Susan Howe, for example, used source texts taken from the archives of American history and literature to fashion linguistically complex reflections on national and personal identity. In *Articulation of Sound Forms in Time* (1987), she drew on the historical account of Hope Atherton, a colonial minister who was separated from the militia he was accompanying during an Indian raid in 1676. In her poetic reconstruction of Atherton's adventures, Howe used a number of idiosyncratic poetic forms, expressing through the fragmentation of language both the disorientation of Atherton as he returns to civilization and the inability of the historical record to capture the sense of his lived experience.

Other Language Poets used various kinds of formal operations as a way of determining elements of the poem's composition. In Lyn Hejinian's *My Life* (1980), she adopted a procedural form based on her age at the time of composition. The poem originally consisted of thirty-seven sections of thirty-seven sentences each, and was revised eight years later to forty-five sections of forty-five sentences. The text also plays against the generic structure of autobiography: while each section represents a year in Hejinian's life, a given section will be made up of a mosaic of discontinuous sentences referencing radically different styles and generic conventions. Within a single section, we may find memories, images, historical observations, and personal reflections:

> A urinating doll, half-buried in sand. She is lying on her stomach with one eye closed, driving a toy truck along the road she has cleared with her fingers. I mean untroubled by the distortions. That was the fashion when she was a young woman and famed for her beauty, surrounded by beaux. Once it was circular and that shape can still be seen from the air. Protected by the dog. Protected by foghorns, frog honks, cricket circles on the brown hills. It was a message of happiness by which we were called into the room, as if to receive a birthday present given early, because it was too large to hide, or alive, a pony perhaps, his mane trimmed with colored ribbons.

In the passage from section 4 quoted here, the poet's childhood self is presented within a gender-coded environment, one in which she must be "protected" from the outside world, in which she will become increasingly aware of such traditionally feminine preoccupations as fashion and beauty, and in which she must remain untroubled by societal "distortions." Hejinian plays with gender identifications in such a way as to confuse our assumptions: the girl, lying prone in the sand, is associated metonymically with the urinating doll next to her, but she is also seen playing with a toy truck, typically the symbolic locus of a male child. In the final image, we again experience gender confusion in the form of a male animal coded as feminine: "a pony perhaps, his mane trimmed with colored ribbons."

The passage also exemplifies the sheer play of language which occurs throughout Hejinian's multilayered poem. Hejinian's use of repetitions, puns, and inversions creates a poetic fabric that is at once comforting and estranging. The phrase "name trimmed with colored ribbons" with which the section begins mutates into a "mane trimmed with colored ribbons." The relationship between "name" and "mane" is left ambiguous: it comes to represent the way in which language can shift, through sonic or orthographic resemblance, into different discursive and semantic registers. The "name" trimmed with colored ribbons, perhaps something a four-year-old girl would bring home from a friend's birthday party, is transfigured into a "mane," the mark of an animalism that works in semantic opposition to the social world.

David Antin's talk poems

David Antin was not associated with any particular school of postwar American poetry, but he was an important participant in the postwar poetic avant-garde and a leader in the international performance poetry movement.

Antin's most famous innovation was the "talk poem," a form of free-flow prose poem based on the recorded texts of his unrehearsed talks. Antin's talk poems represent an attempt to eliminate the distinction between thought, utterance, and text, thus enacting in more literal terms the poetics of spontaneity articulated by postwar poets such as Ginsberg, Olson, and O'Hara.

The format of Antin's talk poems is radically different from that of other postwar poetry because it is not only spontaneous but improvisatory. In other words, where the poems of Ginsberg and O'Hara are part of a movement toward a more spontaneous discourse (a discourse that is at once less constrained by tradition and less filtered through the poet's sense of artistic self-consciousness), Antin's texts are improvised spoken performances *before* they are written texts. In the conventional poem (and even the experimental poem), an idea or observation leads to a written text, which can then be read or recited aloud; for Antin, on the other hand, an idea or group of ideas leads to a live "talk" which is then transcribed into a written text. This text is not always a verbatim rendering of the spoken discourse – Antin will sometimes make changes when he transcribes at the typewriter – but the basis for the final printed text is always the spoken performance. One might argue that these texts are no longer "poems" in any conventional sense, since in many respects they bear a closer resemblance to oral forms such as the lecture, the stand-up comedy routine, the sermon, or the dramatic monologue than they do to the traditional poem. The more we read Antin's talks as spoken "improvisations," the more problematic they become as "poems," since the idea of poetry generally presupposes a certain effort on the part of the writer to shape the text into a formal object that is more than simply a recording of speech.

Yet if Antin's language in his talk poems is not traditionally literary, it is also not exactly the language of ordinary American speech. Just as a lifetime of working with poetic language prepared poets like Frost or Williams for writing the seemingly effortless lines they were able to produce, a lifetime of writing and thinking about ideas prepared Antin for the verbal performances he was to give. Further, Antin's talks are formulated with an acute awareness of the poetic conventions within which and against which he is working. Antin's relation to "poetry" is made clear in *talking at the boundaries* (1976):

if robert lowell is a
poet i dont want to be a poet   if robert frost was a
poet i dont want to be a poet   if socrates was a poet
          ill consider it

Antin's awareness of his relationship both to the tradition of American poets and to the theoretical framework of poetic composition makes his talk poems postmodern instances of the tendency toward metalanguage: he uses the talk poem to talk about his rejection of more traditional notions of poetry (represented by Frost and Lowell) in favor of more experimentalist or philosophical notions of poetry. In "a private occasion in a public place" (1976), Antin suggests that the traditional function of poetry is not essentially different from that of his talk poems:

> and im doing what   poets have done for a long time
> theyve talked out of a   private sense   sometimes from a
> private need   but theyve   talked about it in a rather
> peculiar context   for anybody to eavesdrop

Antin goes on to link poetry with other occasions in which we share the private details of our lives with strangers, such as bartenders and taxi drivers. This comparison suggests that poetry – far from being elevated to some sanctified realm apart from everyday life – is similar to other forms of communication that involve sharing "some aspect of [our] humanness." This more egalitarian concern with the "humanness" of poetry is one that Antin shares with other members of his generation, such as Creeley, O'Hara, and Ginsberg. For Antin, however, the sense of immediate contact between him and his audience that would make such "humanness" possible is not available in the printed poem: it can only occur in the live performance or "talk." In an ironic inversion of W. H. Auden's famous statement that "poetry makes nothing happen," Antin claims that "talking is making something happen": what the talk poem makes happen is the emergence of the self in a particular moment and the communication of certain important aspects of that self (its memories, thoughts, feelings, and observations) to an audience. The talk poem involves not just random talk, or even the kind of specialized talk we might hear in a lecture, but, as Antin claims in his poem "a more private place," "those linguistic acts of invention and discovery through which the mind explores the transformational power of language and discovers and invents the world and itself."

Such a claim does not sound fundamentally different from the claims for poetic language that have been made by poets of the post-Romantic tradition – Frost and Stevens, for example. In fact, Antin's talk poems can easily be reconciled to the traditions of high lyricism. The postmodern form of Antin's talk poems is so flexible, so indeterminate, that they can be read in any number of ways: as miniature epics, as syncopated jazz poems, as examples of site-specific performance art, or as meditative lyrics. Each of these descriptions in some way fits Antin's work, and the number of different generic categories into which the talk poems can be put indicates the complexity of his project. Like Pound's *Cantos* a half-century earlier, and like Whitman's "Song of Myself" before that, the talk poems belong to that American tradition of poetic works that resist easy classification. If Antin's talk poems are strongly avant-garde in conception, they are at the same time typical of American poetry, expressing a tremendous openness to the range of human experience.

Notes

Introduction

1. James Longenbach, *Modernist Poetics of History: Pound, Eliot, and a Sense of the Past* (Princeton: Princeton University Press, 1987), 44.
2. Roy Harvey Pearce, *The Continuity of American Poetry* (Princeton: Princeton University Press, 1961), 4.

1 A new century: from the genteel poets to Robinson and Frost

1. David Perkins, *A History of Modern Poetry*, vol. II: *Modernism and After* (Cambridge, Mass.: Harvard University Press, 1987), 4.
2. Henry Adams, *The Life of Henry Cabot Lodge* (Boston, 1911), 9.
3. Larzer Ziff, *The American 1890s: Life and Times of a Lost Generation* (New York: Viking, 1966), 313.
4. Marie Borroff, *Language and the Poet: Verbal Artistry in Frost, Stevens, and Moore* (Chicago: University of Chicago Press, 1979), 27.
5. Frank Lentricchia, *Modernist Quartet* (Cambridge and New York: Cambridge University Press, 1994), 107.

2 Modernist expatriates: Ezra Pound and T. S. Eliot

1. Hugh Kenner, *The Pound Era* (Berkeley: University of California Press, 1971), 187.
2. James Laughlin and Delmore Schwartz, "Notes on Ezra Pound's 'Cantos': Structure and Music," in *Ezra Pound: the Critical Heritage*, ed. Eric Homberger (London and Boston: Routledge and Kegan Paul, 1972), 340.
3. Michael Alexander, *The Poetic Achievement of Ezra Pound* (Berkeley: University of California Press, 1979), 136–7.
4. Piers Gray, *T. S. Eliot's Intellectual and Poetic Development, 1909–1922* (Brighton: Harvester Press, 1982), 56.
5. A. Walton Litz, "Ezra Pound and T. S. Eliot," in *Columbia Literary History of the United States* (New York: Columbia University Press, 1988), 963.

210

6. David Perkins, *A History of Modern Poetry*, vol. I: *From the 1890s to the Modernist Mode* (Cambridge, Mass.: Harvard University Press, 1980), 514.

3 Lyric modernism: Wallace Stevens and Hart Crane

1. A. Walton Litz, *Introspective Voyager: the Poetic Development of Wallace Stevens* (New York: Oxford University Press, 1972), vi.
2. Denis Donoghue, *Connoisseurs of Chaos: Ideas of Order in Modern American Poetry* (New York: Macmillan, 1965), 194.
3. Frank Kermode, *Wallace Stevens* (London: Oliver and Boyd, 1960), 24.
4. Joseph Riddel, *The Clairvoyant Eye: the Poetry and Poetics of Wallace Stevens* (Baton Rouge: Louisiana State University Press, 1965), 27.
5. Stevens, *Opus Posthumous*, ed. Samuel French Morse (New York: Knopf, 1957), 161.
6. Riddel, *Clairvoyant Eye*, 12.
7. Stevens, *Opus Posthumous*, 270.
8. Riddel, *Clairvoyant Eye*, 84.
9. Warner Berthoff, *Hart Crane: a Re-introduction* (Minneapolis: University of Minnesota Press, 1989), 75.
10. Lee Edelman, *Transmemberment of Song: Hart Crane's Anatomies of Rhetoric and Desire* (Stanford: Stanford University Press, 1987), 135.
11. Edelman, *Transmemberment*, 190.

4 Gendered modernism

1. Alicia Ostriker, *Stealing the Language: the Emergence of Women's Poetry in America* (Boston: Beacon Press, 1986), 44.
2. Sandra Gilbert and Susan Gubar, *No Man's Land: the Place of the Woman Writer in the Twentieth Century*, vol. III: *Letters from the Front* (New Haven: Yale University Press, 1994), 69.
3. Cheryl Walker, *Masks Outrageous and Austere: Culture, Psyche, and Persona in Modern Women Poets* (Bloomington: University of Indiana Press, 1991), 20.
4. Adelaide Morris, "The Concept of Projection: H. D.'s Visionary Powers," in *Signets: Reading H. D.*, ed. Susan Stanford Friedman and Rachel Blaue DuPlessis (Madison: University of Wisconsin, 1990), 276–7.
5. Ostriker, *Stealing the Language*, 212.
6. Elizabeth Dodd, *The Veiled Mirror and the Woman Poet: H. D., Louise Bogan, Elizabeth Bishop, and Louise Gluck* (Columbia: University of Missouri Press, 1992), 34.
7. Susan Stanford Friedman, "Modernism of the Scattered Remnant: Race and Politics in the Development of H. D.'s Modernist Vision," in *H. D.: Woman*

and Poet, ed. Michael King (Orono, ME: National Poetry Foundation, 1986), 116.

8. Eileen Gregory, "Rose Cut in Rock: Sappho and H. D.'s Sea Garden," in *Signets*, 146.
9. Cristanne Miller, *Marianne Moore: Questions of Authority* (Cambridge, Mass., Harvard University Press, 1995), 17, 27, 93.
10. Miller, *Moore*, 28.
11. Miller, *Moore*, 118

5 William Carlos Williams and the modernist American scene

1. J. Hillis Miller, ed. *William Carlos Williams: a Collection of Critical Essays* (Englewood Cliffs, N.J.: Prentice Hall, 1966), 3.
2. James Breslin, *William Carlos Williams, an American Artist* (New York: Oxford University Press, 1970), xix.
3. Joseph Riddel, *The Inverted Bell: Modernism and the Counterpoetics of William Carlos Williams* (Baton Rouge: Louisiana State University Press, 1974), 50.
4. Tim Hunt, ed. *The Selected Poems of Robinson Jeffers* (Stanford: Stanford University Press, 2001), 89.
5. Williams, *Autobiography* (New York: Random House, 1951), 264.
6. George Oppen, Interview in *Contemporary Literature* 10.2 (1969), 161.
7. Perkins, *History*, vol. II, 273.
8. Riddel, *Inverted Bell*, 15–16.
9. Riddel, *Inverted Bell*, 21.
10. Breslin, *Williams*, 171.
11. Breslin, *Williams*, 273.
12. Paul Mariani, *William Carlos Williams: a New World Naked* (New York: McGraw-Hill, 1987), 672.

6 From the Harlem Renaissance to the Black Arts movement

1. Alain Locke, *The New Negro* (New York, 1925), Foreword (n.p.).
2. Gary Wintz, *The Emergence of the Harlem Renaissance, 1920–1940* (New York: Garland, 1996), 51.
3. Shelly Eversly, "Paul Laurence Dunbar," in *Encyclopedia of American Poetry: the Nineteenth Century*, ed. Eric Haralson (Chicago: Fitzroy Dearborn, 1998), 138.
4. James Weldon Johnson in *New York Age*, Jan. 10, 1920.
5. Maureen Honey, *Shadowed Dreams: Women's Poetry of the Harlem Renaissance* (New Brunswick: Rutgers University Press, 1989), 1–2.
6. J. Lee Greene, *Time's Unfading Garden: Anne Spencer's Life and Poetry* (Baton Rouge: Louisiana State University Press, 1977), 133.

7. Greene, *Time's Unfading Garden*, 134.

8. Perkins, *History*, vol. II, 605.

9. Rita Dove, "Introduction," *Harlem Gallery and Other Poems of Melvin B. Tolson*, ed. Raymond Nelson (Charlottesville: University Press of Virginia, 1999), xix.

10. Stephen Henderson, *Understanding the New Black Poetry: Black Speech and Black Music as Poetic References* (New York: Morrow, 1973), 16.

11. Henderson, *Understanding the New Black Poetry*, 21.

12. Jerry Gafio Watts, *Amiri Baraka: the Politics and Art of a Black Intellectual* (New York: New York University Press, 2001), 228.

13. Werner Sollors, *Amiri Baraka / Leroi Jones: the Quest for a "Popular Modernism"* (New York: Columbia University Press, 1978), 198.

14. Watts, *Amiri Baraka*, 177.

15. Günter Lenz, "Black Poetry and Black Music; History and Tradition: Michael Harper and John Coltrane," in *History and Tradition in Afro-American Culture* (Frankfurt and New York: Campus Verlag, 1984), 282–3.

7   The New Criticism and poetic formalism

1. Terry Eagleton, *Literary Theory: an Introduction* (Minneapolis: University of Minnesota Press, 1983), 49.

2. Louis Rubin, "The Serpent in the Mulberry Bush," in *Southern Renascence: the Literature of the Modern South*, ed. Louis Rubin and Robert Jacobs (Baltimore: Johns Hopkins University Press, 1953), 360.

3. Don Adams, *James Merrill's Poetic Quest* (Westport, Conn.: Greenwood Press, 1997), 26.

4. James Breslin, *From Modern to Contemporary: American Poetry 1945–1965* (Chicago: University of Chicago Press, 1984), xv.

5. Breslin, *From Modern to Contemporary*, xiv.

6. Robert Lowell, "The Art of Poetry," in *A Collection of Critical Essays* (Englewood Cliffs, NJ: Prentice-Hall, 1968), 19.

7. Robert Creeley, *A Quick Graph: Collected Notes and Essays*, ed. Donald Allen (San Francisco: Four Seasons Press, 1970), 42.

8. Breslin, *From Modern to Contemporary*, xv.

8   The confessional moment

1. Joseph Conte, *Unending Design: the Forms of Postmodern Poetry* (Ithaca: Cornell University Press, 1992), 2.

2. Thomas Travisano, *Midcentury Quartet: Bishop, Lowell, Jarrell, Berryman, and the Making of a Postmodern Aesthetic* (Charlottesville: University Press of Virginia, 1999), 34.

3. Jed Rasula, *The American Poetry Wax Museum: Reality Effects, 1940–1970* (Urbana: National Council of Teachers of English, 1996), 58.

4. Travisano, *Midcentury*, 259.
5. Diane Wood Middlebrook, "What Was Confessional Poetry?" in *Columbia History of American Poetry* (New York: Columbia University Press, 1993), 636.
6. Breslin, *From Modern to Contemporary*, 138.
7. Charles Altieri, *Enlarging the Temple: New Directions in American Poetry during the 1960s* (London: Associated University Presses, 1979), 67–8.
8. Jon Rosenblatt, *Sylvia Plath: the Poetry of Initiation* (Chapel Hill: University of North Carolina Press, 1979), 42.
9. M. H. Abrams, *A Glossary of Literary Terms*, seventh edition (New York: Harcourt Brace, 1999), 45.
10. Dodd, *Veiled Mirror*, 109.
11. C. K. Doreski, *Elizabeth Bishop: the Restraints of Language* (New York: Oxford University Press, 1993), 58.
12. Brett Millier, "Elusive Mastery: the Drafts of Elizabeth Bishop's 'One Art,'" in *Elizabeth Bishop: the Geography of Gender*, ed. Marilyn Lombardi (Charlottesville: University Press of Virginia, 1993), 235.

9   Lyric as meditation

1. Cited in Perkins, *History*, vol. II, 370.
2. James Dougherty, "North American Sequence," in *Encyclopedia of American Poetry: the Twentieth Century*, ed. Eric Haralson (Chicago: Fitzroy Dearborn, 2001), 629.
3. Perkins, *History*, vol. II, 373–4.

10   The New American Poetry and the postmodern avant-garde

1. Paul Hoover, *Postmodern American Poetry: a Norton Anthology* (New York: Norton, 1994), xxix.
2. Fred Moramarco and William Sullivan, *Containing Multitudes: Poetry in the United States since 1950* (New York: Twayne, 1998), 77.
3. Michael Davidson, *The San Francisco Renaissance: Poetics and Community at Mid-Century* (Cambridge and New York: Cambridge University Press, 1989), 132.
4. Lynn Keller, *Re-making it New: Contemporary Poetry and the Modernist Tradition* (Cambridge and New York: Cambridge University Press, 1987), 146.
5. Altieri, *Enlarging the Temple*, 175.
6. Davidson, *San Francisco Renaissance*, 64.
7. Paul Breslin, *The Psycho-Political Muse: American Poetry since the 1950s* (Chicago: University of Chicago Press, 1987), xiii.

Glossary

alliteration: the repetition of the same consonant sound within a poetic line or in consecutive lines.

assonance: the repetition of the same vowel sound in a poetic line or consecutive lines.

allusion: a passing reference, usually without explicit identification, to a person, place, event, or literary work.

anaphora: the repetition of the opening word of the poetic line.

caesura: a rhythmic break in the middle of a poetic line.

diction: the type of words used in a poem. In discussing the diction of poems, we use terms such as *formal diction*, *literary diction*, *abstract diction*, or *colloquial diction*.

dramatic monologue: a poem in the form of a speech by the speaker (not the poet) to one or more people. The form is often associated with the British poet Robert Browning.

elegy: a poem written in mourning of a death.

enjambment: a place in the poem in which one line runs into the next with no syntactic or rhythmic pause.

figure of speech: a rhetorical device used to heighten the language of a poem through a departure from standard usage. The most commonly used figures of speech include *hyberbole*, *metaphor*, *metonymy*, and *simile*.

free verse: a form of poetry in which the lines are of varied length and have no regular pattern of rhyme.

hyperbole: a figure of speech involving a bold overstatement or exaggeration.

image/imagery: poetic imagery involves the description of objects through the appeal to one or more of the senses. The most commonly used images are visual, though imagery can appeal to other senses as well, as in *auditory images*, *olfactory images*, *tactile images*, and *gustatory images*.

lyric: lyric poems are often distinguished from *narrative*, *dramatic*, or *epic* poems in being shorter in length and more focused on the speaker's feelings or states of mind. The term *lyrical* can also be used to refer to poems which contain a more musical, emotional, or meditative quality.

metaphor: a figure of speech involving an implicit comparison of two disparate things without the use of "like" or "as."

meter: any regularized rhythmic form in a poem. The study or use of meter is called *prosody*. In English-language poetry, the most common metrical forms involve a recurrent pattern of stressed and unstressed syllables. Each unit of meter is called a *foot*. There are several basic meters in English-language poetry: *iambic* (an unstressed syllable followed by a stressed syllable), *trochaic* (a stressed syllable followed by an unstressed syllable), *anapestic* (two unstressed syllables followed by a stressed syllable), *dactylic* (a stressed syllable followed by two unstressed syllables), and *spondaic* (two stressed syllables). The most common form of meter in English is *iambic pentameter* (a line consisting of five iambic feet).

metonymy: a figure of speech involving a comparison based on association or resemblance (i.e. the crown for the king, the waves for the ocean).

paysage moralisé: literally, a "moralized landscape." A device often used by Robert Frost, among other poets, to present human feelings or attributes through the presentation of a natural landscape.

persona: the fictionalized speaker of a poem. A *persona poem*, unlike most other lyric poems, is spoken by a speaker who is clearly not the poet himself.

rhyme: in its most familiar form, rhyme involves the matching of sounds at the end of lines, though some poems also use *internal rhyme*. While the most straightforward rhymes are exact or perfect rhymes, many poets also use various kinds of imperfect rhyme (*slant rhymes* or *off-rhymes*).

simile: a figure of speech involving a comparison using "like" or "as."

stanza: the basic formal units into which traditional poetry is divided. There are many kinds of stanzas, which are named according to their length and the kind of rhyme-scheme they contain.

symbol/symbolism: the term applied to an object or event which signifies something beyond itself. Symbols differ from images, which have a more concrete and limited meaning. Symbols can be either *conventional symbols* (the cross, the dove of peace), or *private symbols* which have a particular resonance in the work of an individual poet.

syntax: the poet's use of syntax – the ordering of words and phrases within each sentence – is crucial to the expressive power of the poem. Poetic syntax often stretches the rules of conventional word order for dramatic effect or in order to emphasize certain words. Poets use syntax in conjunction with other formal structures such as meter and the poetic line.

terza rima: a poetic form composed of three-line stanzas rhyming aba, bcd, cdc, and so on. The terza rima is most commonly associated with its use in Dante's *Divine Comedy*.

villanelle: a fixed form of nineteen lines, composed of five tercets (three-line stanzas) and one quatrain. Each tercet repeats the initial aba rhyme and the quatrain rhymes abaa.

Index